45p

D1325912

The Gospel According to John

By G. CAMPBELL MORGAN

Studies in the Prophecy of Jeremiah . . .	8/6
The Gospel According to Matthew . . .	10/6
The Gospel According to Mark	10/6
The Gospel According to Luke	8/6
The Gospel According to John	7/6
The Acts of the Apostles	15/-
Searchlights from the Word	12/6
The Teaching of Christ	12/6
The Crisis of the Christ	12/6
Living Messages of the Books of the Bible. Two	
Vols. . . . . Each	8/6
The Analyzed Bible . . . . . Each	7/6
Genesis to Esther.	
Job to Malachi.	
Matthew to Revelation.	
Genesis.	
Job.	
Isaiah I.	
Isaiah II.	
Matthew.	
John.	
Romans.	
Hosea: The Heart and Holiness of God . .	3/6
The Spirit of God.	6/-
The Ministry of the Word	2/6
Wherein Have We Robbed God? . . .	3/-
The Study and Teaching of the English Bible .	3/6
The Ten Commandments	3/6
The Bible in Five Years. Outlines . .	1/6
The Bible and the Child	1/6

DEVOTIONAL

God's Perfect Will	4/-
The True Estimate of Life	4/-
Categorical Imperatives of the Faith . . 5/- and	2/6
The Practice of Prayer	3/6
Simple Things of the Christian Life . . .	3/6
The Life of the Christian	2/6
Life Problems	3/-
Discipleship	3/-

226.5
M848g
withdrawn

THE GOSPEL
ACCORDING TO JOHN

By
G. CAMPBELL MORGAN, D.D.

SECOND EDITION

2213

MARSHALL, MORGAN & SCOTT, LTD.
LONDON :: EDINBURGH

Made and Printed in Great Britain
by
Hunt, Barnard & Co., Ltd.
London & Aylesbury.

First Edition . . . *November* 1933.
Second Edition . . . *February* 1934.

BRITISH ISLES NAZARENE LIBRARY COLLEGE

FOREWORD

T HIS is not a Commentary on John, in the usually accepted sense of that word. It is rather a series of Meditations, as given in The Church of the Open Door in Los Angeles, Tabernacle Presbyterian Church, Philadelphia, and finally in Westminster Chapel, London. The addresses, as given, were stenographically reported, and then condensed, so as to omit much that was merely incidental, retaining the general line of thought followed.

Dr. Robertson, of Louisville, Kentucky, has described the Gospel according to John as " the Profoundest Book in the World," and none who has studied it will be inclined to challenge that designation. To attempt to plumb its depths in a series of thirty-nine Lectures would be absurd. What I have attempted to do, with those who have gathered with me around its pages, has been to breathe its atmosphere, and indicate the paths which lead to those depths.

"The Word Became Flesh—We Beheld His Glory." If we have caught some vision of the many-coloured glories merging into the white light of the Revelation, that may help to fuller understanding of the writing in days to come, and in private individual study.

To that end these Meditations are now sent out in this form to a wider circle, and they are committed to the Grace and Truth of God—Who is forever patient with the short-comings of those who seek to serve Him, and Who wondrously resolves the discords of such into the harmony of His own mind and will.

G. CAMPBELL MORGAN.

Westminster Chapel, London.

CONTENTS

	PAGE
THE WRITER'S ACCOUNT OF HIS BOOK - - - - -	9
John xx. 30, 31	
THE THESIS - - - - - - - - -	17
John i. 1, 14, 18	
THE PARENTHESES - - - - - - - -	25
John i. 2–13, 14b, 15–17	
FIRST YEAR OF MINISTRY. "SIGNS."	
WITNESS OF THE HERALD. INTRODUCTION OF JESUS - -	32
John i. 19–34	
FIRST DISCIPLES AND FIRST SIGN - - - -	40
John i. 35–ii. 12	
JERUSALEM. THE SECOND SIGN. NICODEMUS - -	50
John ii. 13–iii. 21	
LAST MESSAGE OF HERALD, AND WRITER'S COMMENTS -	60
John iii. 22–36	
SAMARIA - - - - - - - - -	69
John iv. 1–42	
GALILEE. THIRD SIGN. NOBLEMAN'S SON - -	79
John iv. 43–54	
JERUSALEM. THE FOURTH SIGN. THE DERELICT - -	87
John v.	
CENTRAL PERIOD OF MINISTRY.	
THE FIFTH SIGN. FEEDING 5,000.	
THE SIXTH SIGN. STILLING STORM - - - - -	95
John vi. 1–21	
DISCUSSION AND TEACHING. FIRST "I AM."	
THE BREAD OF LIFE - - - - - - -	104
John vi. 22–40	
CONTINUED DISCUSSION AND SIFTING.	
A PERIOD IN GALILEE - - - - - - -	113
John vi. 41–71	
FINAL PERIOD OF MINISTRY.	
JERUSALEM. FEAST OF TABERNACLES.	
HIS BRETHREN AND RULERS - - - - -	122
John vii. 1–24	
JERUSALEM. FEAST OF TABERNACLES.	
CITIZENS AND PHARISEES - - - - - -	129
John vii. 25–36	
JERUSALEM. THE FEAST OF TABERNACLES.	
THE GREAT INVITATION AND DIVISION - - - -	136
John vii. 37–viii. 1	
JERUSALEM. THE WOMAN. SECOND "I AM."	
THE LIGHT OF THE WORLD. DISCUSSION - - -	145
John viii. 2–30	
CONTINUED DISCUSSION. THIRD "I AM."	
BEFORE ABRAHAM - - - - - - -	154
John viii. 31–59	
JERUSALEM. (LATER) SEVENTH SIGN.	
MAN BORN BLIND - - - - - - -	162
John ix. 1–38	

CONTENTS

PAGE

FINAL PERIOD OF MINISTRY—*Continued.*

JERUSALEM. TEACHING. FOURTH "I AM."
THE DOOR. FIFTH "I AM" GOOD SHEPHERD - - 171
    John ix. 39–x. 21

JERUSALEM. (STILL LATER.) FEAST OF DEDICATION. MES-
SIANIC CHALLENGE. OVER JORDAN - - - - 177
    John x. 22–42

BETHANY. SIXTH "I AM." RESURRECTION AND LIFE - 187
    John xi. 1–27

BETHANY. EIGHTH SIGN. LAZARUS - - - - 104
    John xi. 28–53

IN EPHRAIM. BETHANY, THE SUPPER.
JERUSALEM. THE ARRIVAL - - - - - - 204
    John xi. 54–xii. 19

JERUSALEM. THE GREEKS. TEACHING - - - - 211
    John xii. 20–36

THE WRITER'S COMMENTS, AND LAST APPEAL OF JESUS - 220
    John xii. 37–50

JERUSALEM. WITH HIS OWN. PASSOVER - - - 227
    John xiii. 1–20

JERUSALEM. WITH HIS OWN. NEW FEAST - - - 234
    John xiii. 21–35

JERUSALEM. WITH HIS OWN.
SEVENTH "I AM" WAY, TRUTH, LIFE - - - 241
    John xiii. 36–xiv

JERUSALEM. WITH HIS OWN.
EIGHTH "I AM" VINE. ALLEGORY - - - - 249
    John xv

JERUSALEM. WITH HIS OWN.
LAST TEACHING - - - - - - - - 258
    John xvi

JERUSALEM. WITH HIS OWN.
COMMUNION WITH THE FATHER - - - - - 266
    John xvii

JERUSALEM. THE BETRAYAL.
BEFORE THE PRIESTS - - - - - - - 275
    John xviii. 1–27

JERUSALEM. BEFORE PILATE - - - - - - 283
    John xviii. 28–xix. 16

JERUSALEM. THE CRUCIFIXION - - - - - 291
    John xix. 17–30

JERUSALEM. THE BURIAL - - - - - - 298
    John xix. 31–42

JERUSALEM. THE RISEN LORD.
THE FIRST DAY OF THE WEEK. MORNING - - - 306
    John xx. 1–18

JERUSALEM. THE RISEN LORD.
THE FIRST DAY OF THE WEEK. EVENING - - - 315
    John xx. 19–29

EPILOGUE - - - - - - - - - 324
    John xxi

The Gospel According to John

The Writer's Account of His Book

John xx. 30, 31.

A QUESTION asked long ago, and often repeated is as to why we have four Gospels. The answer to that enquiry was given by Origen when he said, There are not four Gospels, but a four-fold Gospel. This means that to an understanding of the Person and mission of our Lord, each evangelist, inspired of the Holy Spirit, has given one phase of revelation. This being so we cannot compare them in the sense of discriminating between their values. Each has its own distinctive revelation.

Nevertheless, there is a common and justifiable consciousness that in the Gospel according to John we arrive at an ultimate unveiling. Dr. Arthur T. Pierson once suggested that the four Gospels in the order in which we now have them, follow the line of the old Hebrew encampment. Matthew surveys the Theocracy in its entirety. In other words, the whole camp is seen surrounding the King. In Mark we find ourselves in the outer court, in the place of service and sacrifice. In Luke we have passed into the Holy Place, where stood the seven-branched candlestick of witness, and the table of shewbread, or communion. In John we enter within the veil, into the Holiest of all. If this warranted figure of speech be allowed, it at once becomes evident that any approach to this Gospel must be that of reverence and awe.

The work is evidently that of a poet, but it is none the less remarkable for its systematic structure; and we begin by recognizing that structure. The complete treatise is found in the first twenty chapters, so far as verse twenty-nine. This is immediately followed by a foot-note in chapter twenty, verses thirty and thirty-one, in which the writer accounts for his own book. Then there is an Epilogue, a Postscript

[9]

in chapter twenty-one. The terms epilogue, or postscript, do not suggest anything of secondary value, but refer merely to the literary structure. In the last analysis, chapter twenty-one continues and completes the movement ending in verse twenty-nine of chapter twenty. Our first study is concerned with the writer's account of his book, as found in the foot-note, chapter twenty, verses thirty and thirty-one. Every one will agree that when a writer interprets his own book, we must give attention to his interpretation if we are to hope to understand his book.

The foot-note runs thus :

> " Many other signs therefore did Jesus in the presence of the disciples, which are not written in this book ; but these are written, that ye may believe that Jesus is the Christ, the Son of God ; and that believing ye may have life in His name."

In these words the writer gives the reason for the writing, and incidentally reveals the method. Why did he write it ? " These are written, that ye may believe that Jesus is the Christ, the Son of God ; and that believing ye may have life in His name."

Then incidentally he shows how he did his work, or rather, reveals the principle underlying the writing. From many signs he has made a selection.

Three words then will help us to gain the value of this foot-note. One of them is found in the foot-note itself, and the two others result from the finding of the one. The first word is the word " Signs." The next word is Selection. The word is not used by the writer, but the fact is revealed. John is careful to point out that he has not told all the story of Jesus. This does not profess to be a life of Jesus. Neither does it profess to give all the signs available. " Many other signs . . . not written " ; but " these are written." Notice the contrast. Many not written ; these written. John has made a selection. Selection then reveals the method of John. The third word I would use is the word Significance. The significance of the signs, as John saw it. The signs were selected to produce conviction, "*that* ye may believe," and a spiritual result, "and that believing ye may have life."

The word "signs" is arresting. We must understand what that word means, as we find it here. There are three words used in the New Testament in the realm of what we commonly designate the supernatural; "Powers, Wonders, Signs." On the day of Pentecost, Simon Peter preaching, employed them. I will not quote them from the King James Version, nor from the Revised. The Old Version began with the word "miracles," which is not correct. The second word may be so rendered, but not the first. The Revised has it "mighty works," and then puts in the margin the true rendering "powers." "Jesus of Nazareth, a Man approved of God unto you by *powers* and *wonders* and *signs*." In writing his second letter to the Corinthians, Paul, referring to apostolic work, names "signs . . . wonders . . . powers." The same three words, but in another order. In his second letter to the Thessalonians, referring to Satan, he uses the same three words. He says he wrought with powers and signs and wonders falsely. Note that little word "falsely." It qualifies the activity of Satan. But we are in the same realm of ideas. The things that Jesus did; the things His apostles did; the things that the devil does.

Now what do the words mean? "Powers" refers to operations producing results. "Wonders" describes the effect produced by the power when it operates. "Signs" refers to the value of the thing done, which has produced wonder. We have in these three words a complete revelation, a complete philosophy of what we are pleased to call the supernatural.

The word miracles comes from the Latin *miraculum*, derived from the Latin *mirari*, which simply means to wonder. In the life of our Lord, we may take anything which we describe as miraculous,—turning water into wine, that is John's first; the raising of Lazarus, that is his last,—and they were operations which could only produce wonder or astonishment. In the presence of every such manifestation the astonished observer would recognize power, or energy. The wonder would be created by ignorance of the power producing the result. Therefore, it is a miracle, a wonderful thing. The last word reveals the value of it ; it is a sign, proving something. Jesus went about, and God through Him wrought powers, that is the fact ; wonders, that is the effect ; signs, that is the value.

A sign then is something that proves something else. A sign is infinitely more than a symbol. A symbol can be capriciously chosen to represent that with which it has no inherent connection. That is never true of a sign in the New Testament sense of the word. Let me illustrate that. The maple leaf is the symbol of Canada. But the maple leaf is not the sign of Canada. Why not ? Because we have seen maple leaves in other lands. But if we could find a plant which grows in Canada, and nowhere else, that would be a sign. That is the meaning of sign in the New Testament, always. Moreover, a true sign is always a proof of God ; while false signs prove Satan.

In John's Gospel he never uses the word " powers," never calls the things Jesus did, " powers." In the Book of Revelation, he does use the word ; but in the Gospel, and the letters he never employs it. It is also true that he never uses the word " wonders." He does record in the fourth chapter of the Gospel that Jesus once said to the men in Cana, " Except ye see signs and wonders, ye will in no wise believe." John's use of the word implicates powers and wonders, but he does not use the words. As he calls to mind all the things that Jesus did and said, noting their power, noting their wonder, he is emphasizing their significance and value.

In this statement there is an arresting limitation. The writer speaks of " Many other signs therefore did Jesus *in the presence of the disciples*, which are not written in this book." The things done and said were done and said, for the most part, in the presence of the crowd. John is referring to the fact that there were those who saw and understood.

It is possible for Jesus to perform a miracle, and for the crowd to see it, but not to understand it. John was emphasizing the fact that there were other witnesses, who did see the signs, and grasped their meaning.

John—who certainly was an old man when he wrote the Gospel—was going back in memory over the three and half marvellous years with Jesus, remembering the crowded days, and the incidents of all those wonderful days ; and from them all he made a selection of signs, and grouped them in this marvellous piece of writing, and that with a very definite purpose.

And so we come to the declaration of purpose. Why did he write ? " These are written that ye may believe." There are two uses of the same verb in that passage. " That ye may *believe* that Jesus is the Christ, the Son of God ; and that *believing* ye may have life in His name." In this double use of the verb, we have revealed the two sides of the faith that brings men into life. The first quite patently is intellectual conviction, " that ye may believe " ; that is that you may be convinced. Of what ? That Jesus is the Christ, the Son of God. But more ; " And that believing ye may have life." That implies more than intellectual conviction. That is belief as volitional surrender to the thing of which the mind is convinced. As a matter of fact, we never really believe anything until we surrender ourselves to it. It is possible to say every Sunday, " I believe in God the Father Almighty." Do we ? Saying it in the sanctuary does not prove it. The life through the week proves the reality of the faith affirmed, or disproves it. Intellectual conviction is not saving faith ; but apart from it there can be no saving faith. We must have the facts, and grasp them intellectually, and then yield to them.

Begin with the intellectual. What does he say is to be believed ? In order that we may believe something about Jesus. It is very arresting that John uses that name for our Lord more than any other writer. In the Revised Version we find that Mark calls our Lord, " Jesus " only thirteen

times. Luke calls Him " Jesus " eighty-eight times. Matthew
calls Him " Jesus " one hundred and fifty-one times. John
calls Him " Jesus " two hundred and forty-seven times.
That is quite mechanical, but it is revealing. In other words,
all through this Gospel, John is keeping us face to face with
the human Jesus, Jesus as He was known. His eyes were
ever on Jesus as known in the days of His flesh. This is
admittedly the Gospel of our Lord's Deity, and yet this
Gospel keeps me close to His humanity more than either of
the other Gospels does. Matthew ? I am in the presence of
government all the way through. I am impressed with
authority. Mark ? I am in the presence of the suffering
Servant stripped of His dignity. Luke ? I am in the presence
of Man in an ideal perfection that almost frightens me. But
in John I feel I can handle Him, and get close to the human.
He never lets me get away from the human.

But in Him there was more than the human. " These
are written that ye may believe that Jesus is the Christ."
Let us pause there. In this Gospel he calls Him Christ
twenty-one times, three of them in connection with the name
Jesus. Where he says the law came by Moses, grace and
truth by Jesus Christ, he links them. He never links them
again until recording the prayer of our Lord in chapter
seventeen, verse three, " Him Whom Thou didst send, even
Jesus Christ." He does so finally in this foot-note, " that ye
may believe that Jesus is the Christ." Three times only they
are thus linked together.

The first purpose of the writing is to prove that Jesus is
the Christ. That was the question in all the years of our
Lord's public ministry to the people among whom He exercised that ministry. Is He the Christ ? There came a day
when they asked our Lord specifically ; " If Thou art the
Christ, tell us plainly." It was the question that divided
men ; some saying, Yes, and others, No. John now says,
I have gathered up these things to prove that Jesus is the
Christ, that you may believe it.

What else ? " The Son of God." The title Christ refers to

His office. The designation Son of God, refers to His Person. He speaks of the Man of Nazareth, and remembers that he had looked into human eyes, been conscious of the touch of human hands, had put his head on the bosom of Jesus, and felt the beating of His human heart. Yes, but he had gathered up signs that prove the deepest fact, that this Jesus is the Son of God. Not *a* Son of God, but *the* Son of God.

That phrase, occurring here in the foot-note, must be interpreted by the writer's use of it in the earlier part of his book. In that book we find the first reference to the Sonship of Jesus in the eighteenth verse of chapter one, at the close of the prologue. " No man hath seen God at any time " ; but " the only begotten Son Who is in the bosom of the Father, He hath declared Him." That is the first reference of John to the Sonship of Jesus.

There are two renderings of that reference to Sonship. Admittedly it is difficult to decide between them ; and the difficulty is created by a difference in the manuscripts. There are many which read, " the only-begotten Son Who is in the bosom of the Father." But there are also many which read, " God only-begotten." In either case the significance is the same. The word " begotten " marks Sonship, even if the manuscripts which read, " God only begotten " are correct. It is Sonship, and Sonship of a peculiar nature. Every subsequent reference to the Sonship of Jesus must be interpreted by this. He is repeatedly referred to as the Son, or Son of God, in fact twenty-four times ; and always we must interpret by that strange, mystic word, " the only-begotten Son of God," or " God the only begotten." That is what John means at the end.

Now, if the great question of the hour in the ministry of Jesus was that of His Messiahship, the profounder question was the one that Jesus asked, What do you think of the Messiah, Whose Son is He ? They told Him, " The Son of David." Then He said, How did David call Him Lord ? when he said ; " Jehovah said unto my Lord." How did David call Him Lord, if He was only his son ? Christ's great

[15]

question was that, Whose Son is He ? The question of men was, Is He the Messiah ? But the deeper question was, Whose Son is the Messiah ? John says, I have gathered these signs that you may believe that Jesus is the Messiah, and that He is the Son of God. That was the purpose intellectually of this book.

We may state this in another and arresting way. John says in effect : " Many other signs therefore did Jesus in the presence of His disciples, which are not written in this book ; but these are written that ye may believe " that Simon Peter was right at Caesarea Philippi. What did Simon Peter say at Caesarea Philippi ? Jesus had asked, Who do you say that I am ? Peter replied : " Thou art the Christ, the Son of the living God." " Blessed art thou, Simon Bar-Jonah, for flesh and blood hath not revealed it unto thee, but My Father Who is in heaven." Long years after John, the poet, the friend of Simon, sat down, and said in effect, Simon was right that day. Let me gather out the signs. He gathered them, and grouped them ; and wrote his treatise and said, These are written that you may believe that Simon was right, that Jesus is the Christ, the Son of the living God.

And so we reach the end, " that believing ye may have life in His name." If being intellectually convinced, we act in accordance with the conviction, what then ? We have life. That is the way into life ; life in His name. Intellectual conviction is not enough. By volitional surrender only, can we pass into life.

Finally, this word life is arresting. The word John uses for life is the Greek word *zōē*. There are other words which stand for life. There is the word *pneuma* for spirit ; *psuchē* for mind. There is another outstanding word, *bios*. But John uses neither of these. Moreover, it is true that all the New Testament writers, when referring to the life that comes through Jesus, use that word *zōē*. In classical Greek, *zoe* simply means the life principle. It is used of insects, of worms, of men, or of God. *Bios* was supposed to be a higher word, meaning life on a higher level. We have the thought

of the two words in our words biology and zoology. When
we speak of zoology to-day we are referring to animal life.
The other word we use of human life, and all its higher forms.
The New Testament employs the word which refers to life
simply. In Greek there are two words that stand in antithesis, *zoe* and *thanatos*, life and death. In the New Testament
throughout *zoē* is used for life. The Bible recognizes that
death is the result of sin ; so when sin is absent, or dealt with
and put away, life is restored, in which there is no room for
death. *Zoē* therefore becomes sinless life, life completely
realizing the ideal, with no *thanatos*, no death. That is what
Jesus meant when He said, " He that believeth on Me . . .
shall never die." Thus Christianity has taken hold of the
word which is of the simplest in its original intention, and
filled it with sublimity. We enter into life that has no
antithesis in death, that is, eternal life. We enter into that
when we are convinced that Jesus is the Christ, the Son of
God ; and when we answer our conviction by trusting everything that is suggested by that, trusting the great and eternal
implicates that are there.

Thus we have considered the writer's account of his book,
and so are prepared to study it in harmony with its declared
purpose.

The Thesis. i. 1, 14, 18.

HAVING considered the writer's account of his book as
found in his foot-note in verses thirty and thirty-one of chapter
twenty, we turn to the systematic writing, which begins at
i. 1, and runs to xx. 29. In it there are two movements, first
a summary, or summation, or summing up, in the first eighteen
verses of chapter one. We usually call it the prologue. I am
not quarrelling with that word, provided that we do not
think prologue means preface. It is far more than a preface.
In these eighteen verses we have an explanation of everything

that follows from the nineteenth verse of chapter one, to the twenty-ninth verse of chapter twenty. All that follows is intended to prove the accuracy of the things declared in the first eighteen verses. Possibly John wrote those eighteen verses last. Having made his selection of signs, and written them, he made a summary, writing it last. On the other hand, of course, he may have written his summary first, and then the things that proved it. Whether the summation was written first or last, it is a summation ; everything is found in those first eighteen verses. The whole truth, as John saw it, concerning " Jesus Christ the Son of God," is found in these first eighteen verses.

So, I say, we have two movements in the system ; a summary, summation, or summing up of everything. That constitutes the thesis of John. He states his thesis in what we now call the prologue. Then, having stated his thesis, from verse nineteen of chapter one, to the twenty-ninth verse of chapter twenty, he gives the selection of signs, which prove the accuracy of the things stated in the summary.

In this statement of thesis there are two parts ; first the essential declarations which are found in verses one, fourteen, and eighteen ; then certain statements which are parenthetical. In verse fourteen, the King James and English and American translators have put certain words in brackets. They have done so because the words so enclosed do constitute a statement interpolated upon the main movement. But that applies equally to all that is found in verses two to thirteen, and again in verses fifteen to seventeen. Thus there are three parentheses.

This is the structure of the prologue. A statement is made, verse one. That statement is illustrated by a parenthesis, verses two to thirteen. A second statement is made, verse fourteen, and in the middle of it there is a second parenthesis of illumination. This is followed by a third parenthesis of illustration, verses fifteen to seventeen. Finally a third statement is made, verse eighteen.

We are now dealing with the essential declarations of verses

[18]

one, fourteen, and eighteen. In verse one we have three statements. In verse fourteen we have three statements. In
verse eighteen we have two statements.

Let us set out the statements in verse one :

> " In the beginning was the Word ; "
> " And the Word was with God : "
> " And the Word was God."

There are also three statements in verse fourteen. They
are not so clearly marked. The first statement in verse
fourteen is clearly made. The second is made, but the subject
of the sentence is not named ; it is understood. The third
statement is a phrase only, but with subject and predicate
understood. Supplying the subject in the second case ; and
subject and predicate in the third, let us set out these
statements :

" The Word became flesh ; "
" And (the Word) dwelt among us ; "
" (And the Word was) full of grace and truth."

In the eighteenth verse there are two statements. Let us
set these in order :

" No man hath seen God at any time ; "
" The only begotten Son, Who is in the bosom of the
    Father, He hath declared Him."

Now let us observe that the three statements in verse one,
and the three statements in verse fourteen are closely related.
This will be seen if we read them alternately. That is to
say, instead of reading verses one and fourteen straight
through in each case, we will read the first statement in one,
and then the first statement in fourteen, and so on through.

> " In the beginning was the Word."
> " And the Word became flesh."
>
> " And the Word was with God ; "
> " And the Word dwelt among us."
>
> " And the Word was God : "
> " Full of grace and truth."

Then in verse eighteen we have two declarations. Of these, the first belongs to verse one ; and the second belongs to verse fourteen. Once more let us set them out :

"In the beginning was the Word, and the Word was with
    God, and the Word was God."
"No man hath seen God at any time."
"And the Word became flesh, and pitched His tent among
    us . . . full of grace and truth."
"The only begotten Son, Who is in the bosom of the Father,
    He hath declared Him."

Now let us take the statements of verse one.

    "In the beginning was the Word,"
    "And the Word was with God,"
    "And the Word was God."

So much has been written about that verse that it seems almost unnecessary to stay to say very much about it. There are, however, some general facts which should be recognized.

If we had those three statements only, apart from their connection with all that follows, there are two things of which we should be conscious ; first that of the truth of the ideas ; and secondly that they are inexplicable. That is a paradoxical statement, but none the less true.

Glance at the three statements in themselves. First we have a noun that arrests us, "The Word." This is coupled with a verb which does not arrest us in our English translations, but it does arrest us at once in the Greek, not in the essence of the verb, but in the tense employed.

We begin with the noun, "the Word." What is meant by that ? In the realm of Greek philosophy the term ὁ *logos*, was very familiar. While that is true, I do not personally believe it explains John's use of the term. I do not believe that John was influenced by Greek philosophy when he employed it. He was influenced rather by Hebrew philosophy, which is a very important distinction. I recommend to every student, Dr. Burney's book, *The Aramaic Origin of the*

Fourth Gospel. I do not agree with Dr. Burney in some points, but he has established, without dispute, that the Gospel of John in its thinking is Aramaic, not Greek; and his findings are that the book must have been the work of a Palestinian Jew; and that he could not have written it later than A.D. 75. Thus he maintains that the thinking of the writer is Hebrew. When John used the Greek term ὁ *logos*, unquestionably he would do so in the Hebrew sense as found in the Hebrew word *Memra*. The term would have the Greek significance, qualified by Hebrew philosophy.

What then did the Greek mean by it? It referred to the whole realm of thought, the abstract conception lying at the back of everything concrete. Perhaps the idea may be expressed in the word Wisdom. The Greek philosopher recognized wisdom as antedating all works, noumena as preceding phenomena.

The Hebrew philosopher said, Things postulate thought. Wherever there is a thing, it proves a thought. The thing is the outcome of the thought. The Hebrew philosopher went further, and said, If things postulate thought, thought postulates a thinker. The Greek philosopher did not go so far as that. The Greek philosopher said, Behind all things there must be thought, but the thought is abstract. The Hebrew philosopher said; You cannot have an abstract thought unless you have a thinker. Therefore the Hebrew philosopher said, "The fear of God is the beginning of wisdom." The Hebrew philosopher said there is no unsolved problem of the universe finally. It is solved in the mind of the Thinker. "In the beginning God created the heavens and the earth." The Thinker, God; the thought therefore; and then the thing as the result of His thought and His action. So much for the noun.

Now look at the verb. "In the beginning *was* the Word, and the Word *was* with God, and the Word *was* God." Now that, as I have said, is not arresting to us, because our language is not inflected as is the Greek language. The tense in Greek

in every case is the imperfect tense, and the imperfect tense
suggests not something past, or something present, or something future; but something continuous. The word " was "
there suggests a continuous state. " In the beginning *was*
the Word," a continuous fact; " and the Word *was* with
God " continuously; " and the Word *was* God " constantly.
The imperfect tense thus described an age existence which
cannot be measured by what we call time. Time is merely
the marking off of eternity, to help finite beings until they
reach the glory of eternity. The verb as here employed,
takes us into the realm of the timeless. " In the beginning
was the Word," Wisdom postulated as existing. " And the
Word was with God "; Wisdom vested in a Personality, if
I may use the word; only as we use it, do not let us think of
ourselves, but think of Infinite Personality. Personality as
I think of it in the realm of the human, is limited. Again,
" the Word was God "; or to translate in the Greek idiom,
" God was the Word." That is to say that the nature of the
wisdom, was the nature of the Personality, in Whom all
wisdom was found.

Let it at once be admitted that while in some senses these
statements are self-evident truths, they nevertheless are
finally inexplicable. The one quantity is inexplicable; and
therefore all the statements are also inexplicable. The one
Quantity is God. We cannot explain God; consequently
His thought is a mystery; it is beyond us; and the fact of
it being with Him is necessary, but inexplicable.

Glance on for a moment to verse eighteen. " No man
hath seen God at any time." That is as far as philosophy
can go, whether Greek or Hebrew. A recognition of Wisdom,
and of personality; of the thought and the Thinker, and no
more. " No man hath seen God at any time." That is as
far as verse one takes us. But how far is that? The fact of
existence, " In the beginning was the Word "; the law of
existence, " the Word was with God "; the nature of
existence, " God was the Word." All is still in the realm of
the abstract. Yet here the Hebrew philosopher transcends

Greek philosophy, which never rose to the height of affirming the personality of God.

So we pass to verse fourteen. Again notice the noun and the verb. The same noun is here : " the Word." But the verb is different, not " was," but " became." The word refers, not to the beginning of something new, but to that which already had existence, as it became new in manifestation. " The Word *became*," that is one verb. There is another. " Dwelt," literally, pitched a tent.

Whatever is meant in the first verse by the noun " The Word," is meant in the fourteenth. But here are new verbs, no longer marking the continuity that defies all thinking in terms of past, present, and future ; but declaring that something happened, something new, something fresh. " The Word became," and that same Word " dwelt."

Now take the statements, " The Word became flesh." The word " flesh " is used to cover the whole fact of human nature. Having become flesh, the Word pitched His tent among us, dwelt among us. And then merely a phrase, revealing the things that were seen when that thing happened, that new thing happened, " full of grace and truth."

Once again, mark the relationship between verses one and fourteen. " In the beginning was the Word," existence ; " the Word became flesh," a new form of existence ; a new form, not a new existence, but a new form of the same existence. Writing to the Philippians Paul said : " Have this mind in you, which was also in Christ Jesus ; Who, existing in the form of God, counted not the being on an equality with God a prize to be snatched, and held for His own enrichment, but emptied Himself," of what ? Of His Deity ? No, but of one form of manifestation. " Emptied Himself, taking the form of a servant " ;—a new form,— " made in the likeness of men." " The Word became flesh," a new beginning. " In the beginning was the Word "— timeless existence. " The Word became flesh," a new form of existence.

Again, " The Word was with God." In this new form of

[23]

existence, He " pitched His tent among us." Who? The same One. So the things we could not see, we began to see ; and the things we could not know, we began to know ; the things we had never heard with clearness of enunciation, were now finding utterance.

Finally John summarized all he saw through that new manifestation, " full of grace and truth."

That is Christianity in a flash ; and nothing else than that is Christianity. If men try to build up Christianity on an examination of the Man Jesus, they fail. Christianity takes hold of Hebrew philosophy, accepts its accuracy, but declares a new fact in the economy of God, that carries us much further than Hebrew philosophy ever did. " The Word became flesh, pitched His tent among us, . . . full of grace and truth." " The only begotten Son, Who is in the bosom of the Father, He hath declared Him." That is what Christianity is in its sum totality ; it is the revelation of that which was undiscoverable, in order to apprehension and obedience.

So we come to the last statements. " No man hath seen God at any time," or more literally, " No man hath ever yet seen God." But now, " the only begotten Son Who is in the bosom of the Father, He hath declared Him." Many very ancient authorities read, instead of " the only begotten Son," " God only begotten." No man can be dogmatic as to which John wrote, because some old manuscripts read one way, and others the other. It does not matter, because " begotten " marks Sonship and relationship ; and the idea is the same whichever form John may have written. The Son of God means One sharing the nature. He hath declared Him.

But how ? " The Word became flesh," and that becoming flesh was the method of declaring God. Now observe something peculiar and arresting. John wrote, " The only begotten Son Who is in the bosom of the Father." That phrase, " Who is in the bosom of the Father " marks limitation. It declares that what the Son has revealed of the Father has to do with that which is represented by that most beautiful and tender expression, " the bosom of the Father." The revelation He came to make, is the revelation of the heart of God. He did not come to reveal the wisdom and the might and the majesty of God. These things are revealed in Nature, although we have never understood them in their fulness. These things are not possible of apprehension yet. We have eternity to investigate them. But Jesus came to speak from the heart of God. He hath revealed Him from the bosom of the Father. In that sense it is a limiting expression. It is illimitable, because who can measure or fathom the heart of God ; but it is from the bosom of the Father He hath spoken.

Here John employs a revealing verb, " He hath declared Him." " Declared " is a beautiful word. In some senses we cannot improve upon it for the common understanding of ordinary men and women ; but if I take the Greek verb, and instead of translating, transliterate it, it reads, " The only begotten Son Who is in the bosom of the Father, He hath exegeted Him." What is exegesis ? The word means bringing out from into visibility ; to bring forth authoritatively into visibility. Exegesis is the authoritative bringing forth into visibility of that which was there all the time, but which was not seen until so brought forth.

Jesus is the Exegesis of God. He is the One through Whom there is brought forth authoritatively into visibility the things men had not seen. " No man hath seen God at any time ; the only begotten Son Who is in the bosom of the Father, He hath exegeted Him."

That is John's summary. John, who, according to the records, in the days of the flesh of our blessed Lord, laid his head on His bosom. When he did so, he was conscious not merely of the beating of a human heart, but distinguished the reverberations of the eternal compassion.

The Parentheses. i. 2-13, 14b, 15-17.

WE now turn to the parentheses in the summary of the first eighteen verses. The first is found in verses two to thirteen. In verse fourteen certain words are in brackets. They constitute the second. Then in verses fifteen to seventeen we have the third.

In the first parenthesis, having written the first facts about the Word, " In the beginning was the Word, and the Word was with God, and God was the Word," or " and the Word was God," beginning with the words, " The same was in the beginning with God," the writer turned aside to show the relationship of the Word to two creations.

In the middle of verse fourteen we find an interpolated exclamation, " And we beheld His glory, glory as of the Only begotten from the Father." That parenthesis summarizes what John and the rest of them saw.

In the third parenthesis, verses fifteen to seventeen, we have the testimony of two witnesses ; first that of John the herald ; and then that of the writer, John the apostle ; John, the Hebrew prophet, the last voice of the old economy ; and John, the Christian apostle, the first voice of the new.

To summarize yet more briefly. Three parentheses. Number one, the Word and two creations ; Number two, the Word as it was beheld ; Number three, the Word and two witnesses.

In the first parenthesis there are two movements. The first of these deals with the relation of the Word to the first creation (verses two to five) ; while the second deals with the relation of the Word to a new creation (verses six to thirteen).

As to the first creation. Here the writer surveyed the stream of history from the beginning, as recorded in Genesis, to the moment of writing. In doing so he referred to original creation. Of that, he wrote, " The same was in the beginning with God." " The same," that is the One to Whom he has already referred as " the Word." The first declarations moved in the realm of the abstract, and may be impersonal. Now " the same," or more literally, " this One," was " in the beginning with God," brings the consideration into the realm of the personal.

The Greek preposition rendered " with " in verse one, and

in verse two, is arresting. It is the preposition *pros*. It is not *meta* ; it is not *sun* ; it is not *para*. All these can be translated in our language accurately by the one preposition *with*. Yet there is a distinction between them. *Meta* means "in the midst of," or "after." *Sun* means "in closest association." *Para* means "by the side of." *Pros* suggests not merely nearness, but a processional nearness, and united activity. He was with God, that is, facing God ; and the suggestion is that of facing Him, in a perpetual approach of nearness, and co-operation of activity ; facing God, approaching God, acting *with* God.

That was the relationship of the Word with God in original creation. So, "All things were made through Him." The word *panta*, rendered "all things" means exactly that, but recognizes things separately, not only sum totality, but each thing separately. All "were made through Him." That is to say, the Word was the Agent of God's action, through Whom all things came into being.

But there is more to say. "And without Him," that is, "apart from Him was not anything made that hath been made." This declares that processional creation has also been through Him. Originally, through Him all was caused to be ; and without Him there has been no progress or development.

This is the same truth as declared by Paul in his letter to the Colossians, "In Him were all things created in the heavens and upon the earth, . . . and in Him all things consist." That which was from the beginning, with God, and of the very nature of God, is the One through Whom God acted, and still acts ; through Whom everything was originally created ; and processionally, nothing further has appeared, except through Him.

Proceeding, the writer now makes a summarizing declaration, and recognizes a distinction. The summarizing declaration is contained in the words, "In Him was life." What life ? All life. What do we know about life ? We recognize the fact of life. It may be that of an arch-angel or a butterfly. In that inclusive sense the declaration is made, " In Him was life " ; He is the Fountain-Head of life ; all life is from Him.

Then a distinction is recognized. " And the life was the light of men." Life everywhere, super-abundant life, life infinite, mysterious ; but in man, life became light. Man, as distinguished from everything beneath him in the earthly creation, has this element of light. Man is the first, and the only one who, being created, understands ; who can look back into the face of God and commune with Him. Humanity is seen as thus distinguished from everything beneath it in all the realm, or scale, if you like, of life. " The life was the light of men."

Then follows a brief, but arresting declaration. " And the light shineth in the darkness." Darkness, only a word ; but a word recognizing all human failure. In writing of the great conflict of the soldier saints of Jesus, Paul referred to " the age-rulers of this darkness." That is how Paul saw the world. So did John. He saw that darkness persisting through all human history. But he says, " The light shineth in the darkness, and the darkness apprehended it not." The word " apprehended " as we now use it, might mean " understood." But that is not the thought of the writer. It is rather that the darkness has never extinguished the light. It is everywhere, but men have not walked in it. This is not ancient history only, it is true to-day. The light is everywhere, but men are walking in darkness, not obedient to that light. The human consciousness is universal in recognizing a distinction between right and wrong. That is the shining of a light. We read in the Wisdom literature, " The spirit of man is the lamp of the Lord." Not the Spirit of God, but the spirit of man, is the lamp of the Lord. In that spirit nature of man the consciousness exists of the distinction between right and wrong. That light the darkness has never extinguished. Whether men obey it or not is another question.

Having thus dealt with the relation of the Word to the first creation, John turns to another matter, breaking in with the words, " There came a man." He is still viewing the stream of history. In that stream, " There came a man, sent from God, whose name was John. The same came for witness, that he might bear witness of the light, that all might believe through Him. He was not the light, but came that he might bear witness of the light."

This marks a new departure. It began with prophetic foretelling. " There was a man, whose name was John " ; and he came, not to bring some new message, but to talk to men of that which was already with them, the light. This man was not the light, he was bearing witness to it. " There was the true light, even the light which lighteth every man, coming into the world." This is the second creation. The Light that lighteth every man, was coming into the world, was coming into observation, was coming into focussed visibility.

The phrase, " coming into the world," may refer to the word " light," or the word " man." It can mean either grammatically. It can mean, There was the Light which lighteth every man who comes into the world ; or it may mean that the Light that lighteth every man, was coming into the world. The whole movement of the thought here gives little room for doubt that the reference is to the fact that the Light was now coming into the world. It recognizes that there is a light lightening every man ; but the emphasis here is upon the fact that this Light was now entering human history in a new way. A new beginning was being made ; a new creation was taking place.

Then the writer looks back, and looks around. " He was in the world." There was a sense in which He was in every man. " The world was made through Him," and yet " the world knew Him not." Then " The Word became flesh," so " He came unto His own." The Greek there is neuter, and we are sometimes told that it means that He came to His own country, Palestine. I think it has a wider meaning. He came into His own world. Then " they that were His own received Him not." There the reference is to men, not Jews only, but the men of His creation. That is the story of His coming, and of His rejection.

But that is not all. "But as many as received Him, to them gave He the right," the authority, "to become children of God." Here we may pause for a moment with a technicality, upon which no man can be dogmatic. The question has to do with the words, "who were born." Some manuscripts read "who was born." The question is, does that passage mean that the people who believed on Him, were born; or does it mean that He was born, not of blood, nor of the will of the flesh, but of God. It is an open question. Dr. Burney in his book, *The Aramaic Origin of the Fourth Gospel*, argues that it should be "Who was born," referring to the Word; and he says, moreover, that there is to be found John's recognition of the Virgin birth. He gave authority to those who believe on Him, to become children of God. Who did? He Who was born,—mark the words very carefully,—not by the will of the flesh, not of the will of man, but of God.

Take it either way, the main thought is not interfered with. Here is a new beginning. The light that was in every man, which darkness could not put out, came into the world; and when He came, they that were His own did not receive Him. The world that was His own, did not recognize Him, and those that should have received Him did not. But He started a new creation, and to everyone who did receive Him, who did believe on His name, He gave the authority, the right, to become children of God; and, either He Who did so, was the One born Himself, not by the will of man, nor by the will of the flesh, but of God; or those who from Him received that right, were so born. This is the relationship of the Word to the second creation.

In the parenthesis of verse fourteen, John says, "We beheld His glory." The Word . . . pitched His tent amongst us, and "we beheld." The Greek word means we inspected, we saw completely. What was seen was "Glory, as of an only begotten Son of a Father." The Greek preposition here is para, " an only begotten Son WITH a Father," the thought is that of the perfect fellowship of being between the Father and the Son.

Then in a phrase he described that glory,—" Full of grace and truth." In the signs recorded presently in the realm of works, John begins with the turning of water into wine at Cana. That was the glory of God in creation. The last sign he records is that of the raising of Lazarus from the dead. That was the glory of God in restoration. It was the glory of God that shined, when the water blushed into the fruit of the vine. It was the glory of God that was seen, when the body of the dead was reanimated, and came forth restored to strength and activity.

So we pass to the last of the parentheses, verses fifteen to seventeen. " John," that is the herald, " beareth witness of Him, and crieth, saying, This was He of Whom I said, He that cometh after me is become before me ; for He was before me." That is the last word of the old economy. It declared that the Word made flesh, takes precedence in rank, because of eternal precedence. On a later day Jesus Himself said, " Before Abraham was, I am."

Then follows the first word of the new, the witness of the new. John the apostle says, " For of His fulness we all received, and grace for grace. For the law was given through Moses ; grace and truth came through Jesus Christ." Literally, out of the fulness of Him we all received, and grace for grace ; grace in the place of grace, grace succeeding grace.

The first dispensation was of His grace, but the measure was not complete. The law was given through Moses. It was temporary. Now " Grace and truth came through Jesus Christ." The idea of that is not that grace and truth supersede law, except as the law was a temporary application of truth ; and not the final enunciation of it. This passage is often quoted as though it drew a distinction between Law and Grace in essence. As a matter of fact it does not do so ; but it does draw a distinction between them in method. The Law was an expression of Grace, temporary, transient, fitting the need of the time. Every provision of it was a requirement in the interest of man, and inspired by the love, that is the grace of the heart of God. It was given through Moses.

Now that same grace in union with truth came through Jesus Christ. All the requirements of the Law are lifted on to a higher level of interpretation through the Incarnation, both in a moral code, and in the interpretation of human realization. But now the grace which inspired law has come into visibility of action which brings to man a new ennoblement, by way of the cleansing of the nature, and a new birth.

Thus we have three parentheses. " In the beginning was the Word, and the Word was with God, and the Word was God." That Word was related to the first creation, originating ; and processionally continuing, the very Fountain-Head of life, which in man was light. That Word is related to a new beginning. There came a man from God named John, bearing witness to light ; and there was the Light, coming into the world. For those who received Him He established a new creation. Those who receive Him, become the children of God. As He tabernacled in flesh, " we beheld His glory."

Two witnesses speak, John the herald, the last of the Hebrew line ; John the apostle, the messenger of the new. The old came out of the Older, for " in the beginning " before Law, " The Word was with God." Now that Word—the Original in every way—has " become flesh " ; He is the One Who was " before John," and so the New is related to the Eternal.

Now that the Original has come in a new way, the one who was related to the period of the Law, and the herald of the New retires ; and the apostle of the New bears his testimony.

John i. 19-34.

WE have considered the great summarizing declarations ; and the illuminating parentheses, dealing successively, with the relation of the Word to two creations ; the fact of what men saw, glory as of the Only-begotten of the Father ; and the testimony of two witnesses, John the herald, the last of the old economy, retiring ; and John the evangelist, the representative of the new, advancing.

We now begin the main section of the writing. The book consists, as we saw in our first meditation on the writer's foot-note (xx. 30, 31), of a selection of signs from the life and the ministry of our Lord. We now commence a consideration of those signs. As we proceed, we shall find eight in the realm of works, and eight in the realm of words. The present paragraph is introductory. In it no sign is recorded.

At this point it is important that we call to mind the course and method of the public ministry of our Lord. It was divided quite clearly into three periods. That has always been recognized. The three periods have been often described geographically ; as the Judæan ministry, the Galilean ministry, and the Peræan ministry. Now whereas that may be permissible, it is not strictly accurate, because in the first period He was not wholly in Judæa, He was sometimes in Galilee ; and in the second period He was not wholly in Galilee, He was also in Judæa ; and in the third period He was not wholly in Peræa, He was occasionally also in Judaea and Galilee. A better division is this. He commenced His ministry at His baptism. That was the hour of His dedication to Messianic work and consecration therefor, as the Spirit fell on Him. That first period of ministry lasted until the imprisonment of John. When John was put in prison He began the second period. Matthew, Mark, and Luke tell us nothing about the first period. They all begin the story of the ministry of Jesus when John was put in prison. Unquestionably that was a crisis, upon which our Lord entered upon a new period. The second period then lasted from the imprisonment of John to the hour at Cæsarea Philippi, when Simon Peter made his great confession. After that confession the third period commenced, which lasted about six months. As a rule it is said that the public ministry

c   [33]

of our Lord lasted for three years. I am personally convinced that it lasted three and a half years, but it is not worth debating. The first period lasted a year, and it was a quiet year comparatively, in which Jesus alternated between Jerusalem and Galilee. Then John was put in prison, and Jesus immediately went into Galilee, and began quite clearly what was intentionally a public ministry of definite propaganda, intending to draw attention to Himself and His message, as He had not done until that time. When the voice of the herald was silenced, the Lord at once invaded the tetrarchy of the man who had put him in prison, Herod; and caught up and carried on the great message, beginning exactly as John had begun, " Repent, for the Kingdom of heaven is at hand." Then followed the second period, a crowded period, in which we may say His fame grew and increased by leaps and bounds.

Then came the next dividing line when He said to His disciples at Cæsarea Philippi, Who do men say that I am? thus raising His test question. They reported the best things they had heard said concerning Him. Then He made the question personal to them : Who do you say that I am? One of their number, as I always believe expressing the conviction of the rest, made the great confession. Then, says Matthew, " From that time began Jesus to show them that He must suffer, and be killed, and be raised." He had never told them that before explicitly. The last period of six months was still crowded, but the shadow of the Cross was upon them; and as we follow through we see that He was devoting Himself very largely to His own disciples, preparing them for the Cross.

Thus we have the three divisions. The first year, a quiet year, alternating between Jerusalem and Galilee. The next two years crowded years, during which His fame was increasing. The last six months still crowded, largely spent over Jordan in Peræa; and all the way shadowed by the Cross.

Now with that in mind, it is well to notice that John selected his signs mainly from the first period and the last

period. The first five chapters of John have all to do with
the quiet year. Apart from them we should have had no
details of the year between His baptism and the imprisonment
of John the Baptist. Only John gives us incidents, and five
chapters are occupied with happenings during that first period.

Of the crowded two years, so fully accounted for in Matthew,
John gives us only glimpses. Chapter six is the only chapter
that deals with that period. I am not accounting for the
reason of this method, but it may at least be suggested that
John had read Matthew's Gospel, and knew the record was
there of that central period. From chapter seven to the
end, we have the record of things that happened after
Cæsarea Philippi.

We now consider the account of certain preliminary matters
of great significance and importance, those namely of the
witness of the herald ; and the introduction of Jesus in
Person, and His identification by His herald.

Observe in the first place, how John the evangelist, the
writer, plunges in at that nineteenth verse, " And this is the
witness of John." We glance back to verse six, in this same
chapter, and there we read, " There came a man, sent from
God, whose name was John. The same came for witness,
that he might bear witness of the light." Now in verse
nineteen : " And this is the witness of John." Thus he
starts in upon this main section with an introduction which
assumes knowledge concerning John which has already been
written, " a man sent from God " to " bear witness " ; and
" this is the witness."

He records the witness in a very remarkable way. The
witness was given in answer to enquiries, " When the Jews
sent unto him from Jerusalem priests and Levites to ask
him." That is the only occasion where we find that phrase
in the New Testament, the two orders named together,
" priests and Levites." Such were sent from Jerusalem to
ask John, Who are you ? In verse twenty-four we are told
" they had been sent from the Pharisees." John had been
exercising his ministry for a long time, and it was a ministry

that had startled the country-side.   All Judæa had gone
out to listen to him.   Even king Herod had sought him, and
had had conversations with him, and had very nearly entered
into the Kingdom of God ; for it is said that at one time
"Herod heard him gladly."   It had been a marvellous
ministry, but quite evidently the authorities in Jerusalem
were becoming concerned about it, and whereunto it tended,
and who this man really was, who he was officially, who he
really claimed to be.   They sent down a remarkable deputation of those who were priests in the full order, and those
who were Levites, waiting upon their courses in the services
of the Temple.   They sent down a deputation to ask this man
the real meaning of his own ministry.   It may have been
perfectly sincere, or not.   John simply records the fact.
When they came and asked him, " he confessed, and denied
not ; and he confessed, I am not the Christ."   They did not
ask him in so many words if he was the Christ.   They said,
Who are you ?   But John knew what most evidently they were
debating, as to whether, peradventure he was the Messiah,
or wondering whether he claimed to be Messiah.

His answers were first negative and then positive.   His
first negative answer was, " I am not the Christ."   Very
well then, they said, " What then ?   Art thou Elijah ?   And
he saith, I am not."   And then they said, " Art thou the
prophet ?   And he answered, No."   It is interesting how
his answers became shorter in each case.   " I am not the
Christ . . I am not, ... No."

These men were intelligent ; they were sent by the
Pharisees, trained in the lore of their own religion.   They
began by suggesting Art thou the Christ ?   The reply was
clear, " I am not the Christ."   Then they went back to
Malachi, and they said Malachi said that before the Christ
comes, Elijah would come again.   Are you Elijah ?   He said,
I am not.   Then they went back further.   They went to
Moses, and said, " Art thou the prophet ? "   The interpretation of that question is found in Deuteronomy, eighteenth
chapter, fifteenth verse.   Moses had said that God should one

day raise up a prophet like unto him. These men were employing their own Scriptures. Art thou the Messiah? Art
thou Elijah? Well then, art thou the prophet? Every time
the answer was a denial. Then they said, "Who art thou?
that we may give an answer to them that sent us." We cannot go back with negatives. Tell us, "Who art thou? What
sayest thou of thyself?"

Now his reply was very suggestive. Its implicates were
that they had knowledge of their own Scriptures; they had
the Messianic hope; they were familiar with Malachi; and
they knew the prediction of Moses. So he took them to the
great central prophecy of Isaiah; "I am the voice of one
crying in the wilderness, Make straight the way of the Lord,
as said Isaiah the prophet."

Then these men did what men often do when they are
surprised. They raised a ritualistic technicality. They said,
"Why then baptizest thou, if thou art not the Christ, neither
Elijah, neither the prophet?" In reply he interpreted his
mission. "I baptize in water." That is all. They knew what
his baptism in water had meant. They knew what had
preceded it, in his preaching, and what baptism in water at
his hands had signified. He had called them to repent and
be baptized unto the remission of sins; repentance, the
confession of guilt, and baptism, a sign of the need for
remission.

Then he said this amazing thing. "In the midst of you
standeth One Whom ye know not." I think that statement
must be taken quite literally. John knew Jesus was standing
in the crowd that day. Why he did not identify Him that
day I cannot tell. I have no doubt there was some reason.
But he did definitely declare, "In the midst of you standeth
One Whom ye know not, even He that cometh after me, the
latchet of Whose shoe I am not worthy to unloose."

That was the witness of John. I am not the Christ; I am
not Elijah; I am not the prophet; I am the voice, crying in
the wilderness, Prepare ye the way of the Lord; and in your
midst is the One Whose way I am preparing by the uttering

of my voice. He did not then declare what the mission of Jesus was to be. He did not identify Him that day, but affirmed that He was already come, that He was there, undiscovered.

Then, " On the morrow "—mark it carefully. The next day, " he seeth Jesus coming unto him, and saith." Let us remember that these things took place about six weeks after the baptism. When Jesus had been baptized, John had seen the Holy Spirit descending upon Him ; and by that sign had known that He was Messiah. He had not known before. He said he did not know Who the Messiah was, but a sign had been given to him, unquestionably in his communion with God, that upon Whom he should see the Spirit descend, that was He. Now, he said, I have seen it ; I have seen the Spirit descend on Him. In that hour he knew what he did not know before, that Jesus was the Messiah. Between that sign given and these events, Jesus had been into the wilderness, tempted for forty days. Now He had returned. Allowing for the journey to the wilderness and the journey back, six weeks had elapsed. Now Jesus was in the midst of the crowd. On the day of the deputation John saw Him, but did not identify Him.

Now mark the significance of " on the morrow." He saw Jesus coming to him. How are we to interpret that ? I think there can only be one answer, that Jesus was approaching him in order to be publicly identified. Be that as it may, John saw Him approaching, and as He came, he said, " Behold, the Lamb of God, which taketh away the sin of the world."

It was a most remarkable identification in the light of John's previous ministry. I am not undervaluing John's earlier ministry. I am not suggesting that it was in any sense invalidated ; but there was a tremendous change. In all the record of the ministry of John to that point we find nothing like that. That was a new note. He had said He would come with the fan, with the fire, with the axe. He had declared that He was coming to burn up all chaff, and garner wheat ; that He was coming to lower mountains and exalt valleys. Every phrase was suggestive of His coming in majesty and in power ; and it was all true. But something had happened ; and when Jesus was identified, he did not say, Behold, the Man of the fan, and of the fire, and of the axe. He said, " Behold, the Lamb of God, which taketh away the sin of the world." So far as my reading and understanding of the narrative goes, I am quite sure that that conception and vision had broken upon him six weeks before, and had come now to maturity, because of the pondering of those six weeks. Six weeks before, Jesus came to be baptized. John did not know Who He was, but he hesitated about baptizing Him, because though he did not know He was Messiah, he was conscious of His sinlessness. There was no room for John's baptism in His life. Then Jesus had said, " Suffer it to be so now, for thus," *thus* by the very thing from which you are shrinking, the Sinless taking the place of the sinful, by My being numbered with transgressors, " *thus* it becometh us to fulfil all righteousness."

Now six weeks had gone, and when the great herald identified Him, he did it in those words, " Behold, the Lamb of God, which taketh away the sin of the world." Then he gave his proof. " I have beheld the Spirit falling upon Him." That was his reference to the baptism of Jesus.

Then he declared His mission. The day before he had said, " I baptize you with water." Now he said, He " baptizeth with the Holy Spirit." Thus in connection with his identification of Jesus, John revealed the character of His mission. He introduced Him, identified Him, pointed Him out as " the Lamb of God which taketh away the sin of the world," and as the One Who baptized with the Holy Spirit. Thus all the evangelical values were revealed. The twofold mission of the Messiah was that of the taking away of sin, a cleansing process ; and baptizing with the Spirit, an enabling process.

We take a step further. " Again on the morrow," another day, " John was standing, and two of his disciples ; and he looked upon Jesus as He walked." On the day of identification it is distinctly stated that Jesus was approaching John, and he identified Him. On the next day John was talking to two of his disciples, I think undoubtedly in the early hours of the morning. He was not in public, but in private. The crowds were not round about him. He was with two of his own disciples, talking. Inevitably they were talking about what had happened yesterday. Andrew was one, and shall I say without argument, John the writer was the other. Two in the inner circle, two who had heard his message and obeyed it, and had enrolled themselves as being with him. They had heard him say yesterday, " Behold, the Lamb of God," about Jesus ; a Person whom they had known almost surely, though perhaps not intimately, though John after the flesh was related to Him. They had heard the herald declare that He was the Lamb of God. As they talked of these matters, John saw Jesus walking, not towards him, but passing on His way. Then John once more cried, not the full declaration, but an indication of identity, as he said, " Behold, the Lamb of God." In effect he said, There He is. In that moment the two broke with John, and went after Jesus ; and the public ministry of gathering has begun.

The central things that are revealed in these preliminary matters are the words in which John denied that he was Messiah or Elijah or the prophet ; and declared his office, that of " the voice " ; together with his revelation of the two aspects of the Messianic mission of Jesus, those of bearing sin, and baptizing with the Spirit.

John i. 35—ii. 12.

OUR previous meditation was concerned with those preliminary matters ; the witness of the herald, when the deputation came from Jerusalem to enquire as to who he was ; and then his public identification of Jesus as the Messiah. We ran over a little into this paragraph because of its references to the day after the public identification, when John was standing with two of his disciples, and Jesus passed by ; and as He passed, walking evidently on His way, John said—not I think, to the disciples, but so that they heard him,—" Behold, the Lamb of God," the One Whom he had identified in full description on the previous day in the words, " Behold, the Lamb of God, Which taketh away the sin of the world."

So that we come now to the third day in a series. The first day was the day of the coming of the deputation, when John declared, " There standeth One Whom ye know not," but did not identify Him. On the next day came the identification to which we have referred. Now we reach the day following that, when John said, " Behold, the Lamb of God."

That takes us back to the two things he had said about Him on the previous day ; one already twice quoted, " Behold, the Lamb of God that taketh away the sin of the world " ; and the other, " The same is He that baptizeth in the Holy Spirit." Thus He had been described as the Sin-Bearer, and the Spirit-Baptizer.

Now Jesus was seen walking, starting on the pathway of His public ministry ; and we have the story of the first group of disciples gathered to the Messiah ; followed by an account of the first sign, as John names it, the sign at Cana.

With regard to the gathering of this first group of disciples, let us consider two things ; first, the men that were gathered to Him as He began His mighty ministry ; and secondly, how He dealt with them.

As to the men, we take them in rapid survey. They are Andrew and another—and I am going to assume that the other was John, the writer of the Gospel,—then Simon, the brother of Andrew ; and although it is not recorded here, I believe that we may put James in the group. The way the story of Andrew's finding of Simon is told at least suggests that—" He findeth first his own brother Simon." A slight alteration in phrasing gives the thought as I understand it, " He first findeth his own brother." Not, He findeth his own

[41]

BRITISH ISLES NAZARENE LIBRARY COLLEGE

brother first, implying that he was after someone else afterwards. But that he was the first to find his own brother ;
the implicate being that the other man also found his brother.
I have no doubt personally that John found James then.
It seems so natural and beautiful a thing to do. Then Simon
was named, and then Philip. From the standpoint of earthly
position, not a single man of these was of any great note.
I do not know much about Nathanael as to what his position
in the world was. Yet what variety in a little compass.

Andrew. All we know about Andrew is that upon three
occasions he was found introducing someone to Jesus. His
own brother first ; and then a little later on, a lad who had
some supplies, when all the apostles were devoid of them.
And then the occasion when after consultation with Philip,
he came to Jesus with the Greeks. That is how we see Andrew.
If I had to paint his portrait, I would paint the portrait of a
rugged and strong soul. He is the patron saint of Scotland !
I would paint him so ; not dour, for he was not that, but
rugged and strong ; the sort of man who cared for his brother,
and brought him to Jesus. It is good to remember that this
brother was the man who, on the Day of Pentecost, Andrew
heard preach, and lead three thousand into the Kingdom.
How many brothers there have been of that sort. Andrew
was cautious. That is seen in this story. When Jesus said,
What seekest thou ? Andrew said in effect, Nay then, but
where do you live ? He was a man who could not talk easily
out there on the highway. He had to have a time of quietness.

John. He and James Boanerges, sons of thunder ; and
John presently known as apostle of consolation. John, the
dreamer, the mystic, the seer. Two very different men were
these, but they were together with John the Baptist, enrolled
as His disciples, because obedient to his message.

Simon. A great elemental soul, with all the essentials of
humanity strong in his personality ; and yet just as weak as
a man can be, until the day when he was apprehended by
Jesus Christ, and the process began that turned him from
shaly stuff into rock character.

Philip. Certainly a shy and unimpressive man, so shy and unimpressive that Matthew, Mark, and Luke tell us nothing about him, except that Jesus enrolled him as an apostle ; and if I may dare to say so without irreverence, I think they sometimes wondered why the Lord took the man into the apostolate. But John, this man of the seeing eyes, tells us much about Philip. He was the man who at the end, when all the shadows were gathering around that little group of frightened souls, blurted out the whole of human agony in one great cry, " Show us the Father, and it sufficeth us." Those shy men are often the biggest men we have to deal with.

Nathanael. I do not need to describe Nathanael. Our Lord did it. " Behold, an Israelite indeed, in whom is no Jacob." That is exactly the significance of " no guile." Certainly Jacob was in the mind of our Lord, because He made another reference to him presently, about a ladder set up on earth, and reaching to the heavens.

Thus we see them, the first men, the pioneers, strking the trail in the wake of the footsteps of Jesus. Andrew, the cautious ; John, the poet ; Simon, the elemental ; Philip, the shy ; and Nathanael, the guileless.

With what apparent lack of organization the work began. He just moved on, and they came, one by one. Now let us watch Him as He handles them.

The very first thing that He is recorded to have said to one soul on the pathway of His public ministry was the thing He said to Andrew. He knew that those two were following Him, that they had broken with John. There was no rupture. It was the departure from the lower to the higher. Because of John's ministry they had been prepared for this thing. When the hour struck, they went at once after Jesus ; and they were following Him ; and our Lord turned, and speaking to Andrew and the other, said, " What seek ye ? " Mark carefully, He did not say, Whom seek ye ? That was self-evident. They were seeking Him. Yes, but He said in effect, Why are you seeking Me ? What is the meaning of this break with John, and this coming after Me ? What do you want ?

That is the very first word that is recorded as falling from the lips of Jesus as He began His public ministry. As a matter of fact we have only two other earlier words on record ; the first as a Boy of twelve ; and again at the baptism, except such words as are recorded as passing in the hour of temptation. Here then was, and is the first question, the first question of Jesus to a human being ; the first question of Jesus to humanity as He begins His ministry. It is a question that plumbs the deepest thing in human life. What are you seeking ? What are you seeking ? Now, here in the sanctuary, with the open Book in front of us, or to-morrow in the store, the office, the home, that is the supreme question about each one of us individually. What do we want ? What are we seeking ? What is the central inspiration, urge beneath all our lives' activities ?

Then, as I have said, came that very characteristic answer, " Where dwellest Thou ? " which surely did mean that Andrew was conscious of the big thing that had been asked of him, and perhaps he was conscious of his own inability to answer it. As though he might have said, " Well, what am I seeking ? What does lie deep down in my life ? " I do not know that he went through that process, but I think he did. And so he said, I cannot answer it at once. Give me time ; where do You live ? Can't I come and see you, and talk it out ?

And then came the second word of Jesus, " Come, and see," the Old Version had it ; but the Revised gives a more accurate shade of meaning ; " Come, and ye shall see." The two first words of Jesus then in His public ministry, were, What are you seeking ? and Come with Me, and your eyes shall be opened, and you shall see. And they went into the house, " and it was about the tenth hour." We will not enter into any debate as to whether it was the Hebrew or Roman time. If the Hebrew, it was four o'clock in the afternoon. If John used the Roman time, it was ten o'clock in the morning. I do not know. It has been argued with equal scholarship both ways. I think personally that it was the Roman time all through John, and that therefore it was ten o'clock in the morning. In either case several hours elapsed of which we have no record. It was one of those unrecorded private interviews that Jesus had more than once with individual souls.

Then we see Andrew coming out, and hurrying away to find Simon with one message, " We have found the Messiah." Then we see him coming back with Simon, this elemental man ; and again the Lord is heard speaking ; " I know you ; you are Simon. Your father's name is John. You shall be called Rock." It was a most amazing thing to say, and unless I sadly misunderstand human nature, no one was quite so amazed as Simon himself. Rock ? That is the one thing he knew he was not. He knew perfectly well his strength, but he also knew his weakness ; for every man of that kind is conscious of his own weakness. We need not take the trouble to point it out. Men would say ;—" Oh yes, we all know old Simon, he is a good sort, but heavens above ! save us from him. We cannot build on him." That is the expression men use of that sort of man. He knew men could not build on him ; but here were eyes looking into his, and a voice that said, You shall be rock ; you shall be a man men can build on. Our Lord had captured him. He never lost him again. It looked at one time as though he were going to slip out of His hands altogether ; but he never did.

Philip. According to the record, nobody went after Philip. What did I say ? There was One Who went after Philip, and we have that illuminative declaration, " He findeth Philip." Perhaps he had no brother, perhaps no close friend, interested enough to go after him. These other two came from his town, and probably Philip was associated with them in their discipleship of John ; but they had not thought of Philip. But Somebody did. " He findeth Philip," and to Philip He uttered for the first time, so far as the records reveal, the formula of which He so loved. He said to Philip when He found him, " Come and travel with Me " ; for I make no apology in saying that that is the truer translation. That was all ; but He had gained him.

Nathanael. Philip found Nathanael, and when Nathanael came—mark the method of the Master. First of all His word was not spoken directly to him, but to those about him ; " Behold, an Israelite indeed, in whom is no guile "—no deceit, no crookedness, who is transparent and open. The proof of the estimate was at once unconsciously given by Nathanael himself, as he said, How do you know me ? I have known people if you said something like that to them, they would have replied, No, that is too kind altogether ! Guile ! Guile ! This man said, How do You know there is no guile in me ? How do You know about me ?

Then Jesus uttered that word so full of significance. " Before Philip "—He is always before Philip. " Before Philip called thee, when thou wast under the fig tree," in that quiet hour of meditation, possibly reading the story of Jacob and the ladder, " when thou wast under the fig tree, I saw thee." " Before Philip," and that guileless soul saw a glory that amazed him, and at once responded, " Thou art the Son of God ; Thou art the King of Israel." And then once again the words of Jesus. Do you believe simply because I said I saw you under the fig tree ? You shall see greater things than these. You shall see that matter that you have been contemplating under the fig tree, that story of a ladder set up on earth, and reaching to heaven, fulfilled in Me, " Ye shall see the heaven opened, and the angels of God ascending and descending upon the Son of man."

Such was the first group as the story shows ; different men ; different methods. Mark that carefully. Let those who have the cure of souls in any form, not stereotype their methods. If you have somewhere a book giving mechanical instructions as to how to deal with souls, go straight home and burn it ! Why ? Because the next soul you meet will baffle your text books, and laugh at your regulations. Humanity is infinite in variety ; and our Lord is always changing His method.

That is what I see as I read this page of John, with its story of that early group, and how He dealt with it.

Thus we come to the first Sign. On the third day they arrived at Cana. There are three matters to be considered ; first the occasion of the sign ; secondly, that arresting intermission when He talked to His Mother ; and then the sign itself, and its value.

The occasion. The first sign was given at a marriage, at the sacred hour of union, through which there is completed the image and the likeness of God. A significant statement is found in Genesis v. 1 and 2. "This is the book of the generations of Adam. In the day that God created man, in the likeness of God made He him ; male and female created He them ; and blessed them, and called their name Adam, in the day when they were created." I once heard Dan Crawford, reading that chapter at Northfield, say, " Please note that. He called their name Adam, not the Adamses ! " I repeat then that our Lord wrought His first sign in that sacred hour, that sacramental hour, when the two sides of the one image and likeness of God were coming into union, and that for the continuity of the race, and the carrying on of the revelation. In God there is Father—" Like as a Father pitieth His children " ; and there is Mother,—" as one whom his mother comforteth." And even then God is not complete in revelation. There is childhood. The likeness of God is completed in the Son. It was a sacred hour, the hour of joy ; and Jesus went there for His first sign. He was a bidden Guest, John tells us, and He accepted the invitation ; and while He was there the wine failed.

Then came the revealing intermission. Let us attempt to understand what did happen as between Jesus and His Mother. The naturalness of the story first arrests us. His Mother came to Him, and said, " They have no wine." Now what did Mary mean by that ? What did she want ? The easy answer is that of course she wanted Him to provide wine. But the converse reveals a deeper meaning in her words.

We should never have known what Mary meant that day, if it had not been for what He said to her.

What did He say to her? "Woman, what have I to do with thee? Mine hour is not yet come." I do not know a piece of translation which hides the spirit of something said more than that does. To begin with, our word "Woman," may give a false impression. On the lips of Jesus it was a word of intense tenderness. He used it again to Mary from His Cross. Then the question as translated has a harshness quite unjustified. Let us translate literally, even though the idiom is not ours. "Woman, what is there to thee and to Me? Mine hour is not yet come." "What is there to thee and to Me?" It was as if He had said; Mother Mine, I know what you want, but you do not understand; there are limitations to your understanding of Me. Mother of My flesh, dear to My heart, Mother under whose heart My life was enshrined when God prepared for Me My body; there are limitations to your understanding. You have been watching over Me all My years, and now I seem to be moving out into public work, you are anxious I shall do something that will reveal the meaning of My personality and mission. Mary was indeed the blessed Virgin. In her Magnificat she had sung by inspiration "All generations shall call me blessed." She knew the profound secret of His personality, and it was a secret she never could share. Has it ever occurred to you that the Virgin Mother went through life under suspicion, because there are some things which cannot be interpreted to common carnal humanity.

And now the thought of her heart was,—Oh, if only He would show something, and prove!

To that longing He said; Mother, Mine, I know what you want. "Mine hour is not yet come." What did He mean? That He would not perform the miracle? Certainly not. He did it. He turned the water into wine. It was His first sign; but He said in effect; That sign cannot satisfy the hunger of your heart; it will not produce the effect that you desire.

From that point in John's story let us take a rapid glance
on. In the seventh chapter we find that He said to His
brethren, " My time is not yet come." In the same chapter
it is declared that " No man laid his hand on Him because
His hour was not yet come." In the eighth chapter John
tells us He was teaching in the Temple " And no man took
Him because His hour had not yet come." In chapter twelve,
when the end was approaching, the Greeks came, and He
said, " The hour is come that the Son of man should be
glorified," and went on to show He was referring to His coming
Cross, resurrection and ascension. In chapter thirteen we
read, " Knowing that His hour was come that He should
depart out of the world " ; and once more in chapter seventeen
He said, " Father, the hour is come." Thus His first reference
to His hour was made to His Mother, and the last to His
Father ; and the thought of His glory being manifested
through His Cross is discovered throughout.

Then, having said that there were things His Mother could
not apprehend, and that all the infinitely deep desire of her
heart could not be satisfied in the way she suggested, He at
once performed the sign, and turned the water into wine.

Then John tells us that the value as to Himself was that
" He manifested His glory." That does not mean that there
was a full and final and complete manifestation ; but that
He manifested His glory, that is, that He made His glory
shine forth. In chapter twenty-one by and by we read,
" He manifested Himself again " to the disciples. Here the
same verb is employed, with the same idea ; something done
resolutely of His own will and intention. He manifested His
glory. In his summing up John had written, " We beheld
His glory, glory as of the only-begotten Son of a Father,
full of grace and truth." Here then was the value of what
He did. " He manifested His glory." The glory as of the
Only-begotten of the Father, shone through that wonder.

The value so far as His disciples were concerned was that
they believed on Him. The verb employed there is an
arresting one. It means that His disciples made a surrender

to Him in complete confidence. Of course they had believed on Him on that journey up. But now what they saw led them further ; and in that moment, in a way not realized before, they saw His glory, and they believed on Him.

The first sign in the house of joy at a wedding, was a creative act, the turning of the water into wine. Thus the eternal Word is seen, in flesh, sanctifying the marriage relationship, sharing human joy ; acting in essential human experience, and sanctifying human life in that realm of its ever persistent origin and new beginning.

John ii. 13—iii. 21.

AFTER the first sign at Cana, as John records, Jesus tarried a few days in Capernaum ; and then He took His journey to Jerusalem, because the Passover feast was at hand. This was His first recorded visit to Jerusalem, as Messiah. I have no doubt He had been there before in the course of His life. We have the story of a visit when He was a Boy ; and we have every reason to believe He had gone up year after year. But now, coming as Messiah, it was certainly within the Divine order that He made His way to the Temple, which was at the centre of the national life. There He wrought a sign, which is the second in John's selection. It was wrought in the Temple, and it was of the Temple, distinctly a sign in the realm of worship. The first sign at Cana was in the realm of joy at a marriage feast, a revelation of creative power. Now He passed to the centre of the national life in the city, and to the centre of the life of the city in the Temple ; and there He wrought this second sign in the realm of worship.

It was startlingly significant, and produced far-reaching results. It began the action unquestionably, of definite hostility towards Him, which never found its culmination, until they put Him on His bitter Cross. The action is most significant as we consider what He said in connection with it ;

something that was not understood at the moment, which nevertheless does interpret to us His own mind, His own heart, His own outlook, His own understanding, His own purpose. In considering the matter, we will follow two lines ; first, the sign in itself ; and then, those immediate results which John has recorded for us.

We are first arrested by what John tells us Jesus found in the Temple. The word translated Temple here is *hieron*, not the word *naos*, used a little later on, of which more anon. It refers not to the sanctuary, but the outer courts, more or less open and available to all, and especially to the Gentile courts. What did He find in the Temple ? " Those that sold oxen and sheep and doves, and the changers of money sitting." To realize what that means, we must remember the Temple, and what it really signified in the Divine economy ; what it was intended to be in the history of the nation, and through the nation, in the interest of the world. Jesus came, the Messiah, into the Temple ; and He found the Gentile courts with cattle in them, and the changers of money trafficking in them. These men were there to change Roman coins into Jewish coins, because no coin with the effigy of the emperor could be offered within those Temple courts for any purpose. That would have been a desecration. So, for the convenience of the worshippers, there were men there prepared, at a percentage, to change the money. They also were ready to change large coins for smaller ones. This thing, by the way, still goes on. I have occasionally been asked if I could provide some small change before someone was going to service ! These men were there to make religion easy ! There was no need to trouble to rear one's own lamb, or bring one's own pair of pigeons. It could all be done for you. Everything was conveniently arranged for, in the Temple courts. That is what He found. Religion made easy, and so devitalized.

Now with equal brevity, let us remind ourselves of what He did. He first plaited a scourge of cords ; very likely picking up cords that were lying about, which had been bound round the oxen. He plaited them into the form of a whip of action ; and then He advanced upon that whole crowd, and drove them out. There is an anaemic form of thinking that is eager to say He did not smite. I do not know that He did ; but we do not know He did not. In any case I make my protest against that weak idea of Jesus that imagines there was no lightning flashing from His eyes, no wrath manifested upon His face, and no anger in His heart. That is an anaemic Christ Who does nothing for the world. The very symbol at any rate suggested " the wrath of the Lamb." We must not cancel that expression. When we do, we cancel Christianity as a living force. He plaited that cord, and He drove them out, and with splendid iconoclasm turned the money tables over, and scattered the coins across the Temple floor, in every direction.

Why was He doing all this ? Listen to Him, " Take these things hence ; make not My Father's house a house of traffic." He saw the desecration of the House of His Father, " My Father's house." The last thing He called this Temple much later on was, " Your house,"—" Your house is left unto you desolate." He saw the courts, the places where men and women drew nigh to God, desecrated ; and He wrought the sign ; and the disciples remembered that it was written, " The zeal "—do not soften that,—the burning, consuming passion " of Thy house shall eat Me up."

His second sign, in John's selection, was thus a sign in the realm of worship ; and a sign characterized by the revelation of an august and an awful majesty, acting for the restoration of a desecrated House to its true function. I emphasize once more the fact that, as we know from other writings, those money changers carried on their work, and the sellers of oxen, sheep, and doves their work, not in Jewish courts, but in the courts that were supposed to be consecrated or set apart for Gentiles. The supreme iniquity to the heart of Jesus was that the Hebrew people were failing to function as God intended. His intention was always that they should bless all the nations ; but they had now come to that position when they thought only of themselves, and the ease and comfort of their own worship. Gentiles ! What did Gentiles matter ? Certainly use their courts, and desecrate them. Christ thus came, and swept out the whole unholy traffic, the zeal of the House of God consuming Him. Such was the sign.

Now immediately following the sign, we have John's record of the results. There are three things to observe. First, in verses eighteen to twenty-two the challenge that was given to Him, and His answer to it. Then a little paragraph at the close of the chapter, showing in result, belief in Him, and His unbelief in those who did believe in Him. And finally, the story of Nicodemus, in the first twenty-one verses of chapter three.

First then the challenge that they brought to Him after He had wrought the sign. The exact words are found in verse eighteen—" The Jews therefore answered and said unto Him." That is, they answered His action. They saw in His action a challenge. They " answered." It is quite significant. The rulers recognized the startling challenge in what He had done in cleansing the Temple courts. As He stood in lonely dignity, coins scattered, animals dispersed in every direction, and with the animals those who owned them gone, they gathered about Him and they " answered " Him. It was an answer to what He had done. " What sign showest Thou unto us, seeing that Thou doest these things ? " They asked Him for a sign, to authenticate a sign. They had just received a remarkable sign. At any rate there was one man in the crowd had seen it, I feel sure ; and that one man was Nicodemus. Presently we hear him say, " No man can do these signs that Thou doest, except God be with Him." But they said, What sign do You give, which authenticates the sign You have given ?

Thus we come to that which is the most significant thing in all the story. Jesus answered them and said, " Destroy this sanctuary." Here I use the marginal reading, ' sanctuary," to draw a distinction between *hieron*, the word used for the Temple courts that were cleansed ; and *naos*, the sacred enclosure itself, which was the word our Lord used now, " Destroy this sanctuary, and in three days I will raise it up." How many of us would have understood Him, had we heard Him utter those words ? Not one of us. Nobody did understand. The rulers did not. They laughed at Him. " They said, Forty and six years has this temple been building." The Temple was not finished even then ; nor for another ten years after that. They practically pointed, Look at it ; for forty-six years this building has been going on ; and one can hear the ribaldry of their mockery, " and wilt Thou raise it up in three days ? " It was very natural. We might have said the same sort of thing. John is magnificently honest. He tells us that it was not until after His resurrection that they remembered He had said that, and so understood.

We hear the words nineteen hundred years after, and we listen to them, not as the rulers understood them, not as the disciples failed to understand them, but as He meant them. What is Thy sign ? said these rulers ; Thou Who comest up to this Temple, and sweepest out the vested interests that are supposed to be in the interest of religion ? Thou overturnest everything. Thou art an Iconoclast. What is the sign of Thy authority ?

Now very reverently, hear me, if I change the wording, not to improve it, but interpret it. In effect He said ; The sign of My authority will be My Cross and resurrection. The ultimate proof and demonstration of the authority of all I am doing to-day will be discovered in the day when you unloose this tabernacle ; destroy it in that sense, dissolve it ; and I will raise the unloosened tabernacle in three days.

No, it was not intended that they should understand it then ; but right here, in the beginning, in the first sign in the House of God, I discover the thought of His heart, and the sense of His mind, and the centre of His authority. What was it ? His Cross and His resurrection.

Let me turn aside for a moment, and make an excursus

in relation.   Later on in His ministry, another evangelist
records that He said ; "An evil and adulterous generation
seeketh after a sign ; and there shall no sign be given to it
but the sign of Jonah the prophet ; for as Jonah was three
days and three nights in the belly of the sea-monster ; so
shall the Son of man be three days and three nights in the
heart of the earth." That is the same thing, but in other
language. He gave many signs. Yes, but He said, No sign
will carry, no sign will be demonstration, no sign will produce
conviction.   An evil and adulterous generation seeketh a
sign, and no sign shall be given it ; but there will be a sign ;
the sign of death, and of resurrection. In those words then
we find an unveiling of His own heart, and His own thinking
at that moment.

Next, John tells that when He was there in Jerusalem at
the Passover, during the feast, "many believed on His name,
beholding His signs which He did." He did other signs,
which are not recorded. John has given the central one.
He now declares that many believed, not on Him, but " on
His name," that is, accepted His Messianic claim, " beholding
His signs which He did." Then this startling thing follows.
" But Jesus did not trust Himself unto them." The same
verb is employed in both cases. I think something will
be gained if we rendered it so. "Many believed in His
name . . . but He did not believe in them." Or, "Many
trusted in His name, or on His name ; . . . but He did not
trust them." Or to change it yet again, "Many committed
themselves to His name ; . . . but He did not commit
Himself."

Here we are face to face with something arresting. His
signs produced a belief, but it was not a belief to which He
could commit Himself. They committed themselves to Him
in a certain way ; but He could not commit Himself to them.
Their belief was shallow. It was based on wonder. The things
that were necessarily arresting, startling, spectacular, were
all they wanted. Belief that is based upon the spectacular
is always shallow and evanescent. If belief is nothing more

than admiration for the spectacular, it will create in multitudes applause ; but the Son of God cannot commit Himself to that kind of faith.

In that connection John illuminates His personality. He says, " He knew all men, and because He needed not that any one should bear witness concerning man ; for He Himself knew what was in man." He knew all men, generically ; and He knew every man, individually. That is why He could not commit Himself. And yet in that heart there surged the infinite, the eternal compassion of God, and the desire to save. But He could not commit Himself to them. He needed something deeper on which to build.

Then we come to the story of Nicodemus. Notice how it begins ; " *Now* there *was* a man of the Pharisees." The word rendered " Now " may with equal accuracy be translated " But." When I went to school they told me " But " was a disjunctive conjunction ; which means that it indicates a separation of ideas, and a contrast. What then is the meaning of " *Now* there was a man of the Pharisees " ? John was linking the Nicodemus story, with that which had immediately preceded it. Jesus could not trust Himself to some men, but there was a man of the Pharisees named Nicodemus,—and to summarize all the story,—to whom He did commit Himself, whom He could trust, in whom He did believe.

Here then is a man to whom Jesus could commit Himself. It has become almost an expository habit to abuse Nicodemus, and to say that he was a coward. It may be well to remember that he and Joseph of Arimathaea were so-called secret disciples ; but when all the loud-shouting crowd ran away, those were the two who buried Him. Sometimes there is more courage in quietness, than in noise.

Then follows the matchless story of the converse between Jesus and Nicodemus. It was night, and Nicodemus came at night, because he was determined to have Jesus all to himself. He had something of grave importance to say to this Teacher. He did not see Him as more than that. But he did believe Him to be One officially sent from God. The signs he had seen had convinced him of that. He had come to the absolutely correct conclusion, that anyone who wrought those signs must be from God.

The conversation proceeded in three movements. In verses two and three we have the first movement, in which we see Nicodemus and Jesus face to face. Then the second movement is in verses four to eight, in which we see Nicodemus and Jesus mind to mind. The last movement is in verses nine to twenty-one, in which we see Nicodemus and Jesus heart to heart.

Face to face. " Nicodemus, a ruler of the Jews, a Pharisee." He addressed Jesus as " Rabbi." The title was one of respect, but it was not the highest. Rab ; Rabbi ; Rabban. Such were the degrees. Rabbi was the middle title. But it was respectful. " Rabbi, we know that Thou art a Teacher come from God ; for no man can do these signs that Thou doest, except God be with Him." He was perfectly right. He had not asked for anything. He had simply made a statement, and then stood quietly waiting. But unquestionably the statement was a suggestion. What was it ? That he wanted the latest word from God. He was a ruler. Jesus presently said to him, " Art thou *the* teacher of Israel ? " I believe at that moment Nicodemus was—to use the word perhaps in its higher and better sense—the most popular teacher in Jerusalem. He knew the Torah ; was familiar with the Nebiim ; and was acquainted with the Kethubim, or Sacred Writings. He knew too that there had been no authentic voice until that of John had sounded, the herald ; and now this Teacher, authenticated by signs, demonstrating that He was from God. So he came, waiting to hear this latest word from God.

Then, in the history of that man, that wonderful man, that fine man, that courageous man, there crashed across all human thinking, all its religions, all its philosophies, and its theologies, the revealing word. " Except a man be born from above, he cannot see the Kingdom of God." Human

[57]

intellect is entirely at fault. There must be a new birth, a
new life principle, before the Kingdom of God can be seen,
to say nothing of entering into it.

Thus they are seen face to face, the seeker standing in the
presence of a Divine Teacher, wanting the last word ; the
one final and authoritative Teacher saying, What you need
is not to graduate, but to backslide further back than baby-
hood ; you need to be born anew. No psychology will ever
effect conversion. Regeneration must affect psychology.
" Except a man be born *anothen*, from above, he cannot
see."

Now mark the second movement, mind to mind. Nicodemus said, How can this thing be ? He was not contradicting
Jesus. I believe that in a flash he saw what a marvellous
thing it would be if that could be ; what a glorious thing
it would be if a man could begin all over again. But how
could it be ? Then he used the physical as an illustration,
" Can a man enter a second time into his mother's womb,
and be born ? " He was only illustrating, but it was a very
powerful illustration. Nicodemus meant to say, Born again !
Here am I, and what I am is the result of what I was an
hour ago, and yesterday, and all the days of the past. My
personality is the result of processes. Can this body of mine
be turned back into embryonic form in my mother's womb ?
And if that cannot be, then how is the more difficult thing
to be done, that of remaking my personality, spirit, mind,
and body ?

Then Jesus went on, very beautifully answering him in the
realm of interpretation. Listen to Him. He said, " Except
a man be born of water and the Spirit, he canot enter into
the Kingdom of God." Mark the continuity. You have been
attending the ministry of one who baptized you in water,
and told you Another would baptize you in the Spirit. Except
you are born of all that the water baptism signified, repentance ; and that which the Spirit baptism accomplishes,
regeneration, you cannot enter into the Kingdom of
God.

Then correcting the illustration He said, " That which is born of the flesh is flesh ; and that which is born of the Spirit is spirit." That is to say, Nicodemus, your illustration won't do ; it only applies in the realm of the flesh, and it is impossible in the realm of the flesh ; you cannot enter into your mother's womb a second time and be born. That is the flesh. Do not confuse flesh with spirit. The spirit of a man can be completely regenerated ; he can be born again. That which is born of the Spirit is spirit. Do not confuse the two things, said Jesus in effect.

And then He gave an illustration. You cannot understand the blowing of the wind, but you obey the law and gain its force ; so with the Spirit. Do not postpone relationship with the possibility, Nicodemus, by intellectual struggle. Obey the law of the wind, and the wind obeys you. Obey the law of the Spirit, and you will know the new birth.

Then Nicodemus came with his last question. I am sure this question had an entirely different significance. Nicodemus said, " How can these things be ? " His first question meant, Can they be at all ; the second question meant, What is the process ?

Then with tender, gentle playfulness Jesus said, Are you the teacher in Israel, and don't you know these things ? If I told you earthly things, the things I have told you so far, and you don't believe ; how are you going to believe if I tell you heavenly things ? But He went on, and did tell him of the heavenly.

His answer to the last " How " of Nicodemus is found in three movements. " As Moses lifted up the serpent in the wilderness, even so must the Son of man be lifted up ; that whosoever believeth may in Him have eternal life." That is how.

Let us go further. " God so loved the world, that He gave His only begotten Son." That is how.

And yet a little further, " God sent not the Son into the world to judge the world ; but that the world should be saved through Him " He has sent the light. That is how.

How? said Nicodemus. Jesus said, Life through My death; love from the heart of God through His gift; light through My mission in the world. That is How. Because God so loved, He gave; and life comes through that gift; and now the light is shining.

John iii. 22-36.

IN the orderly sequence of this book of selected signs in proof that Jesus is the Christ, the Son of God, this paragraph constitutes an interlude, both as to the course of our Lord's ministry, and in the system of the book.

After the sign wrought in the Temple, and the things immediately following, including the night of converse with Nicodemus, Jesus left the city of Jerusalem, and went into the country of Judæa, and "there He tarried with" His disciples, "and baptized," possibly for some considerable time.

The arresting thing is that during the period thus referred to, He was co-operating in John's ministry, rather than more definitely carrying on His own. The evangelist is careful to record the fact that while Jesus was in the Judæa country-side with His disciples, baptizing, John was doing the same thing in another locality, not very far away. It is quite evident that he continued to do this until he was arrested and cast into prison. John practically reveals this when he says, "For John was not yet cast into prison." That statement chronologically synchronizes with Matthew's statement in the fourth chapter, and with Mark's in the first, that it was after the imprisonment of John, that Jesus began His more definitely public propaganda.

The situation then is arresting in that it reveals John and Jesus carrying on, at the same time. John, the voice, the herald, had publicly identified the Messiah, in the remarkable words, " Behold, the Lamb of God, Which taketh away the sin of the world." Moreover, on the very next day, after that identification, he had again pointed Jesus out to two of his disciples, as our Lord was seen passing along His way, evidently starting upon His public ministry ; and at once, by a natural and beautiful sequence, those two who were with him, left John, and went after Jesus. He had identified Messiah. It would have seemed as though his work was completed, and yet we find him still carrying on that preparatory work. His disciples came to him presently with a question, which shows that Jesus was also doing that work. They said, " Rabbi, He that was with thee beyond Jordan, to Whom thou hast borne witness, behold, the Same baptizeth, and all men come to Him."

We can easily see how a difficulty would arise in the minds of some, and perhaps those the more intelligent. They had listened to John during all his ministry, had enrolled themselves as his disciples ; and then there came that moment when he had, in answer to a deputation, said he was not the Christ, he was not Elijah, he was not the prophet foretold by Moses ; he was a voice. The day after that he had pointed out the One Whose coming he had announced. But he was going on, and going on evidently with the same work ; still preaching as he had preached, and still receiving those who, conscious of their need of repentance, confessed their repentance and their sins ; and practising still the rite of baptism. At the same time Jesus had moved into the country-side, and was doing exactly the same thing.

Then John tells us that " There arose *therefore* a questioning on the part of John's disciples." The word " therefore " is significant, showing that the facts we have been considering accounted for the questioning. The discussion was on the subject of purifying, between John's disciples and—the Old Version reads—" the Jews." The New Version with accuracy says, " a Jew." That was the local situation ; a discussion arose on the subject of purifying. We must understand that word as used at the time. It referred to the whole subject of moral and ceremonial purifying. That exactly described the realm of John's ministry, and of the ministry which our Lord was now carrying on. The ministry of John was not concerned with matters political or economic, save indirectly. It was a moral ministry. So was that of our Lord. The question of purifying, as to how there could be cleansing from moral defilement, and what part or place ritual took in the work, was the question under discussion.

I think we are warranted in going further, and saying that the discussion was the result of a comparison between John's work and that of Jesus. I do not mean in the burden of teaching between John and Jesus, but in the matter of the success of each. When John's disciples came to him, this is how they told the story. " Rabbi, He that was with thee beyond Jordan, to Whom thou hast borne witness, behold, the Same baptizeth, and all men come to Him." There is no meaning in that except that it suggests some little feeling of resentment at the fact that Jesus, this new Teacher, He that was with John beyond Jordan, and to Whom John had witnessed, was apparently more successful than their master, " Behold, the Same baptizeth, and all men come to Him."

Now all that is preliminary, and leads to the account of the answer which John gave to those men. From verse twenty-seven to thirty we have the record of that answer. There are differing opinions as to whether from verse thirty-one to the end of the chapter, John the herald is still speaking or whether he ends with the great words, " He must increase, but I must decrease " ; and then John the evangelist adds his comment. I am personally quite convinced that John the evangelist is making his own comments from verse thirty-one to the end. What we have here then is this, the testimony of John the Baptist in answer to the enquiry raised by his disciples as the result of a discussion with a Jew. John the evangelist having thus recorded the testimony of the herald, proceeds to make certain comments of his own on the whole situation.

Thus we have in this section an interlude of witness;

first from the lips of the herald, we have the witness to Jesus, that may be described as the great Recessional. The whole of the old economy had come to its climax. The last messenger of that economy, God-called, God-equipped, had done his work. Thus we find the final words of the old economy. Immediately following, the New Testament writer, this apostle of Jesus, this evangelist, makes his own comments; and so we have in the last part of the paragraph the great Processional. John, the herald, uttered the Recessional, concluding the old economy. John, the apostle, uttered the Processional, marking the order of everything that was now beginning, that which was superseding the old, in order that it might pass away. The difference marks continuity; the great Recessional of John the herald; the illuminating Processional of John the evangelist; both in the presence of the Incarnate Word.

Let us then first consider the Recessional of the herald. He first uttered a great principle; "A man can receive nothing, except it have been given him from heaven." To understand this we must get our background. The men who came to John knew him. They believed in his ministry. They had been influenced by it. They were his disciples. They knew also about Jesus; and they found He was carrying on along exactly the same lines as John, proclaiming the same message, and performing the same rite through His disciples. They knew too that men were crowding to Him. So they went to John with a little feeling of jealousy for him. He answered first by the declaration of a principle which precluded the possibility of any idea of rivalry between himself and Jesus. "A man can receive nothing, except it have been given him from above." This principle applied equally to John as herald, and to Jesus as Messiah. It was a principle to be recognized by these disciples of John, and by all men at all times.

Its teaching is perfectly simple. It calls for a recognition of the final, ultimate authority of heaven. A man receives nothing, whether it be the call to, and the power for, a preliminary ministry such as John's; or whether it be the call to, and the power for, the Messianic fulfilment of eternal purpose, save by the authority of heaven. The ultimate authority of heaven is the principle. It is of abiding importance and application. It for evermore sweeps out all possibility of rivalry, and all sense that some piece of work is more important than some other within the authority of heaven, however much it may seem to be so when judged by human statistics. It becomes all the more arresting when thus stated by John in reference to his own work, and that of the Messiah. There was no room for any thought of competition or rivalry. For what a man receives he is responsible; and to have any share, under heaven's authority, whether it be that of a voice crying, or of the Word Incarnate, is of itself supreme majesty and dignity. Between those thus authorized, there can be nothing in the nature of rivalry. Having laid down the principle, John applied it.

He applied it first to himself. "Ye yourselves bear me witness, that I said, I am not the Christ, but, that I am sent before Him." He thus claimed that his work had been authorized from heaven. He had received from heaven his call, his gift. He employed no terms that could be construed as derogatory to the splendour of his own work. He was magnifying his office. He was claiming he was sent, not as the Christ, but before Him, a voice.

Then he applied the principle to the Messiah Himself, "He that hath the bride is the bridegroom; but the friend of the bridegroom, which standeth and heareth him, rejoiceth greatly because of the bridegroom's voice; this my joy therefore is fulfilled."

John was addressing Jews, people familiar with their own literature; and with his mind, thinking of Jesus as Messiah, he fell back upon a remarkable figure of speech with which they were familiar in their own writings. He had already in differing ways described the Messiah, the varying tones all being needed to reveal His glory. He had spoken of Him as coming with the fan, coming with the fire, coming with the axe ; and as " The Lamb of God, which taketh away the sin of the world." Now he spoke of Him as the Bridegroom. That was figurative language taken from the Old Testament. In Hosea the language of God concerning His people, was, " I have betrothed thee unto Me for ever." In Ezekiel the same figure of speech is found, and yet again in Malachi. This figure of the bridegroom and the bride, always suggested the relationship between Jehovah and His people. Believing too that in the Song of Solomon, though an Eastern love-song, there are mystical intentions and suggestions ; the same idea is present. So John catches up that idea, in the poetry and the prophecy of the Old Testament, and applies the figure to Jesus, as he speaks of Him as the Bridegroom.

In that connection he describes his relation to Him, and shows what it meant to him. He speaks of himself as " the friend of the Bridegroom." That was a great office in the Eastern lands. The friend of the bridegroom was the one who ceremonially handed the bride to her groom ; and until he had done it, the groom's voice was not heard. As he handed the bride to her bridegroom, the voice of the bridegroom accepting her was heard. John, recognizing the relationship between Jehovah and His people, said, I am " the friend of the Bridegroom." It has been my business to lead the Bride to Him. Now I have heard His voice. That is my joy, " now my joy is fulfilled."

Then followed the last great statement. I never read these final words of John without feeling their dignity and majesty. None greater ever fell from human lips. " He must increase, but I must decrease." That expressed the perfect content of a man who knew he had received from heaven his authority, who had carried out his great mission. He had heard the voice of the Bridegroom welcoming the bride he had introduced, in that first group of disciples he had pointed to Jesus. Then the quiet, restful, triumphant content, as, conscious of heaven's authority, and all of his mission fulfilled, he said, " He must increase . . . I must decrease." There was no unwarranted derogation of his own personality or work ;

E   [65]

but the content of the star as its lustre is lost in the rising glory of the sun. " He must increase, but I must decrease." Such was the Recessional.

Then we have the comments of the writer, constituting the Processional. He begins, " He that cometh from above is above all ; he that is of the earth is of the earth, and of the earth he speaketh ; He that cometh from heaven is above all."

John the evangelist was thus showing the difference between the voice and the Word ; the friend of the Bridegroom, and the Bridegroom Himself ; pointing out the infinite distance between John and Jesus the Christ, the Son of God. He speaks of Him as the One " that cometh from heaven " ; " *cometh*," not *came*. The eternal present tense is used, always coming from above. Jesus " cometh from heaven." What of John ? He " is of the earth, and of the earth he speaketh." Again, that is not the language of disrespect to John. It is language, recognizing the limitation of John's ministry. He is of the earth. Jesus is the One " that cometh from above " ; and because He " cometh from above," He " is above all." Mark the contrast. John, of the earth, as to his *birth* and his being. Jesus, from above, as to His *begetting* and His Being. The contrast is quite sharp. John of the earth, speaking of the earth, Divinely authorized so to do, but having no more to say than that. But now the One Who is always coming from above, Whose begetting and Being can only be accounted for in that way, and Who therefore is for ever " above all."

So much for the two personalities. Then, running on, he described the mission of the One Who comes from above, and the language is in itself so simple that if we are not attentive, we miss the sublimity of it. " What He hath seen and heard, of that He beareth witness." In the statement there is a double idea. What He has seen, are the eternal facts, the facts out of the midst of which He has come from above, the things with which He is familiar because of His eternal relationship to them. " In the beginning was the

Word, and the Word was with God, and the Word was God."
" What He hath seen " in those relationships.

" And heard." What does that mean ? The first statement,
" What He hath seen " refers unquestionably to the eternal
facts. " What He hath heard " refers to His mission, the
Evangel with which He has been charged. The eternal
verities, He sees ; the counsels of God, He has heard. These
are the things to which John says He has come to bear
witness.

Again we go back to the prologue, and link up the great
themes.

> " In the beginning was the Word, and the Word was
> with God, and the Word was God."

> " And the Word became flesh, and pitched His tent
> among us (and we beheld His glory, glory as of the
> only begotten Son of the Father), full of grace and
> truth."

> " No man hath seen God at any time ; the only begotten
> Son, Which is in the bosom of the Father, He hath
> declared Him."

These things which no man had seen, the Word has seen,
and now He " Who is in the bosom of the Father, hath
declared Him." He bears witness to the eternal things, the
things He has seen. But more, He bears witness to the
counsels and purposes of God, through which He has come,
the things He has heard. Seen things, the eternal facts ;
heard things, the evangel.

Then follows that admittedly startling and strange parenthesis " and no man receiveth His witness." Surely that
was a superlative utterance, not intended to be taken literally.
Evidently so, because the next thing he says is this, " He
that hath received His witness, hath set his seal to this, that
God is true." Years after he wrote ; " The whole world
lieth in the evil one," while writing to those who were no
longer under the control of the evil one. We find a similar

parenthesis in the words of Jesus recorded by Matthew, " All things have been delivered unto Me of My Father ; and *no one knoweth the Son save the Father*,"—a parenthesis expressing a difficulty of the moment.

He went on, " He that receiveth His witness, hath set his seal to this, that God is true." He that " cometh from above " has seen the eternal facts ; has heard the counsel of God, and He bears witness to these things ; and the man who accepts that witness, sets his seal to the fact that God is true ; that all the old economy, finding its culmination in the magnificent words of John, was true. In Jesus such a man finds the Yea and the Amen to every message of God, and to every covenant of God.

Then, still running on. " For He Whom God hath sent speaketh the words of God ; for He giveth not the Spirit by measure." What does this mean ? That God does not give His Spirit by measure to the One Whom He has sent ? Or that the One He has sent, does not give His Spirit by measure to those to whom He is sent ? Perhaps no dogmatic reply to that enquiry is warranted. My own conviction is that both the things are involved. The primary meaning is that the Son came, sent of God, and God did not give the Spirit by measure to Him, for in Him dwelt all the pleroma of the Godhead. I think it is equally true of what He does for us ; He gives the Spirit, not in measure, but in fulness, having received that Gift from the Father.

Then John comes to a statement in which he gives the secret for the authority of the Son. " The Father loveth the Son, and hath given all things into His hand." Now go back and listen to the herald. " A man can receive nothing, except it have been given him from heaven." He was sent ; he received his commission and carried it out. He has done. " I must decrease." Now says the evangelist, of the One to Whom John had pointed, " The Father hath loved the Son, and delivered all things into His hand." That accounts for the final authority of the Son.

Then the question of human responsibility is revealed, and

needs no comment in the light of its clarity of statement. " He that believeth on the Son hath eternal life ; he that obeyeth not the Son shall not see life, but the wrath of God abideth on him."

Thus we have the interlude of witness ; the merging of the old and the new. There is no conflict, but continuity. In the words of the epistle to the Hebrews, " He taketh away the first, that He may establish the second." The final word of the old economy, the fitting final word is, " He must increase, but I must decrease." The appropriate annunciation of the new is, " The Father loveth the Son, and hath given all things into His hand."

John iv. 1-42.

In this paragraph no specific sign is recorded either in the realm of works, or of words. Nevertheless it has profound significance in John's account of the ministry of our Lord. The chief interest of the story is Samaria. To put the whole matter into a sentence by way of introduction, our Lord is seen crossing the boundary line of prejudice, and supposed privilege, as He went through Samaria. Jews, says John in a comment, have no dealings with Samaritans, but this Jew went through Samaria.

The section has three movements. In the first four verses we have the occasion of His journey ; in verses five to twenty-six, His conversation with the woman ; and in verses twenty-seven to forty-two the things issuing therefrom, the results that were immediate.

Let us first carefully look at what John tells us about the occasion. He says, " When therefore the Lord knew." Something that He knew, accounted for this particular journey. What was it ? " That the Pharisees had heard that Jesus was making and baptizing more disciples than

[69]

John." Then " He left Judæa, and departed again into
Galilee. And He must needs pass through Samaria." The
statements are so sun-clear that one need not tarry with
them long, yet it is well to look at them. First of all, the
Lord knew that the account of His success was reaching
the Pharisees. Quite evidently remarkable success was
attending that ministry of Jesus, which we were considering
in our last study as collateral with that of John. That
success was evidenced by the fear expressed by John's
disciples when they said, " All men go after Him." The
account of this success was now reaching the Pharisees.
On that account, He left Judæa. The implicate is quite
self-evident, that this knowledge was precipitating conflict
between Himself and the Pharisees. Already we have seen
how in connection with His second sign,—His first in the
Temple, when He cleansed it,—that He came into conflict
with them. Now news came to these men, that the One
Whose action in the Temple had raised their objection,
was marvellously successful in His ministry, even more so
than John. The Lord knew that this would mean conflict ;
and on that account He left Judæa.

Again notice, " He left Judæa." The word here translated
" *left* " is a singularly strong word, not occurring anywhere
else. It marks a definite and intentional break. We should
not misinterpret the thought if we said He abandoned Judæa.
He did go back, but very seldom. He had been to Judæa.
He had gone to the Temple. He had exercised His ministry
in the surrounding country with marvellous success ; but
hostility was stirring there, and He left Judæa ; He broke
with it.

This brings us to the arresting statement ; " He must
needs go through Samaria." Why " must " ? That is a
very old question, and all sorts of answers have been given,
all of them more or less correct. Let us consider it simply.

If we did not know anything about the times in which our
Lord lived, and we looked at the map, the answer to the
question would be quite easy ; Judæa was in the south,

Galilee in the north, and Samaria lay between. It was the direct road. " He must needs pass through Samaria."

Yes, but that was not the usual road, for the Jew. Those of Judæa practically never travelled to Galilee through Samaria. " Jews have no dealings with Samaritans." It is a very significant statement. Those of proud Judæa, held Samaria almost in abhorrence, and if they had to go to Galilee, they generally crossed the Jordan, travelled up through Peræa, and entered Galilee that way. But " He must needs go through Samaria."

Geographically it was the straight way, but it was not the usual way ; and I do not think we can escape from the conviction that the " must " means that He was making His protest against the false reason for the usual way, and so refusing to take it ; and in doing so, He was, by this very action, in the moment when Judæa was refusing Him, and Jerusalem was rising against Him, indicating the universality of His Messianic mission. " He must needs pass through Samaria."

The " must " may be geographical, but I think it has a deeper note. Instead of taking the road of the Judæan, He chose the road they did not take, as a protest against their reason for not taking it, and a protest against their prejudice and pride ; and an indication of the inclusiveness of His Messiahship.

He arrived, John tells us, " He cometh to a city of Samaria, called Sychar, near to the parcel of ground that Jacob gave to his son Joseph ; and Jacob's well was there." So it reads in the Authorized ; so it reads in our Revisions ; " Jacob's well was there." In the margin of the Revisions this note is found ; " *Greek, spring.*" There is a remarkable distinction between a " spring " and a " well." When the woman talked about it she did not say " spring." She said " well." When Jesus presently spoke of the water that He should give, He did not say " well," He said " spring." The difference between a spring and a well is that a spring is a source of living water, that is, water that is always coming and bubbling

up ; and a well is a hole in which stagnant water is kept.
" Jesus therefore, being wearied with His journey, sat thus
by the spring. It was about the sixth hour."

That story of the parcel of ground that Jacob had given to
Joseph, is found in the Old Testament. Jacob bought it.
He gave it to Joseph. Presently Joseph was buried there.
There Jesus arrived, weary ; and it was the sixth hour.
There are differences of opinion as to whether John in his
Gospel used the Hebrew reckoning of time, or the Roman. I
leave it. It is an open discussion. It is not vital. I personally
believe that he used the Roman time, which means that
this was six o'clock in the evening. There had been the
long journey from Judæa to Sychar, and He was tired. Do
not let us miss these revealing touches. " In the beginning
was the Word, and the Word was with God, and the Word
was God . . . And the Word became flesh," and travelled
from Judæa through Samaria until He came to Sychar,
and was tired. God incarnate experiencing the limitations
of human life.

Now we have these verses, seven to twenty-five, and the
way in which we will glance at them is that of following the
dialogue. That dialogue is clearly marked in the repetition
of the sentences, " Jesus saith . . . the woman saith."
Jesus opened the conversation ; Jesus closed the conversation.
He opened the conversation by asking a favour on the human
level. He closed it by the supreme claim to Messiahship,
" I that speak unto thee am He." Between that opening
human request, and that final august statement of claim,
we have the record of the conversation.

He opened the conversation with a request on the human
level, the level of His own human necessity. He asked her
to give Him to drink. He knew her. He knew all about her.
The sequel proves it. He knew her past history ; He knew
her present life ; nevertheless He began by asking her to do
Him a favour. That in itself is arresting and revealing.
Some people would not have asked a favour of such a woman.
In that measure they are unlike their Master. He gained

admission to the soul of a sinning woman, by asking her to do Him a favour.

In her reply there was nothing of respect. An old Puritan commentator says it was a woman's pertness; "How is it, that Thou, being a Jew, askest a favour of me, which am a Samaritan woman?" Perhaps it was pertness, but I think it was more. I think it was astonishment. She knew that "Jews have no dealings with Samaritans"; and I think she was surprised to see a Jew in that neighbourhood at all. She was more surprised that He, a Jew evidently, a Jew perhaps by the very form and fashion of His countenance, and certainly by His dress, should ask a favour of a Samaritan woman. But there was no title of respect, in her first question. It was curiosity, astonishment; perchance astonishment expressing itself as the Puritan divine said, in pertness.

Then our Lord said to that woman that remarkable thing; "If thou knewest the gift of God, and Who it is that saith to thee, Give Me to drink; thou wouldest have asked of Him, and He would have given thee living water." This was a suggested offer. He has asked a favour. I wonder if she ever gave Him a drink. I do not know. I do not think she did, because I read presently, "She left her waterpot." I do not think she had filled it. But whether she responded or not, whether her astonishment halted her in responding or not; He came straight to the central spiritual need of the woman, as He made a suggested offer of living water.

She replied, and there was evidently something about that word of Jesus, that took away the pertness, if pertness it was. The casual, ordinary manner of her speech at first, the speech of a stranger to a stranger, ended. She said, "Sir." It was a word of respect, "Sir, Thou hast nothing to draw with, and the well is deep; from whence then hast Thou that living water? Art Thou greater than our father Jacob, which gave us the well, and drank thereof himself, and his sons, and his cattle?"

In that reply there was incredulity, and yet wonder. Her curiosity had been aroused, and she wondered what

He meant. She was confused in her thinking. She could not understand how He could give her living water. But evidently the phrase " living water " arrested her. She went back to the history of her people, and said ; " Art Thou greater than our father Jacob, which gave us this well ? " I do not think there was anything very clear in her apprehension ; but she was arrested. She spoke to Him with respect, but there was incredulity in her mind, and yet she was wondering, " Art Thou greater ? "

Then He answered her, " Everyone that drinketh of this water shall thirst again ; but whosoever drinketh of the water that I shall give him shall never thirst ; but the water that I shall give him shall become in him a spring of water, bubbling up unto eternal life." He thus interpreted His meaning to her, not perfectly, but suggestively. He had first said He was able to give water, and that if she had known Who He was, she would have asked water from Him. But said she, How can You get it ? The well is deep, and You have nothing to draw with ? Art Thou greater than Jacob ? To which He replied that the water He would give would be water which would spring up in her own life. He was indicating to her that His intention was a spiritual intention.

Now listen to her. " Sir "—still respectful,—" Give me this water, that I thirst not, neither come all the way hither to draw." Mark the confusion in her thinking. The first part of her word to Him was a recognition of the fact of the dissatisfaction at the core of her personality. " Give me this water that I thirst not." Then, " neither come all the way hither to draw." She was confused. She had caught something of the spiritual significance of what He had said, " Give me this water that I thirst not " ; but continuing, " neither come all the way hither to draw," she swung back to the material. She had grasped something of the significance of what He had said, and then there was a reaction of perplexity. First, " Give me this water that I thirst not."

I do not think that I am doing any violence to the story

if I suggest that if she had said all she thought at that moment, it might have been,—Never thirst ? How thirsty I am, how disillusioned I am, how disappointed I am, how restless I am. Give me this water that I thirst not ; but perhaps He does not mean anything of that sort. Then give me something to prevent this toilsome journey in order to draw. Now, " Give me this water, that I thirst not," was the sigh, the sob of a discontented, disappointed, thirsty woman.

How did He reply ? " Go, call thy husband." Why that ? If she was to have that well of water springing up in her, there must first be moral investigation and correction. She had said, Give me this water. In effect He said, I hear the cry of your soul for this water. I have this water to give, but there is something in your life that has first to be set right. " Go, call they husband."

Immediately she was evasive, when He touched the moral realm. " I have no husband." It was a sort of supercilious dismissal. She used no title of respect now, but bluntly said, " I have no husband," as though she would say, I am an emancipated woman ; I want no interference.

But the Lord had not done with her. Very beautifully, He continued. There was nothing contemptuous or bitter in what He said, but the simple statement of facts. That is quite true ; you have had five ; and the man you are living with now is not your husband. He had thus invaded the moral realm, and torn the mask away, that she was proposing to fling over the story by her evasion. That little sentence, " I have no husband " was an evasion, an intended dismissal of the question. It meant, That is none of Your business ; what is that to do with You ? To which the Lord replied, You cannot hide from Me. I know all about you.

Now watch her next word, " Sir, I perceive that Thou art a prophet." The term of respect was again employed, and more. Her words proved conviction, and constituted a tacit confession. A moment ago there was evasion. Now there was admission. " Sir, I perceive that Thou art a prophet," which meant, You evidently know all.

Then listen, " Our fathers worshipped in this mountain ; and ye say, that in Jerusalem is the place where men ought to worship." She had been unmasked. She had been compelled to own up ; and then she adopted a method that is very constantly adopted. She tried to evade the issue once more, by raising a theological discussion. And yet was there not something more in it than that ? Had there not come up out of her life the question which had often puzzled her in her girlhood and young womanhood ? I have been brought up here. I belong here. All my people, my father's people, have said Gerizim is the place for worship ; but you Jews say Jerusalem. Which is right ? It was a very vital question.

The marvellous thing is the way in which Jesus answered. He consented to enter into her discussion. He told her first of all the Samaritans were still in ignorance of the worship of God. The Jew was the one who did know the truth about worship, and through the Jew had come salvation. But then He went right on, and said to her that marvellous thing, " Woman, believe Me, the hour cometh, when neither in this mountain "—Gerizim ; " nor in Jerusalem, shall ye worship the Father " ; and, " The hour cometh, and now is, when the true worshippers shall worship the Father in spirit and truth ; for such doth the Father seek to be His worshippers. God is Spirit ; and they that worship Him must worship Him in spirit and truth."

Thus He answered her, in statements so profound that sometimes I think we hardly yet grasp their significance. He revealed the fact that there is no value in Mount Gerizim ; there is no value in Jerusalem, apart from reality and spiritual intention. The hour cometh and now is, when they that worship God, worship in spirit and truth. It is not a question of locality in worship. Moreover it is not a question of intellect merely. To worship, men must get down to the deepest thing in their personality, spirit and truth. There must be honesty ; there must be reality. As though He had said to her, I have been trying to help you there, by tearing off the mask, and compelling you to face your own life. If you are prepared to do that, you need not discuss locations. Gerizim is nothing; Jerusalem is nothing; spirit and truth are everything.

And then she said; " I know that Messiah cometh . . . when He is come, He will declare unto us all things," and He replied in the final claim, " I that speak unto thee am He."

The story reveals a woman with a remarkable religious background. She spoke of " Our father, Jacob." Most probably she had not referred to that relationship for years, but it recurred in the presence of Jesus. Then presently she revealed the fact of the hope of her people in which she had been trained; the coming of Messiah. As our Lord dealt with her, we observe first her almost flippant address; then there came respect, and a recognition of a Man of God, a prophet. Presently we find her not affirming, but out of a sincere soul asking, " Can this be the Christ ? "

The last movement in this section reveals the issues of this Samaritan visit. First the effect on the disciples. They came back. They were astonished to see Him talking to a woman; for remember according to Jewish law, no Rabbi must ever hold conversation with a woman alone. He was doing it. He was always trampling upon the foolish traditional conventionalities that were blasting human life. However, though they were astonished, they kept silence! It is a great gift that of silence !

Think of that day again, and so understand their concern about Him. The long journey, eventide, a tired Master and thirsty. They knew He ought to be hungry. Rabbi, they said, Eat. Then He revealed His heart. " I have meat to eat that ye know not. . . . My meat is to do the will of Him that sent Me, and to accomplish His work." May we not with very great reverence say, It is as though Jesus had said : There are times when the physical does not count at all. There is a hunger deeper than the physical ; and there is bread that will satisfy that ; and I have been having that bread. What was that doing of the will of God? Dealing with that human soul, leading that woman into the light. Perfect sustenance for His whole life for the time being was found in the wooing and the winning of a sinning woman.

Then He looked at them, and He said, You say four months, and then cometh harvest. He was still thinking in the realm of the spiritual. "Behold, I say unto you, lift up your eyes, and look on the fields, that they are white already unto harvest." Now in a few brief sentences let us get the sense of that. If those disciples had been appointed a commission of enquiry as to the possibilities of Christian enterprise in Samaria I know exactly the resolution they would have passed. The resolution would have been; Samaria unquestionably needs our Master's message, but it is not ready for it. There must first be ploughing, then sowing, and then waiting. It is needy, but it is not ready. That is exactly what He said, "Say not ye, There are yet four months, and then." Four months meant ploughing and sowing, and waiting. But He said, You are wrong. These fields "are white already unto harvest." The region that looks most hopeless is ready if you will reap.

To-day we speak of some field as difficult, and almost hopeless. Christ still says that such fields are white to harvest. The most difficult fields are white to harvest. Our business is to put in the sickle, and reap.

He said the same thing on another occasion. When He saw the multitudes distressed and scattered, He was moved with compassion, and He called His disciples and said, "Harvest!" The trouble is not that the fields are not white. The trouble is that the labourers are not ready.

Then we return to the woman and the Samaritans. The woman had left her waterpot. She forgot all about it. She did not get her water. She went. Something had happened to her, a revolution. She had come face to face with a Jew, that was a prophet, and possibly the Messiah. She left her waterpot, and she went to the men of the city, and she said, "Come, see a Man, which told me all things that ever I did;

can this be the Christ ? " They were evidently impressed, because they came with her, back to Jesus. Then I do not quite know what He said to them, but it so impressed them that they begged Him to stay with them, and He stayed two whole days.

Then listen to them ! John tells us, " They believed on Him because of the word of the woman." Then presently they said, " Now we believe, not because of thy speaking ; for we have heard for ourselves." They had believed because of her word, but now they had got beyond that, they had heard Him. Belief on her testimony brought them to enquire ; and the result was they believed on His word.

Then it was in Samaria that He was given that full and final title, " The Saviour of the world." He crossed the boundary line of prejudice. He left the region that boasted in its privilege ; and in the region outside, He had found a human soul, and she a sinning woman, who had burnt out her life until only the ashes were left ; and had opened to her the way to God for worship, by dealing with her moral nature, and satisfying her spiritual thirst. He had seen the fields white to harvest, and had gathered that sheaf. And so, right there in Samaria, it was that they said, " The Saviour of the world."

John iv. 43-54.

AFTER the two days' sojourn in Samaria, the Lord completed His journey to Galilee. John tells us that " After the two days He went forth from thence into Galilee. For Jesus Himself testified, that a prophet hath no honour in his own country." That links the story with what we have at the beginning of chapter four. " When therefore the Lord knew how that the Pharisees had heard that Jesus was making and baptizing more disciples than John, He departed again into Galilee." Then came the Samaritan interlude. Now,

taking the story up again, " After the two days, He went
forth from thence into Galilee." In other words, He completed
His journey, and arrived at the destination for which He
started when He left Judæa.

The parenthesis of John here is arresting ; " Jesus Himself
testified, that a prophet hath no honour in his own country."
Admittedly that statement is a little difficult. What does
John mean there by " His own country " ? There are differing
opinions. There are those who say that it meant Galilee.
In Galilee He had been brought up. In Galilee was the town
which He made the basis of His operations, Capernaum.
But I think that is hardly tenable when we notice what immediately follows. " Jesus Himself testified that a prophet
hath no honour in his own country. So when He came into
Galilee, the Galileans received Him." I do not think it is
possible to understand the reference to be to Galilee. I think
Origen was right that the reference is to Judæa. Judæa
was the country of His birth and registration (Luke ii. 4).
He was of the tribe of Judah after the flesh. Judæa was
peopled largely by the people of the tribes of Judah and
Benjamin. In the returns from captivity, remnants of all
the tribes went back, a great admixture. Still Benjamin and
Judah were the predominant tribes ; and our Lord, in that
sense, belonged to Judah. " His own country " was surely
Judæa.

The sequence in the ministry of Jesus is patent. He had
been in the capital city, the city of the great king, Jerusalem ;
and there we are told, " Many believed on His name, beholding the signs which He did." But He did not believe in
them. He knew that their attitude of supposed acceptance
of Him was superficial, the result of that which was spectacular
only. He could not trust them. He could not commit
Himself to them. Then He had left Jerusalem, and gone
into Judæa itself, and carried on a ministry there. Now,
in the fourth chapter and the third verse we read, " He left
Judæa, and departed again into Galilee. The word employed there for " departed " as we saw, is a singularly strong

one, meaning that He broke with Judæa. That does not
mean that He never went back. He did. But He had not
been received either in the city or the country in any way
other than the superficial. By this time He had a group of
disciples. He had not yet elected apostles. He did so
eventually ; among them He elected those who were in this
first group. It is surely significant that not one of the apostles
came from Judæa. They were all from the district despised
by Judæans. When presently Saul was found, and called
to the apostolate, he was not from Judæa. He was born in
Tarsus. Judæa had refused Him, and now, after the two
days' sojourn in Samaria, He continued His journey ; and He
arrived in Galilee, because the Prophet was not in honour in
His own country.

John emphasized the contrast between the attitude in
Judæa, and that in Galilee. "When He came into Galilee,
the Galileans received Him." Why ? "Having seen all the
things that He did in Jerusalem at the feast." Mark the
force of the next statement, "For they also went unto the
feast." John meant to show that if the Galileans were not
Judæans, they were not alienated from the religion of Israel ;
"*they also went to the feast.*" These Galileans in Jerusalem
had seen what He had done there, and they travelled back.
Before the Lord arrived, they had spread the news of the
things they had seen, and so they welcomed Him. Later He
broke with Galilee also. It was Judæa which first practically
refused Him. So He withdrew from the superficiality of her
crowds, and the crass ignorance and hostility of her rulers ;
and turned to Galilee. At the beginning they welcomed Him.

It was in Galilee that He wrought the third sign. John
says, "this is again the second sign that Jesus did, having
come out of Judæa into Galilee." In the sequence of his
selection this is the third sign, but the second in Galilee.

The story in some senses, is not so spectacular or pictorial
as the turning of water into wine, or the cleansing of the
Temple. In other senses it is one of the most remarkable.

The occasion of the working of this sign was the appeal of

[81]

F

a father, who is called in our translations a "nobleman." The Greek word *Basilikos* means a king's man. The term simply means an officer in the court of a king. This man was an officer in the service of Herod the tetrarch. We really do not know who he was. There have been very interesting suggestions made. Some have suggested this was Chusa, Herod's steward. Others have suggested that he was Manaen, Herod's foster brother.

This man, when he heard that Jesus had come out of Judæa into Galilee, "went unto Him, and besought Him that He would come down, and heal his son, for he was at the point of death." It was the appeal of agony, made by a father. His boy was at the point of death, and he came to Jesus, and asked Him to go down and heal him.

At that point in this story we arrive at an amazing thing. "Jesus said unto him, Except ye see signs and wonders, ye will in no wise believe." We are inevitably startled that Jesus should answer in that way to such a cry as came from that man's heart. It is a very revealing matter. The man came to Jesus in his agony and besought Him—mark the force of it,—"*besought* Him that He would come down, and heal his son, for he was at the point of death." Jesus said, "Except ye see signs and wonders, ye will in no wise believe."

Notice first that our Lord addressed him in the plural number. He did not say, *Thou*, except *thou* shalt see; He said "Ye." He addressed him as one of a crowd. He classified him as among the ordinary and common crowd which our Lord was facing in His ministry, whether in Judæa, or in Galilee. What was true in Judæa, that there was a confidence in Him, to which He could not commit Himself, was equally true in Galilee. Let me here run ahead of my story, and say that our Lord meant to answer the cry of that agony. He could not refuse, being Who He was. But He had purposes deeper than the comfort of sorrow, even of such sorrow as that. He was dealing with a man in the actuality of the deep necessity of his individuality. And so as a surgeon plunges a knife, He said in effect, You have come to Me in

your agony ; but you are only one of a crowd. " Except ye
see signs and wonders, ye will in no wise believe." That is
the truth about you in common with others. That is what you
are all looking for ; and though you have come to Me about
your boy, why have you come to Me ? Because you have
heard that I am performing signs and wonders, and you
hope to get something out of it. It was severe, but He was
dealing with the whole man. He lay bare the underlying
truth about him as He classified him with the crowd. Agony
had driven him to Jesus. He will deal with that presently ;
He will heal the boy ; but He will first deal with the man.

What next ? " The nobleman saith unto Him, Sir, come
down ere my child die." We cannot tell how far that rebuke
of Jesus had really reached him and found him at this point ;
but his reply is very remarkable in that he did not deny the
charge Jesus had made against him that he was looking for
signs and wonders. Indeed, he admitted it, for he said, " Come
down ere my child die." There was no consciousness in his
soul that it was possible for Christ to deal with that boy
unless He was there. He was looking for the material, and
the touch. He had believed that if only Jesus were there,
He could do something, because he had heard of what He had
done. So out of the anguish of his heart, he said, " Sir, come
down, ere my child die." It was as though he had said,
Whether I want to see signs or wonders does not count ;
I want my boy healed, and that can only be if Thou art there.
Thus he was tacitly admitting the truth of what Jesus had
said. But he asked for help, and flung himself out on the
power of Jesus, not understanding.

Then Jesus spoke again ; " Go thy way ; thy son liveth."
That was all. Observe what that meant. He gave him no
sign ; and He did not do what he asked Him to do, which
would have satisfied his feeling that there was a necessity
for something spectacular. The man said, " Come down."
Jesus replied practically : I am not coming. I am not
going to act in the way you think necessary. But I will give
you the help you seek. " Go, . . . thy son liveth." He gave

[83]

him no sign, but He created an opportunity for the exercise of a faith which lacked a sign. Christ said in effect : I will not give you a sign ; I will give you a word. You will get your sign after your faith operates.

Then we read : " The man believed the word that Jesus spake unto him, and he went his way." What made him believe ? Perchance I cannot tell you dogmatically ; and yet I think I know quite well. There was something in the tone of that voice, something in the glance of that eye, something in the majesty and beauty of that face, that made that man say, Well, I do not know how it is going to be done, but I believe Him, He says my boy lives. He believed, and went his way.

Here let us pause and take a backward glance. They believed in Jerusalem because they saw the signs, and He could not commit Himself to them. In Samaria they said at last to the woman, Now we believe, not because of your testimony ; we have heard Him, we have heard His word, and believe. Now we have the same thing again, " He believed the word Jesus spake."

The sign itself was the healing of the boy. At the hour in which Jesus spoke the boy was healed, at a distance. There were at least between twenty and thirty miles separating Capernaum from Cana. At the moment of the word of Jesus distance was annihilated ; the boy was healed.

When the father arrived, his servants met him. They told him " that his son lived." That is exactly what Jesus had said ; " Thy son liveth." He went without any evidence other than the word of Jesus ; and as he arrived, the servants of his household met him, and practically repeated what Jesus had said. He had said it with authority, and the man had believed His word, not understanding. Now the servants stated it as an actual accomplishment, Thy son liveth.

The man is perfectly honest. He is going to enquire, to investigate. This is the time to investigate, when the thing has happened. " He enquired of them the hour when he began to amend." In his question the weakness of his understanding is revealed. He could not imagine that the boy he had left at the point of death could have become well immediately. He enquired when he began to amend. They told him that he did not begin to amend at all. He was well straightway, "Yesterday at the seventh hour the fever left him." Suddenly the boy was well. At what hour? The seventh. The man at once saw the synchronizing of the word of Jesus twenty miles away with a fact in his home. Thy son liveth, at the seventh hour Jesus said that; and twenty miles away, the fever left him, the burning heat passed, and the boy was well.

"The father knew that it was at that hour in which Jesus said unto him, Thy son liveth; and himself believed, and his whole house." Thus this man won to the highest realm of belief. First of all there was the feeling, which amounted to belief, that this wonderful Prophet Who had now come out of Judæa into Galilee, could do something for his boy, when nobody else could. Christ searched him with amazing severity, unmasking the deepest fact in his life. Then He created for him the opportunity for the exercise of faith without a sign. The man saw something in that face, and heard something in that tone, which made him say, I believe that. Then he started, and yet he halted, when he arrived; What were the signs? When did he begin to amend? The reply was that there was no process but immediateness; the fever left him; and it was at the seventh hour. Then the full significance broke upon him, and he went over, the whole of his personality, to Jesus; and not he alone, but all his household.

The first sign recorded by John was wrought in the realm of creation and joy, at the wedding feast, when He turned the water into wine. The second was wrought in the realm of worship, when He went into the Temple and cleansed it. Now in the third, power is seen operating in the realm of disease and sorrow.

In this sign then we have first of all a revelation of absolute power. We use the word supernatural. I am not objecting to it, if it be rightly apprehended. As a matter of fact, however, what we call supernatural, is only super-understandable. All this was perfectly natural to One Who like Jesus, lived in unbroken fellowship with God, so that God could operate through Him, as He could not through others. All the signs which we call miracles, are demonstrations, not of Christ's Deity. The demonstration of that is found rather in His words. As Peter put it on the day of Pentecost, He was " a Man, approved of God unto you by powers and wonders and signs which God wrought through Him in the midst of you." God was operating through Him. Once we recognize that " power belongeth unto God," there is no difficulty at all. In this sign there was a revelation of God's absolute power, healing in a moment at a distance, without contact. Should it seem an incredible thing with you, with any man, with any woman, that there can be healing at a distance, when God is at work, without contact ; if we can listen to someone talking from the other side of the world to-day without any visible contact at all ? It is too late in the day to attempt to laugh the supernatural out of court.

And yet, in the working of this sign, there was a revelation of difficulty, the difficulty of God. " Except ye see signs and wonders ye will not believe." Something spectacular is a wrong basis for faith. In the last hours, Jesus looked into the eyes of His disciples and said, " Believe Me that I am in the Father, and the Father in Me ; or else believe Me for the very works' sake." The works are secondary line of proof ; Himself is the supreme line of proof.

And what a revelation is here of His infinite compassion, and His infinite patience. If a man wants a sign, and is seeking for it, well, Christ will give it to him ; but He will make it possible by a word, for him to exercise faith before he gets the sign.

Here also is a revelation of method. " Go thy way, thy son liveth," a word of command, no evidence ; but when that command is obeyed, the evidence comes in the healing of the boy.

And so as one stands back, and looks at this third sign,

the things that impress one are these : the severity of our Lord in the presence of some weakness of the human soul ; the authority of our Lord by which He appeals even to that weak soul, and gives him an opportunity ; the victory of our Lord in which He so spoke that the man obeyed ; and at last the man was won, with all his household.

John v.

THE chapter begins with an indefinite time note, " After these things." John who, in the beginning of his narrative seemed to be almost meticulous in noting the succession of days, now refers indefinitely to time, so that we do not know exactly how long elapsed before the thing now recorded, took place. But we do observe that He, Who had practically broken with Judæa, went up to Jerusalem. John says, " There was a feast of the Jews." There has been a good deal of interesting discussion as to what feast was referred to. I believe it was the Passover, but it is not of vital importance that we should know.

The story contained in this chapter is one, and in chronological sequence, it is the last incident recorded in the first year of our Lord's ministry. Almost immediately after this, Christ began His definitely and intentionally public propaganda.

This then is the account of the fourth sign in John's selection of signs. The chapter tells the story briefly of the sign, and of the controversy which it raised. On the human level, what Jesus did that day, and what He said that day, cost Him His life. They never forgave Him.

The chapter breaks quite naturally into two movements ; first the story of the sign in itself, verses one to nine ; and then the account of the controversy which resulted from the sign, from the tenth verse to the end.

[87]

The details of the sign in itself are most familiar to all of us. I touch upon them lightly, in order that we may consider the significance of the sign, as revealed in the controversy which resulted.

This sign was spontaneous on the part of Jesus. The first sign He wrought in response to a request, His mother's. The second was spontaneous, when He cleansed the Temple. The third He wrought in response to a request, that of the king's man who came to Him about his boy. Here again is a sign that Jesus wrought without being asked. There was no cry from that man for help. This makes it the more remarkable in revealing His mission, and the purpose of His heart, that for which He was in the world.

Passing through the porches round Bethesda He saw, He knew, He acted. "He saw a man." He "knew that he had been now a long time in that case"; and He acted. The story, merely as a story, is full of dramatic suggestiveness. Jesus only spoke to this man three times, and every time in what may be described as short, sharp, incisive sentences. Looking at him as he lay, He said, Do you want to be made whole? Not "Wilt thou"? as if "wilt" were part of the verb to will; or "Wouldest thou" in the same sense. Our Lord was not asking him if he had decided, resolved, willed to be made whole. It was a question, not of volition, but of desire. Do you want to be made whole?

The man's answer was a protest, as though he had said, Why ask me a question like that? He said, "Sir, I have no man, when the water is troubled, to put me into the pool"; which simply meant, What do you mean asking me that? Of course I want to be made whole, but what chance have I? He had lost hope.

Then came the quick and sharp threefold command: "Arise, take up thy bed, and walk." First, Rise, do the thing you cannot do, because I tell you to do it. Then, Take up thy bed, which Dr. Marcus Dods said meant, Make no provision for a relapse! Finally, "And walk," which I may say means, Do not expect to be carried.

Then Jesus " conveyed Himself away," and the man did not know Who He was. In the same day, later, in the Temple, Jesus found him. The man had not been to the Temple for thirty-eight years at least. Now he had evidently gone straight there, and Christ spoke to him once more, " Behold, thou art made whole ; no longer continue in sin, lest a worse thing befall thee."

Thus we discover that this sign had invaded a new realm. The first was a sign in the realm of creation and joy at Cana. The second was a sign in the realm of worship in the Temple. The third was a sign in the realm of suffering and disease, again at Cana. Now our Lord invaded, in this last incident in the first year of His public ministry, the moral realm. This last word of Jesus to the man shows what was the matter with him radically,—palsy resultantly, but palsy resulting from his own sin. We know this because of what Jesus said to him, " No longer continue in sin ; lest a worse thing befall thee." The physical was the result, and the evidence, of moral malady. Our Lord invaded that realm, and invaded that realm in the case of a man absolutely derelict. For eight and thirty years he had been in that case. The continuity of the suffering was the result of the continuity of the sinning. To that man Jesus came, and wrought this great sign.

The full significance of the sign is revealed in the controversy. This controversy moved in two realms ; first on the question of the Sabbath ; and then, as the result of what Christ had said in the presence of His critics about His action on the Sabbath, the controversy became bitter, and was concerned with the claim that He had made.

The question of the Sabbath. The rulers saw this man carrying his mattress through the streets of Jerusalem ; and they at once charged him with breaking Sabbath. Technically, the law was on their side. Such a thing was certainly forbidden. That which arrests us as we ponder this is that these rulers surely knew this man. It is almost incredible that a man who had been living on charity, a derelict for thirty and eight years, would not be known. But they do not appear to have recognized the fact that the man upon whom they had looked, derelict and undone and in misery, to whom perchance ever and anon they had flung a charitable shekel, was now walking in the full vigour of his manhood. He was carrying a mattress on the Sabbath, and that was all they saw. They ignored the man, and charged him with breaking Sabbath.

His answer to the charge was revealing and conclusive. He said, He that healed me told me to do it. He tried to draw their attention to his new condition. They took no notice of the fact. He was breaking Sabbath ; his healing was nothing. These men have their successors to-day. There is always a tragedy in being blind to some great spiritual and moral victory, while we strain at a gnat, swallowing a camel. That is what they were doing.

How did our Lord answer them ? He had a double answer. He answered first to the man. He gave him, if incidentally, none the less definitely, a revelation of the moral significance of the thing He had done for him. He was in the Temple. Jesus found him, and said, " Behold, thou art made whole ; continue no longer in sin." This certainly meant ; What I have done for you to-day in giving you back your physical health, and enabling you to carry that mattress, and leave it somewhere, and come to the Temple, has a moral intention. I am not concerned, as though Jesus had said to him, first with your body. I am concerned with the moral dereliction which has blasted you. I have delivered you. That is the meaning of the thing that is done to-day. You are made whole. Why ? That you may " no longer continue in sin." That was Christ's answer to the charge, made to the man, an indication of the moral significance of what He had done.

Then He made answer to the Jews who were criticizing. " My Father worketh even until now, and I work." That revealed the religious significance of what He had done. The moral intention was revealed to the man who was healed. The religious significance was revealed to the men who were

supposedly the exponents of religion. In that declaration
He interpreted God. To the man He showed that the healing
was in order to right living. To the religious rulers He declared
in effect : The reason why you see that man carrying his
mattress on the Sabbath day, a healed man, is to be found in
the restlessness of God in the presence of all human agony,
even though it result from sin. " My Father worketh." These
rulers said that the rest of the Sabbath was being violated ;
and Jesus said, God has no rest while a man like this lies where
that man was lying ? Humanity broke in upon the rest of
God, when it sinned against Him, and so against itself, bringing all the blasting and the blighting and the misery of the
years ; and because of that, God is restless. Said Jesus, My
Father works, and I work ; and the work of God, and My work,
is revealed in what that man has now received. The carrying
of a mattress on a Sabbath day is very trivial a thing when we
get a vision of God, and of His action. That man had continued in sin, had known the misery of the continuity ; but
God was after him. There can be no rest for God while
humanity is suffering.

Then began the second phase of controversy. These men
were intelligent. They saw the significance of what Jesus
had said. They recognized that He claimed equality with
God as He called God His Father. They were perfectly right
in their understanding. That is precisely what Jesus had
done. On another occasion He said, " I and My Father are
one." From verses nineteen to forty-seven we have His
answer to their objection and criticism. That answer has
three movements. First of all, in verses nineteen to twenty-
nine, He enforced the very claim to which they had objected.
Then, in verses thirty to thirty-seven, He spoke of witnesses
to the truth of the claim, naming two whom He declined ;
and two whom He claimed as giving final demonstration.
Then, from verses thirty-eight to forty-seven, our Lord in
the most searching and withering way, turned upon those
critics of His, those religious rulers, and condemned them.

In His enforcement of His claims He thrice used the

arresting formula, " Verily, verily," verses nineteen, twenty-four and twenty-six.

The first " Verily, verily " introduced a statement yet more emphatic of the thing He had said, when He had declared, " My Father worketh . . . and I work "; co-operation between Himself and God. " The Son can do nothing of Himself, . . . but the Father loveth the Son . . . the Father . . . hath given all judgment unto the Son . . . that all may honour the Son even as they honour the Father." These are the revealing phrases. He was repeating His claim of co-operation with God, and God's co-operation with Him. He was insisting upon it.

The second " Verily, verily " introduced His declaration concerning His own activity, in which He had claimed that His activity resulted from the fact that He was sent ; thus still enforcing the idea of fellowship and co-operation with God. It is indeed a stupendous claim. According to it, if a man believe His word, he does not only believe Him, he believes the One that sent Him ; and he that does that, has the age-abiding life, " and cometh not into judgment, but hath passed out of death into life."

The last " Verily, verily " introduced a statement in which He went back to what had already been said ; and said it in a new form, again insisting upon the co-operation of the Father and the Son. " Verily, verily, I say unto you, The hour cometh, and now is, when the dead shall hear the voice of the Son of God and they that hear shall live. For as the Father hath life in Himself, even so gave He to the Son also to have life in Himself ; and He gave Him authority to execute judgment, because He is the Son of man."

All this He said to account for what He had done for the man, and for the fact that He had ignored the triviality of a supposed desecration of the Sabbath, when a man was healed, and enabled not to sin.

Then He referred to the witnesses to the truth of what He had been saying, and that in a most remarkable way. First of all, He said, " If I bear witness of Myself, My witness is not true." He might have borne witness of Himself, but He declined to do it. He said, "It is another that beareth witness of Me, and I know that the witness which He witnesseth is true." To whom was He referring? John? No. He referred to John briefly and beautifully; " Ye have sent unto John, and he hath borne witness unto the truth." He told you the truth. John said, I am not the Christ, I am not the prophet, I am the voice in the wilderness. You sent to John. John bare witness unto the truth; " But the witness which I receive is not from man." John's witness was true; he bare witness to the truth; but that was not the witness that proved the accuracy of what He was saying. Said Christ, I receive not witness from John. And then, in an aside of tender and beautiful recognition of the greatness of John, He said, " He was the lamp that burneth and shineth . . . but the witness that I have is greater than that of John."

What witness then did He depend upon? The witness of the works. " The works which the Father hath given Me to accomplish, the very works that I do, bear witness of Me." His works demonstrated the fact that He was sent from the Father, and therefore He had the witness of the Father through the works. That derelict man was such a work. Christ thus claimed that the healed man, restored not only to physical strength, but to the possibility of worship within the Temple courts, by moral cleansing, demonstrated the activity of God.

Then as He closed, He turned upon those men. I do not think it is possible to read this, without feeling the stirring of His anger in the presence of the men who put more value on the technicality of a ritual observance, than the restoration of a man to life and righteousness. He began by saying, " Ye have neither heard His voice at any time, nor seen His form." He thus charged them with ignorance of God. " Ye have not His word abiding in you ; for Whom He sent, Him ye believe not." Mark the magnificence of that claim. When One comes, sent from God, you do not know Him, and you do not receive Him. " My Father worketh even until now, and I work." You say I am a blasphemer, claiming equality with

God. But you never knew God ; you never heard His voice, or saw His form. Consequently you do not know Me !

Then with fine satire, He uttered the words so constantly misquoted. He did not say, " Search the Scriptures." It was not a command. It was a statement. " Ye search the Scriptures." They were doing it, but in a wrong way, and from a wrong view-point, because they had got a wrong idea of their own Scriptures. " Ye search the Scriptures, because ye think that in them ye have eternal life." That is where they were wrong. It is possible to search these writings, and never come into the realm of eternal life.

He had not done. " And these are they which testify of Me." Yes, that is the truth. There is no life in the Scriptures themselves, but if we will follow where they lead, they will bring us to Him, and so we find life, not in the Scriptures, but in Him through them.

Then mark the biting satire of the next words. He said, " I " and the " I " is emphatic, " *I* receive not glory from men. But I know you, that ye have not the love of God in yourselves." What was the proof ? The proof was that they were more concerned with a sabbatarian ritual, than with a derelict man restored to manhood and purity. He said, You lack God's love. It is God's love that makes Him restless and makes Him work. If they had known Him, they would not have raised this objection.

And still the satire. " I am come in My Father's name, and ye receive Me not ; if another shall come in his own name, him ye will receive." And so the final word, " How can ye believe, which receive glory one of another, and the glory that cometh from the only God ye seek not."

And so He ended. " Think not that I will accuse you to the Father ; there is one that accuseth you, even Moses, on whom ye have set your hope. If ye believed Moses, ye would believe Me ; for he wrote of Me. But if ye believe not his writings, how shall ye believe My words ? " The emphasis there is on " his " and " My." If you believe not *his* writings, how will you believe *My* words ? That is to say, our Lord in those final words to those rulers, claimed the authority of Moses. He revealed the fact that the ultimate in the authority of Moses could only be discovered in Him. He wrote of Me, said Jesus.

So far we have had four signs; the first in the realm of creation and joy in answer to the request of His mother; the second in the realm of religion and worship, a stupendous action of His own volition; the third in the realm of disease, in response to the agonized cry of a father; and now as the first year was closing, and He was about entering upon that wider ministry of propaganda and declaration, in the realm of the moral, here was a sign, spontaneously wrought. He went to the lowest deeps, and entered the moral realm, and touched sin in its effects upon man; and then interpreted His action by the declaration that He was working together with God.

John vi. 1–21.

In the ministry of our Lord, the central period commenced with the imprisonment of John the Baptist, and found its culmination in the confession of Peter at Caesarea Philippi. That period lasted for about two years; and it is the period to which John gives least attention. All he has to tell us about it is found in chapter six, running over into the first verse of chapter seven, which marks the end of the period. From this period John selected two signs in the realm of works, and one in the realm of words.

In this chapter we have the record of these three signs, and they are closely connected. The two signs in the realm of works followed each other in sequence; and the first sign in the realm of words, grew directly out of the sign wrought in the realm of works, when He fed the multitude.

In these twenty-one verses we have two signs in the realm

of works ; in the scheme of John the fifth sign, the feeding of five thousand ; and the sixth, the stilling of the storm.

The importance of the sign of the feeding of the five thousand is evidenced by the fact that it is the only miracle of Jesus, using the common word, recorded by the four evangelists. Mark, the writer of the first Gospel unquestionably from the standpoint of time, tells the story. Matthew who follows him, repeats it. Luke who came a little later, gives it ; and now John, writing much later, records the story also. What its significance is, will be discovered when we consider the discourse that grew out of it. Now we look at the sign in itself ; and at the first effects which were produced ; and at the fact that it was immediately followed by another, the stilling of the storm, which had its relation so far as His disciples were concerned, to the sign of the feeding.

What was the occasion upon which Jesus wrought this sign ? I ask the question, because John does not tell us. He simply says, "After these things," and nothing is told us as to the occasion. Moreover he omits many details supplied by Matthew, Mark, and Luke. He omits nothing that is essential to the value of the sign, but only details which are helpful in our thinking about it. So I am going to refer to the other records, in order that we may see when it occurred.

Such reference shows first that this sign was wrought after the twelve returned from their first mission. We learn secondly that it occurred almost immediately after the death of John the Baptist. And finally we discover that the sign was wrought about the time when Herod had expressed his desire to see Jesus. Filled with fear after the death of John, he heard of Jesus and His wondrous doings. In all likelihood he had heard a good deal about Him before then, but had passed it off as having no particular value. Herod had passed under the influence of the preaching of John, and as I believe, at one moment had very nearly yielded his life to his preaching. It is a significant statement that Herod " had heard him gladly." Then he had yielded to lust and passion.

Now John was dead, murdered at the behest of a dancing wanton ; and Herod heard about Jesus, and he sought to see Him, for, he said, John Baptist was risen from the dead. That creates the atmosphere of this sign.

John does not give us particulars of the immediate circumstances. " After these things Jesus went away to the other side of the sea of Galilee, which is the sea of Tiberias. And a great multitude followed Him, because they beheld the signs which He did on them that were sick." Again this is a translation which misses the point a little. The tenses of the verbs are suggestive. Let us read it, slightly changed. " And a great multitude were following Him, because they were beholding the signs which He was doing." It is not merely the record of an occasion, but of a constant thing. The time had now come when these people were constantly and habitually following Him.

It was at that time that " Jesus went up into the mountain, and there was sitting with His disciples." Thus the occasion is revealed from John's standpoint. The hour had come when Jesus practically had no rest. The multitude was following Him. Wherever He went they were beholding the signs He did. Constant activity on the part of our Lord. Constant interest on the part of the crowd. Because of those conditions, " He went up into the mountain, and there He was sitting with His disciples," seeking retirement, seeking rest. " The Word became flesh," and entered into all the experiences of human life ; among the rest, felt the weariness that comes from the pressure of the crowd.

In that connection John tells us, " The passover, the feast of the Jews, was at hand," thus emphasizing the greatness and eagerness of the crowds that were round about Him ; and continuing, says " Jesus therefore lifting up His eyes, and seeing that a great multitude cometh unto Him, saith unto Philip."

Here again the narrative by John is condensed. Once more then, we refer to the other Gospels ; and our reference here is pertinent and important. From them we learn that He had

G [97]

spent a whole day teaching those crowds. Luke tells us that
He was teaching them concerning " the Kingdom of God."

John records the desire of Jesus to feed the crowd. He
was teaching them concerning " the Kingdom of God " ; and
yet, understanding their hunger, He desired to satisfy it.

Then comes the story of the discussion with Philip and
Andrew. Desiring to feed the crowd, the Lord turned to
Philip, and He said, " Whence are we to buy bread, that
these may eat ? " What an amazing question. Five thousand,
as the event turned out, of men ; and Jesus said, Philip, where
shall we buy bread to feed them ? Philip did not answer the
question, as to the " where." He said in effect, What is the
use of talking about " where " when we have no money to
buy. Two hundred pennyworth of bread would not be
sufficient for everyone to have a little.

In that connection John makes a revealing declaration ;
" He Himself knew what He would do." It is sixty years
ago that in the city of Bristol I was taken by my father to
Bethesda to hear George Muller preach. I can see him yet,
that wonderful old man. That was his text. " He Himself
knew what He would do." He could not pronounce it in
good English ; he had a quaint and picturesque German
accent. Sixty years have gone, and I have never lost the
effect of that sermon, for it helped me to understand the ways
of my Lord.

That is the only occasion on record when Jesus is said to
have asked anyone for any kind of advice. We never find
Him consulting with anyone except here ; and here John by
inspiration has written, " He Himself knew what He would
do." He asked the question to prove Philip. He did it to
give Philip his chance. Philip's answer was the answer of
calculation, with no sense whatever of the significance of the
question from the standpoint of the ability of his Lord.

There was one man who went a little further. It was
Andrew. He said, " There is a little lad here, which hath five
barley loaves and two tiny fishes." The word for lad and
the word for fishes are diminutive.

But observe the reaction in Andrew's word, almost the reaction of amusement, " but what are these among so many ? " Five loaves and two wee fishes. Andrew did make a venture of faith, and then half laughed at his own suggestion. Philip's answer was an answer to a direct challenge, and was perfectly honest. Andrew, perhaps looking into the face of Jesus, said, Well, there is a wee bit of a laddie here who has five barley loaves, and two tiny fishes, but, what is the good ? " What are these among so many ? "

Thus the disciples around their Lord, interested and sincere and honest. Neither of them said, Thou canst deal with the situation. Why not ? Because they did not see it. Such honesty is far preferable to making a profession of apprehension, while in the heart there is questioning.

Then the sign was wrought. He did not criticize either of His disciples. He had no unkind thing to say to them. He had asked and received from Philip an answer of perfect honesty. He had heard Andrew's suggestion, and He fastened upon it. Our Lord said in effect, Very well, I will take your suggestion, Andrew, " Make the people sit down." Mark says they were sitting in companies. There was orderliness about it. John says it was on the grass. Look at that crowd. Then look at the supply. The lad and the Lord. As to the lad, the supply was absolutely inadequate ; but as to the Lord, the lad's inadequacy is sufficiency, plus. Plus ? Yes, twelve baskets full presently. It is a revealing story in every way. Our inadequacy is patent. But He will take our five loaves, and two little fishes, and make them suffice.

> " 'Twas spring time when He blessed the bread,
> And harvest when He brake."

Mark tells us of the multitude that " they were all filled." Philip said, If you spent two hundred pence you would not give everyone a little. But when Jesus gets down to the business, it is not a snack that tantalizes, but a meal that satisfies.

So the great sign was wrought. Its real significance we

shall discover presently. It is well here to remember that
Mark tells us concerning the disciples, " They understood not
concerning the loaves, for their heart was hardened." They
were not yet keen and sensitive enough spiritually and
emotionally to apprehend the real significance of what Jesus
had done.

What were the immediate issues ? These are revealed in
verses fourteen and fifteen, and are most suggestive. " When
therefore the people saw the sign which He did, they said,
This is of a truth the prophet that cometh into the world."
In our course we have come across that expression before.
They had asked John on a memorable occasion, " Art thou
the prophet ? " We saw then that the reference was to that
stupendous word of Moses that a day should come when a
prophet should arise like unto himself. Now these people
said of Jesus, " This is of a truth the prophet that cometh
into the world." Through Moses, God had fed the people
in the wilderness with manna. Now here was Another, Who
had fed them when there seemed to be no resource. They
said, Surely this is that prophet. In the discussion which
followed they referred to the manna. Well now, if the prophet
had appeared, what did the crowd propose to do with Him ?
They decided to make Him King. " They were about to
come and take Him by force, to make Him King," on the
basis of this sign.

Thus we are brought into the atmosphere of the false
materialistic conception these people had of Messiahship,
and of the Kingdom of God. Their own thinking about their
own Scriptures showed how completely they were at fault.

What happened ? " He withdrew " ; in other words, He
declined Kingship on that basis. Matthew and Mark tell us
that the first thing He did was to send His own disciples
away. John does not tell us about their being sent. He
simply referred to the fact that they went over the sea.
Matthew and Mark tell us also that He dismissed the crowd,
and then went to the mountain to prayer.

To summarize. He had fed the crowd. They were impressed by the wonder of that feeding. They were filled with food. I sometimes think that the biggest mistakes in the world are made when men and women get filled with food. They were filled; they were impressed. Why, they said, this must be the prophet. The time has come; we will take Him by force; we will compel Him to be King, He Who can, without labour, fill our bellies, must be Messiah.

Jesus got His group of disciples, and said, Get into that boat and go to the other side. And then, somehow, I am not told how He did it, but perhaps with some word of august authority, He dismissed the crowds. They went, and He went to the mountain to pray. He went for communion with His God. So it ended. The scattering crowds, the dismissed disciples, the retired Lord to the mountain side.

And now we see the little boat making its way across, and when it is about twenty-five or thirty furlongs from the land, that is, quite literally, about half way across the sea, the storm broke upon them. Jesus had sent them there, out of the danger created by the popular movement to make Him King. What those disciples longed for above everything was to see Jesus King. Of course they did. Their love and loyalty made them desire it, and now the people were about to do it. They did not understand any better than did the crowd. They knew more about Him, but they had not grasped the significance of His Messiahship. I can imagine the joy on the faces of the little band when there was a popular movement to make Jesus King. I have seen the same kind of look on the rapt faces of a crowd in this country when a speaker has told them of the wonderful fact that a man in Hyde Park flung his cap up in the air, and said, "Hurrah for Jesus!" Most likely the man who flung his cap up was making the same mistake about His Kingdom, that it is a Kingdom dealing first with material things, and bringing in a new social order on a bread basis. Jesus, the Incarnate Word, would have none of it. He sent His disciples out of the danger zone, and He went to the mountain for communion with His Father.

Then it was dark, and the sea was rising, and the disciples were at their wits' end. There is much to be said for them. They were loyal. The wind was contrary. These men were accustomed to handle boats. They knew how to manage a boat from the standpoint of mere craftsmanship. If the wind is contrary, there is only one thing to do from the craftsman's point ; put the boat about. A little dangerous perhaps. The moment of real peril occurs when the boat is broadside ; but a skilful manipulator of a boat can do that, and then run with the wind, and the wind that before was contrary, now blows the boat back to safety. Why did they not go back ? He had said the other side, and they never dreamed of going back. Though they were ignorant of the spiritual significance of the Master's mission, they did not dream of going back. They kept on, and then something happened, the sign was given.

They saw a Figure approaching them, walking, head against the contrary wind, for He was overtaking them. The wind which was holding them back, was not holding back that approaching Figure. The seas were raging, and threatening to engulf them ; but this strange, mysterious Figure coming after them, seemed to be walking on adamant, was not sinking. What they saw—let us put it bluntly—was a ghost, an apparition ; and the fear of the apparition was greater than the terror of the storm. It always is. We may say we do not believe in ghosts. No, but if we saw one, we should be frightened ! And they really did see one. They saw this on-coming spectre, this apparition.

Then came a voice that was familiar, " It is I ; be not afraid." And the Lord was with them. They received Him into the boat, and the boat reached the other side in safety.

Now mark this carefully. None saw that sign but His own disciples. It was a sign for them only. Why ? I can only answer suggestively. It seems to me that when He sent them in that boat across the sea, He knew the keenness of their disappointment, and their perplexity, that He would not be made King. Perhaps they wondered and questioned as to whether after all, He had Kingly power and authority. So He gave them a demonstration of His present Kingship, and that in the realm of Nature. It was as though He had said, I have refused to be crowned King upon the basis of bread, but make no mistake, I am King in every realm ; King in the realm of Nature, contrary winds cannot hinder Me ; the tossing sea cannot overwhelm Me. I am King.

Mark says, " They were sore amazed in themselves." " They understood not concerning the loaves." The connection is self-evident. " They understood not concerning the loaves." The fineness of what He had done did not penetrate their understanding.

This statement of Mark should be closely linked to that of Matthew, who tells us that " they worshipped Him," and they said, " Of a truth Thou art the Son of God." There is no contradiction. Amazed, not understanding, yet they worshipped, and recognized that He was indeed the Son of God. It was a sign for His own, and so full of significance that we might deal with it for the comfort and correction of our own hearts, and the revelation of the glory of our Lord.

What do we find in these two signs ? False and true ideas of Messiahship brought into sharp contrast. The false idea was that of a Kingship on a bread basis, a material basis. That was their conception of Messiahship, and of the Kingdom of God, of which He had been teaching them. It was that conception that put Him on His Cross. It was that conception that blasted the Hebrew people ; and it seems to me, is still holding some people in thrall to-day. Bread, and all material things, are within His Kingdom. But He will not begin there. He will not be made King on the basis of being a wholesale food provider. True Kingship must rest on a spiritual basis. Because the disciples understood not the loaves, in great tenderness He gave them the sign of His Kingly authority and power in the natural and the material realm. In so doing He certainly intended to strengthen them at the moment of their wonder and disappointment ; and so eventually to lead them to the fuller understanding.

John vi. 22–40.

HERE once more, John introduces a very definite time note, " On the morrow," thus linking the sign of the feeding of the five thousand, with the discussion which followed on the next day, and with the superlative claim that our Lord made in connection with that discussion.

This paragraph has three movements. First, the occasion is clearly revealed, that is, the occasion, leading to the uttering of the claim. At the commencement of our studies we saw that the scheme of John is the selection of signs, which he claims prove that Jesus is the Christ, the Son of God ; and that the selection consists of eight signs in the realm of works, such things as we commonly designate miracles, and eight signs in the realm of words, the great central and superlative utterances of Jesus, all of them in the nature of personal claims, and every one introduced by the formula " I am." The first of these now occurs. The occasion is revealed in verses twenty-two to twenty-five.

The second movement in verses twenty-six to thirty-four, records the way in which Jesus rebuked the crowds.

The final movement in verses thirty-five to forty, brings us to the great sign in words, consequent upon the miracle wrought in the realm of works, and the address which He had delivered to them in rebuke.

Verses twenty-two to twenty-five, revealing the occasion, are confessedly a little difficult to read. All expositors agree that the passage is a complicated passage. Nevertheless the sequence of events can be clearly stated. Two days are referred to ; the day on which our Lord fed the five thousand, and the day following. On the day of the feeding of the five thousand, the people saw the disciples enter the boat, and start across the sea ; and they saw that Jesus did not go with them in that boat. That was the first day.

The day after, the people who perhaps had scattered far and wide for the night, gathered together again, as they were so constantly doing in those days in the public ministry of our Lord. They found Jesus and His disciples still absent. They had seen the disciples go across the sea the previous evening, and they had seen that Jesus had stayed behind. In the meantime other boats had arrived, and some of the multitude entered into those boats, and went across where the disciples had gone. They did not at all know where Jesus was, but only that He had not gone with the disciples. Presumably He was still on this side of the sea. When they arrived, they only found one boat there, that in which the disciples had gone, but they found Jesus there. The natural question was, How did He get there ? So they came to Him and said, " Rabbi, when camest Thou hither ? " That is the setting of the story.

Then we come to our Lord's answer. He began with that solemn formula, which He so often employed, when there was something He would specially emphasize :—

" Verily, verily I say unto you, Ye seek Me, not because ye saw signs, but because ye ate of the loaves, and were filled. Work not for the meat which perisheth, but for the meat which abideth unto eternal life, which the Son of man shall give unto you ; for Him the Father, even God, hath sealed."

Notice first that He did not answer their question. They asked Him *when He* came there. He told them *why they* had come. He ignored their curiosity, and went straight to the business that was on His heart. He said, You are not seeking for Me because you saw signs. But they had seen signs. No, that is exactly what they had not done. They had seen the wonder wrought, and the power put forth ; but they had not caught the significance of the thing. He said, You are not here because you have seen the sign. You ate of the loaves, and you were filled, and that is what brings you here; but you do not understand; you do not see the sign. He thus revealed and rebuked their false interest.

Because they ate and were filled, they had tried to make Him King, and He would have none of it. In what He now said He revealed the reason of His refusal. Their interest was not created by any understanding of His teaching concerning the Kingdom of God, but because they ate of the loaves, and were filled. He then made a great appeal to them in those wonderful words: "Work not for the meat which perisheth, but for the meat which abideth unto eternal life, which the Son of man shall give unto you; for Him, the Father, even God, hath sealed." He rebuked the reason of their interest, and then appealed, and in so doing repeated claims He had already made, that He was the Son of God, that He was authorized by God, and sealed by God.

These words of Jesus were immediately followed by discussion. They first asked a question. "What must we do that we may work the works of God?" They fastened upon His word *work*. He had said, Do not work for the meat that perisheth. Do not make that the supreme thing. Do not condition life merely within the material. Work for that which is supreme, which the Son of man, sealed by God, is able to give you. They caught His word *work*, and they said, "What must we do that we may work the works of God?"

What did these people mean when they asked Him that question? They certainly had caught a moral intention, if not a spiritual significance, in what He had just been saying. To them the works of God simply meant the Law, and obedience to legal requirements. They saw that in what He had said there was a moral significance. I do not think they had caught the deep spiritual significance. I do not think that they understood, what many men do not yet understand, that the moral is rooted in the spiritual; that if we lose the sense of the spiritual nature of man, we have lost all sanctions of any kind for morality. They were not recognizing the fact that morality is rooted in the spiritual, but they had caught the drift of what He said so far as the moral was concerned, and they said, " What must we do that we may work the works of God ? "

And yet look at it a little more carefully. Their question had a spiritual drift, even if they themselves did not recognize it. They did not say, What are the works of God that we are to do. What they did say was, What shall we do that we may work the works of God ? In other words, it was as though they had said ; Yes, we see what You mean, that the supreme matter in life, is that we should be moral and upright, and keep the law ; but will You tell us how we are going to do it ? Whether they realized it or not, that was the cry that came out of their spiritual nature. That was the question. It is the question of sincere men to-day. Men are not asking what is right or wrong ; but they are asking, if not in actual words, they are asking constantly : Will anyone tell us how we are going to do the right ? That is what they asked Jesus. " What must we do that we may work the works of God ? " Not, What are the works of God we are to do ? but, How are we going to do them ?

Then, " Jesus answered . . . This is the work of God, that ye believe on Him Whom He hath sent." Just as astounding an answer, as the question was an arresting and startling one. " This is the work of God." They had not asked Him what it was, but He declared it ; because involved in the work was the reply to the enquiry as to how the works of God could be done. " This is the work of God, that ye believe on Him Whom He hath sent." In other words, they asked a question which was in the realm of the moralities ; and He said in reply, I will tell you of one spiritual act which, if it be performed, will include the dynamic of all the moralities. " This is the work of God, that ye believe on the Son Whom He hath sent."

It will be remembered that later on when He was talking to His disciples, just under the shadow of the Cross, speaking of the coming of the Paraclete, He said, " He, when He is come, will convict the world in respect of sin, and of righteousness, and of judgment"; and then explaining, "Of sin, because they believe not on Me." "This is the work of God, that ye believe on Him Whom He hath sent."

Because of the coming of the Word in flesh, sin itself found a new centre and a new interpretation. They were asking how they were to do the works of the law. His answer was, Believe on Me. To do that is to find the dynamic of holiness, and the ensurance of morality.

In what follows there is an arresting unveiling of human nature. "They said therefore unto Him, What then doest Thou for a sign?" That, in spite of the sign of the day before in the feeding of the five thousand. As our Lord had said, they had not sought Him because they had seen the sign. They had not. This is proved as they now asked Him, "What then doest Thou for a sign, that we may see and believe Thee?" "See and believe"! It is still often affirmed that "Seeing is believing." Well, it is never true. Seeing is seeing. Believing is being sure without seeing. But they had not done. They were still thinking about yesterday, and that feeding. "Our fathers ate the manna in the wilderness; as it is written, He gave them bread out of heaven to eat." They were really going back on what they had seen yesterday; and saying in effect, Yes, it was a wonderful thing that Thou didst yesterday, and we thought to make Thee King; but after all, it was not so much the feeding of five thousand on one occasion. Moses fed the people in the wilderness for forty years on manna. Can You do anything as big as that? That is what they meant. They were going back upon their own experience. They had not seen the sign. They had not understood its significance. They did not definitely say that Moses had fed then in the wilderness, but that is what they meant, as we learn from our Lord's reply. "Verily, verily I say unto you, It was not Moses gave you the bread out of heaven." He did not go any further than thus to deny the suggested comparison between Moses and Himself. He simply dismissed it. And then continuing returned to the real significance of the sign of yesterday ; " But My Father giveth you the true bread out of heaven. For the bread of God is that which cometh down out of heaven, and giveth life unto the world."

To that they replied, " Lord, evermore give us this bread." Had they apprehended ? I think not. The woman in Samaria had said, Give me to drink of this water that I come no longer hither to draw. Human nature is just the same, whether in a Samaritan woman or a crowd of Jews. The same blindness is manifest. They were still material in their thinking. They swung back, and puzzled, said, Moses fed the people for forty years, and You say that through You God is sending bread out of heaven. Let us have it. They are still on the level of the material.

So we reach the great word. " Jesus said unto them, I am the Bread of life ; he that cometh to Me shall not hunger, and he that believeth on Me shall never thirst."

Keep these things together. They said, " Lord, evermore give us this bread " ; with a half tone of mockery, He replied, " I am the Bread of life, he that cometh to Me shall not hunger, he that believeth on Me shall never thirst. But I said unto you, that ye haves een Me, and yet believe not."

No words of exposition of which I at least am capable, can do justice to that marvellous claim. He had warned them against thinking in the realm of the material ; He had warned them against thinking of dust only ; He had warned them against attempting to reach the deepest necessity of life through material things. He had told them to work for the bread out of heaven which will meet the deepest necessity of human life. And then He said ; I am that ; " I am the Bread of life ; he that cometh to Me shall not hunger ; he that believeth on Me shall never thirst." All the craving of desire, the underlying clamant cry of human necessity, I am here to meet.

They had been talking about Moses. In the prologue, the writer of this Gospel had referred to Moses. Now He went back to the great call of Moses, to the day when, eighty years of age, he came in the wilderness upon a bush that burned with fire, and was not consumed, and heard the voice that bade him put his shoes from off his feet, that the place whereon he stood was holy ground ; to the hour in which Moses spoke to the Dweller in the bush, and said, Tell me, what is Thy name ? Moses had heard the answer, " I AM," and as probably he was waiting for a further word, which would interpret the " I AM," it recoiled upon itself in the declaration, without interpretation, " I AM THAT I AM." Centuries had passed away. Moses did not send you the bread from heaven. That manna in the wilderness met your physical necessity, but it did not meet your deepest need. Moses did not send you bread from heaven. God has now sent you bread from heaven. He took the name of the burning bush, and linked it with the symbol of perfect sustenance for human life. " I am the Bread of life." Thus He employed the simplest of terms, with sublimest significance.

Then He uttered their condemnation in that He said to them, You have seen Me, and yet you have not believed on Me ; and gave them this word of assurance, " All that which the Father giveth shall come to Me ; and him that cometh to Me I will in no wise cast out. For I am come down from heaven, not to do Mine own will, but the will of Him that sent Me."

Thus again He was insisting upon the thing that had been under discussion before. Having claimed to be the Bread of life, He uttered their condemnation in that they saw and did not see ; having eyes they failed to see. They had not apprehended. They saw the wonder, the power, but did not get its significance. Now He made His great claim, and in great tenderness said, All that the Father has given Me shall come to Me, and the Father gives Me all who come ; and him that cometh, I will in no wise cast out. Then again linking Himself with the Father, He said, " I am come down from heaven, not to do Mine own will, but the will of Him that sent Me." And what is that ? " This is the will of

Him that sent Me," that everyone that beholdeth the Son, and believeth on Him, should have the age-abiding life, " and I will raise him up at the last day."

Strange, that last word ? Yet not strange at all. The resurrection is the ultimate issue of eternal life ; and so He said, " I will raise him up at the last day."

There is a sense in which at this point we arrive at the beginning of the deepest notes in this Gospel according to John. Not the signs in the realm of works were most wonderful and stupendous ; but the signs in the realm of words. Not the things He did, marvellous as they were, arresting as they were, supreme as they were, but the things He said mark Him for evermore as either the supreme imposter of all time, or One Who is infinitely more than human.

Taking this whole narrative, notice again that as in the desire of the crowd to make Him King, and His refusal, there was a sharp contrast between a false conception of Messiahship, One Who shall provide for the material; and a true conception of Messiahship, One Who deals first with the spiritual, and then with the material; so here again we find a sharp contrast. The quest of the crowd and the mission of the Christ stand remarkably in contrast. What was the quest of the crowd ? Life. What was the mission of the Christ ? Life. The crowd wanted life. Christ was there to give them life. Wherein then is the contrast ? In the interpretation of life. Of course they wanted life, and so they wanted to crown Him. Life, they said, comes when we are fed, when the physical is satisfied ; when our bellies are full we are living. Many people think that to-day. Paul once with tears said of certain people, " Whose god is the belly." We do not say that kind of thing very often to-day, and therefore the pulpit is weaker than it ought to be.

Some few years ago I heard an American preacher say things about the Parable of the Prodigal, which I will here repeat. He asked, Why did the prodigal leave home ? He wanted life. How did he interpret life ? If we may judge

[111]

by to-day, he wanted clothes, and shoes, and jewellery, and plenty to eat and drink.

Life interpreted by the material. That is what these people were after. Christ came along, saying, I am come that you may have life, the very bread of life, that which meets the clamant cry of your human nature. Do not work for the meat that perishes. Do not make your life revolve around your belly. Work for the bread that cometh down from heaven, that which reaches the deepest necessity of your life.

And now to complete my reference to the American preacher's interpretation of the prodigal. All the things he sought, he found when he got home. His father said, Bring forth the best robe and put it on him. He went to get clothes, and lost them, but the father had them. Put shoes on his feet. That is what he went to get, and he came back bare-footed. But his father found them. Put a ring on his hand. He wanted jewellery, but he lost his jewels when he was away, and found them when he returned. He wanted to have plenty to eat, and found starvation. It was his father who said, Bring forth the fatted calf and let us eat. He wanted a good time, and found misery. It was the father who said, "Let us be merry."

And so all these things people are trying to get are really, in the last analysis, in the Father's house ; and if they get them apart from the Father's house, they blast them, and damn them. They wanted life through bread. He was there to give them life through spiritual sustenance.

And so we close by listening to Him, as He uttered the supreme first claim, "I am the Bread of life." From then until now, wherever and whenever humanity has found its hunger satisfied, its thirst quenched, it has been when it has come to Jesus, and at no other time, and in no other place. That first great sign in the realm of words, "I am the Bread of life" is a sentence that on the lips of any other than God manifest in flesh, would have been the supremest folly.

John vi. 41–71.

THIS section is a continuation without break, in the story we were considering last. That is seen in the use of the word "Therefore." "The Jews *therefore* murmured." That is verse forty-one. In verse fifty-two, "The Jews *therefore* strove one with another." And again in verse sixty, "Many *therefore* of His disciples . . . went back."

As we read it, I wonder if we are not inclined to say what the disciples said, "This is a hard saying ; who can hear it ?" not necessarily in the spirit in which they said it, to which I will come presently, and yet honestly. At this part of the Gospel we are face to face with that which is in some senses most difficult of understanding and interpretation. That does not mean we ought to shun it. It does mean that we cannot do more than gain a general impression of it.

Everything here grows out of the claim that Jesus made, "I am the Bread of life." That claim caused difficulties in the minds of the people, and raised controversy ; and it is that story which we have now read.

The paragraph again has two clearly defined movements ; first an account of the controversy arising as the result of the making of the claim, verses forty-one to fifty-nine ; and then that startling and revealing thing, the account of the effect that the claim and controversy had upon the disciples of Jesus.

The difficulties concerned His Person, and His declared Purpose. From verses forty-one to fifty-one we have the story of the difficulties concerning His Person ; and then in verses fifty-two to fifty-nine, the difficulties concerning His Purpose.

As to His Person.

"The Jews therefore murmured concerning Him, because He said, I am the Bread which came down out of heaven." As a matter of fact, He did not say that exactly in that form, but it was a perfectly fair summary of what He had said, that He was the Bread of life, and that He had come out of heaven.

H

" And they said, Is not this Jesus, the Son of Joseph, whose father and mother we know? how doth He now say, I am come down out of heaven? "

We see at once that their difficulty was created by their incomplete knowledge of Him. There is a sense in which it can be understood. The mystery of His Person had not been revealed, nor could be. As He moved amongst them, He was to them a Man, and nothing more. They thought they knew all about Him. They thought they knew His father and His mother. Seeing that they thought they had perfect knowledge, the problem of course presented itself at once as to how He could say that He had come out of heaven.

It was perfectly natural. I think very likely you and I would have said the same thing under the same circumstances. They could not know the mystery of His Person. If Mary had ever attempted to explain it, she would have been laughed out of court. I feel perfectly sure that one element of the sword that pierced her soul was the constant suspicion under which she lived.

But if we recognize that, let us recognize this also. They had no right to come to the conclusion that they knew all about Him. We never have any right, in our judgment of our fellow-beings, to say we know all about them. These men evidenced what our Lord had rebuked, a lack of spiritual apprehension and discernment of any kind. They said, We know all about Him, and therefore His claim cannot be true. It was a false method of approach. They were completely bewildered. Their problem arose because of their ignorance, an ignorance in which they were content to rest, instead of investigating what He was saying. They had sought Him, not because they had seen the sign. They had seen the wonder, but they had not seen the sign, had not caught the significance. In order to direct their minds to the level of the spiritual He had spoken at length to them, and made His claim. They still saw nothing.

Now how did our Lord answer their difficulty? First of

all it is to be observed that He did not correct their blunder. He did not say to them, No, you are wrong at that point. I am not the Child of Joseph and Mary. He ignored it. But He did that which was equivalent in another way. He first of all told them the reason why they could not understand Him.

"Murmur not among yourselves. No man can come to Me, except the Father Which sent Me draw him."

Then He flung in again that little sentence which He had already used, and which He repeated later, with regard to the ultimate,

"And I will raise him up in the last day."

Thus in another way, in different words, He was saying to those people exactly what He had said to Nicodemus in the first year. Nicodemus had said, We know Thou art a teacher come from God; and Christ in effect had said to him, You cannot know anything, you cannot see, you cannot enter into the realm over which God is reigning, the Kingdom of God, unless you are born again. So to these people He said, The reason why you do not apprehend is to be found in the fact that no man can know all about Me, and reach Me in fellowship, except the Father Which sent Me, draw him.

Then notice particularly that while relationship with Jesus Christ depends upon God's action, it is equally true that it depends upon our response. He quoted here this remarkable word,

"It is written in the prophets, And they shall all be taught of God."

Mark the significance. You cannot come to Me, said Jesus, except you are drawn; but that is no excuse for your ignorance, because God is drawing you; "They shall all be taught of God."

Then what follows is full of significance;

"Everyone that hath heard from the Father, and hath learned, cometh unto Me."

Mark the two things; the drawing of God, and learning by

man, which means that on his part there must be response. So, in language full of mystic value, He told these people that the real reason for their blindness was found in the fact that they were not learning, were not responsive to the Divine drawing ; and until they were, there could be no apprehension, " Except a man be born anew, he cannot see the Kingdom of God."

Then going on concerning Himself,

" Not that any man hath seen the Father, save He Which is from God, He hath seen the Father." He was referring to the claim that He had made, that He had come down from heaven. In this connection He said, " He that believeth hath eternal life," and repeated His claim, " I am the Bread of life. Your fathers did eat the manna in the wilderness, and they died." He thus went back to their own reference to the manna, and contrasted it with Himself. " This is the bread which cometh down out of heaven, that a man may eat thereof, and not die." Again, reiterating His claim, He said,

" I am the living Bread Which came down out of heaven ; if any man eat of this Bread, he shall live for ever ; yea, and the Bread which I will give is My flesh, for the life of the world."

Mark the significance of this. What did He mean when He spoke of " My flesh " ? I think we must interpret that by going back to the beginning of the Gospel, to the great central declaration of the Prologue, " The Word became flesh, and dwelt among us." " The Word became flesh " ; was another way of saying, that when He came into the world, God created a new humanity, grafted on to the old by an immaculate conception and virgin birth. His flesh was a new humanity. That is the living Bread, " the Word was made flesh." His flesh was thus given for the life of the world ; and the sustenance and satisfaction of human life can only be found as that life, that new human life, typified under that great word " flesh," because revealed in flesh, is taken, assimilated, and enters into human experience.

And so we come to the second difficulty, growing out of His answer to the first, that of His purpose.

" The Jews therefore strove one with another, saying, How can this Man give us His flesh to eat ? "

This again was a quite understandable question, because they were thinking only in the realm of the physical and the material ; while all the time our Lord was using these things in order to illustrate the realm of the eternal and the spiritual. Spiritual blindness characterized them still. How can a Man impart His own humanity to another man, so that other man shall assimilate it, and find the life of that humanity dominating his own ? How can this be ? It was a pertinent suggestion on their level. They had not caught the significance. They had not understood that He was speaking of His entire personality.

And so we pass to His answer to them. He introduced it again with that formula He used when He would re-arrest attention.

" Verily, verily, Except ye eat the flesh of the Son of man and drink His blood, ye have not life in yourselves."

The term " flesh," standing, as we have said, for the whole fact of His human nature, the term " blood " was at least a suggestion of His death. He was using figurative language, and He said, Unless you eat that flesh, unless you partake of that humanity ; and unless you drink of that blood, unless you enter into the experience that comes by the way of the shedding of blood, you have no life in yourselves.

Then He made again His positive claim :

" He that eateth My flesh and drinketh My blood hath eternal life " ;

and again the reference to the ultimate,—

" I will raise him up at the last day. For My flesh is meat indeed, and My blood is drink indeed. He that eateth My flesh and drinketh My blood abideth in Me, an dI in him." The result of that feeding and that drinking, of that assimilation of that new human nature through the mystery of blood, is that of vital union.

[117]

Thus our Lord, under these confessedly startling figures
of speech, all growing out of His claim to be the Bread of life,
claimed that humanity can find in Him that which will
sustain and satisfy all its deepest need.

And so we come to the record of the results among His
disciples of this teaching.

" Many therefore of His disciples, when they heard this,
said, This is a hard saying."

I said at the beginning of this study that if any of us had
been inclined to say in the presence of these mystic words
and teachings of Jesus—in which through illustration He
was endeavouring to lift men out of their materialized thinking
into the realm of spiritual truth, of the essential fact of human
nature—that it was a hard saying, I hoped that we had
not said it, as they meant it. As a matter of fact the word
" hard " (*skleros*), means harsh, rough, objectionable. Hard
there does not mean obscure, but offensive. Many of His
disciples said, This is a hard saying. Now, we cannot go
any further with Him. They did not mean that what He
said was obscure. It was perhaps obscure, but they did not
mean that. They meant it was offensive, the idea of eating
His flesh, and drinking His blood. They broke with Him
there. I am quite content to leave that without any lengthy
comment, save to say that attitude towards that kind of
teaching, which is central to the record of the earthly ministry
of our Lord, has often raised that kind of objection. It has
been said that the hymn,

> " Not all the blood of beasts
> On Jewish altars slain,"

represented a " religion of the shambles." Horrible phrase,
but revealing the same attitude.

Now what had our Lord to say to them ?

" Jesus, knowing in Himself that His disciples were
murmuring at this, said unto them, Doth this cause you to
stumble ? What then if ye should behold the Son of man
ascending where He was before ? "

What did He mean? Is what I am saying to you about eating My flesh and drinking My blood, causing you to stumble? Is there something objectionable in that? What if you see the Son of man ascending where He was before? Did He mean, If this caused you to stumble, how will you be caused to stumble presently when I go back whence I came? That is certainly what He meant; but involved in it was His recognition of the fact that He was moving ultimately to a Cross, a shameful and ignominious death, the Cross that was to the Jew a stumblingblock, and to the Greeks foolishness. He was about to ascend where He was before, but by the way of the Cross. A little later on, in chapter twelve, He said, " I if I be lifted up from the earth, will draw all men unto Myself." " From the earth " is too weak. *Ek* is the Greek word, " I if I be lifted *up out of* the earth." How was He lifted up out of the earth? By the way of the Cross. Yes, but it was not the Cross alone. It was the Cross, followed by the resurrection, and the ascension. He was going back, but He must go that way; and He was telling them that if they stumbled when they listened to language which they could not perfectly apprehend, how would they do in that dark hour, to human seeming, that was coming to them when He thus ascended?

And now, right in the midst, occurs His statement which illuminates everything;

" It is the spirit that quickeneth; the flesh profiteth nothing; the words that I have spoken unto you are spirit, and are life."

They were listening to what He said about eating His flesh, and drinking His blood, wholly on the level of the material. Then He said, " the flesh profiteth nothing." As though He had said to them, Do not be blinded by the dust of the physical and the material. See through the things I am saying to you. The flesh, as you are thinking of it, profits nothing; the words that I speak to you are spirit, and they are life. It was His appeal to them to recognize that the ultimate was not the flesh, but the spirit.

But the flesh was definite and positive. It was. Yet the
Incarnation itself was of value, and of value only, because
through it men are brought to God Who is Spirit. Not
even the material in the actuality of the flesh of Jesus was
of any value save as it was the means by which men apprehended, and were drawn nearer to God. " In the beginning
was the Word, and the Word was with God, and the Word
was God . . . and the Word became flesh . . . and we
beheld His glory, glory as of the only begotten Son of the
Father. . . . No man hath seen God at any time, but the
Son, . . . hath declared Him." God declared through
Incarnation is the ultimate value of Incarnation. The moment
we take this chapter of John, or take any of these things,
and make them the ultimate in our thinking and our religion,
we are out of touch with the spiritual. It is only as we
pass through them, it is only as we recognize that when we
come to the Table of the Lord, the material is nothing at all,
save as it may be a suggestion of that which lies behind it,
that we find its true value. " The flesh profiteth nothing."
He Who had just said, You must eat My flesh, and drink
My blood, now distinctly said the flesh as flesh alone, profiteth
nothing ; it is the spirit which is life. That is to say that
what is suggested by the flesh, is of supreme value, not the
flesh.

And then come these startling words, " Upon this, many
of His disciples went back, and walked no more with Him."
John has written that as strongly as it can be written. That
kind of thing sifted the ranks of His disciples, and there was
a definite break with Him on the part, not of a few, but of
many.

" Many of His disciples went back, and walked no more
with Him." Jesus said therefore unto the twelve, Would ye
also go away ? " that is, Do you also want to go ?

Then was given Peter's great answer : " Lord, to whom
shall we go ? " That declared the uselessness of going.
" Thou hast the words of eternal life." That revealed the
reason for staying. Peter had caught something of the

significance of the teaching, and the statement, " The words that I have spoken are spirit, and are life." " Thou hast the words." By them we know that " Thou art the Holy One of God."

But the sifting took place. " Many went back, and walked no more with Him." Hard sayings ! They were only thinking on the level of the material. He had fed the multitude, and they had wanted to make Him King. He had rebuked them for working for the meat that perished ; and then had taken the figure of the Bread of life ; claiming to be able to satisfy all the needs of human nature. He had figuratively revealed the method, eating His flesh, sharing in His humanity ; drinking His blood, entering through the gate of sacrifice into life. It was a hard saying, offensive to the carnally minded ; and yet the saying which introduces us to the deepest mystery of spiritual life and religion.

I think the best place to close this meditation is with Peter's question. Jesus said, Would you also go away ? Do you wish to leave Me ? And Peter said, " To whom shall we go ? " Exactly. If we turn our back upon Him, because our intellect is baffled, because we cannot grasp at first all the spiritual significance of what He says, and perhaps never shall on this side of the Glory come to perfect apprehension ; are we to go back, and part company with Him, and leave Him ? To whom shall we go ? Who else would be able to meet our deepest need ?

> " Now none but Christ can satisfy,
> None other name than His."

Mystic, strange, even to us in this hour ; and yet surely, with that central light burning in the chapter, " It is the spirit that quickeneth, the flesh profiteth nothing," we may enter into the meaning of His teaching, and hear Him saying again, " I am the Bread of life," and find experimentally the truth of the claim.

John vii. 1–24.

IN relation to the chronological sequence in the ministry of our Lord, we come now to the commencement of the third and final period, that is, from John's standpoint.

The first verse is a general one.

"And after these things Jesus walked in Galilee; for He would not walk in Judæa, because the Jews sought to kill Him." The tenses there are all imperfects, and I think we gather the sense better if we render it, "After these things Jesus was walking in Galilee, for He did not desire to walk in Judæa, because the Jews were seeking to kill Him."

We find the parallels in Matthew sixteen, in Mark eight, and in Luke nine, all connected with the visit to Cæsarea Philippi. John does not record that visit, nor has he put on record the great confession which Peter made there. There are those who have suggested that at the close of chapter six we have John's account of the confession. I do not think the view is tenable; but there is a marked similarity between the two incidents. At Cæsarea Philippi our Lord asked His disciples, "Who do ye say that I am"; and Simon Peter answered, "Thou art the Christ, the Son of the living God." John tells of an occasion when Jesus said to the twelve,—the same group,—"Would ye also go away? Simon Peter answered Him, Lord, to whom shall we go? Thou hast the words of eternal life. And we have believed and know that Thou art the Holy One of God."

The similarity is self-evident, and yet the difference is so patent that the two occasions cannot be confused. Nevertheless they breathe the same atmosphere. The time had come for the commencement of the final movement in the work of the Messiah, and I think that the incident recorded by John antedated the confession at Cæsarea Philippi. He had been saying strange things, "hard sayings" as they said, and there was a break, "Many of His disciples went back, and walked no more with Him." Then He said to the twelve, Do you also want to go? It was Simon who said, "To whom shall we go? Thou hast the words of eternal life. And we have believed and know that Thou art the Holy One of God." After that they travelled up to Tyre and Sidon, and moving back towards Decapolis, they came to Cæsarea Philippi ; where He said, Who do you say that I am ? and the great confession was made. Then the last six months began.

The first incident which John records in that period is that of the occurrence of the feast of Tabernacles. At the time He was in Galilee, and we are told the reason. He would not, that is, He did not desire, to walk in Judæa because the Jews were seeking to kill Him. The hostility was becoming more and more intense. All the conditions were characterized by unrest. Everything was in turmoil around our Lord. He was the one calm, poised, majestic soul. His friends were perplexed. Some of them had gone back to walk no more with Him. His enemies were becoming more and more bitter. Controversy was surging round Him. He was engaged in discussions with His enemies, discussions with enquirers, discussions presently with His own.

The feast of Tabernacles was the occasion upon which Jesus, although staying almost exclusively in Galilee, broke with that habit, and went back to Jerusalem. This whole chapter, seven, is occupied with the story of that feast.

It is quite evident too that on this visit to Jerusalem, our Lord tarried for some days. The full story occupies chapters seven, eight, nine and ten.

In the story of the feast there are three movements ; first He is seen in connection with His brethren and the rulers. Then the citizens of the city are perplexed, and He is seen in connection with them and the Pharisees. The last movement is the story of what happened on the final day, when He stood and gave His great invitation ; and the account of the division that followed it. We are now concerned with the story of our Lord and His brethren, and the rulers.

As to His brethren. The approach of the feast precipitated an action on their part.

"His brethren therefore said unto Him, Depart hence, and go into Judæa."

Multitudes were going up to perhaps the most joyous feast of all the year. It lasted seven days, plus one. Seven days strictly of ceremony and elaborate ritual; and one final day of less ritual, and probably more rejoicing, completing the octave.

It was as the caravans of pilgrims were travelling to Jerusalem for this feast that His brethren came to Him, and offered Him advice :

" His brethren therefore said unto Him, Depart hence, and go into Judæa, that Thy disciples also may behold the works which Thou doest." Surely a reference to those who had become His disciples in the first year, who were still in Judæa, and had not seen Him much for the past two years. They reinforced their advice by argument as they said :

" For no man doeth anything in secret, and himself seeketh to be known openly. If Thou doest these things, manifest Thyself to the world."

What lay behind this advice of His brethren ? John does not leave us to surmise. " For even His brethren did not believe on Him." That does not mean that they were definitely hostile to Him. There are those who hold that the mother of our Lord bore no other child. There is no warrant for such a view, except what has been called an undue solicitude for God, and a mistaken conception of the high and holy sanctity of motherhood. There is no doubt whatever that these were the actual brethren of Jesus after the flesh, by the same mother, and born subsequently to our Lord. There is no question that He was her Firstborn ; but why Firstborn if there were no others ? Luke says when Jesus began His ministry He was about thirty years. By this time He would be three and thirty probably. We know of His two brethren, James and Jude. Probably one of them would be a couple of years younger, say thirty-one, and the other, say twenty-nine. They had grown up in closest association with Him in all His boyhood's days, and young manhood's days. Now here they appear after three years' ministry. We saw them with Him at the wedding feast in Cana. A little

later they came again, on the occasion when His mother
went for very love of Him, to persuade Him to give up His
work, and go home with her. She had come to the conclusion,
together with them—they were associated with her—that
He was beside Himself. When they came, and one told
Him His mother and brethren were without, seeking Him,
He said, Who is My mother and My brethren ? We do not
see them again till now. And now John says, " Even His
brethren did not believe on Him," that is, they were not
convinced, they were not sure. They had evidently travelled
with Him in those earliest weeks. They had seen the sign
at Cana. They had been interested enough to join their
mother in an attempt to save Him from Himself. But so
far they were not convinced as to His Messiahship. Therefore
they came to Him with the advice of worldly wisdom. Everything they said seemed to be reasonable. What they said
in effect was, Why are You stopping here in obscure Galilee ?
If Your claims are justified, go to the centre of things. Their
whole thought is revealed in the words, " Manifest Thyself
to the world."

With very great reverence let us think of what this advice
meant to Jesus. He answered them quite definitely as we
shall see ; but when pondering this, the words which came
to me were, " Tempted in all points like as we are." It was
such wise advice by the standards of worldly wisdom. Do
not hug the shadows. Get into the limelight. Worldly
wisdom, yes, quite worldly ; and if you want another word,
devilish wisdom. Get out to the crowds ; go into the limelight ; do something that leaves no room for doubt. Tempted,
Oh yes, but without sin. There was no yielding, not for a
moment ; and yet the very affection of His heart on the
human level, must have made Him susceptible to the good
intention of His brethren after the flesh, however mistaken
they were.

What then was His answer ? First He answered in words ;
and then in action.

The answer in words, " My time is not yet come." This

is not quite the same word He had used to His mother when He said, " Mine hour is not yet come," but it is the same thought. The word " time " here means the season, the set season. Whenever reference is made to the hour, the hour is the ultimate, the Cross. Now with the same conception of an arranged programme, He said, My season is not come. They said, " Manifest Thyself to the world." He said, It cannot be done. As for them, He told them their time was always ready. I do not think it was an unkind word, or intended to be an unkind word. It was a recognition on His part, and a declaration to them, that they were not called to His ministry and work. They could go on with their work in the ordinary way. For Him the season was not come for doing that which should prove His claims. As He had said to His mother, " Mine hour is not yet come " ; so now to these His brethren after the flesh He said, " My time is not yet come."

Moreover, He explained the difference between them and Him.

" The world cannot hate you."
There is nothing to prevent you going on. " But Me it hateth, because I testify of it, that its works are evil." A hostile world cannot see Me. The world is hostile to Me, therefore it cannot see. I shall never make the world understand until something is done that breaks down the hostility of the human heart. His hour came for the manifestation of His glory, when He went all the way to the Cross, and through it ; and was lifted up out of the earth. That was the manifestation of redeeming love, which broke the heart of hostile man. That then was the first part of His answer.

What was the next ? He went up. The consistency of Divine action is often obscure to the small consistencies of human wisdom. He said, I am not going up yet ; but He went up. But He did not go up to do something spectacular in order to produce conviction. John tells us that He went up privately, " as it were in secret." I wonder what that really means geographically. I do not know, but I have an idea that when He went up, He did not take the high road where the caravans travelled, the usual route. Possibly He went through Samaria.

At that time He was the centre of interest in Jerusalem. He was the One around Whom the thoughts of all the multitudes were gathered. By this time His fame had spread wider and wider afield, and thousands upon thousands had looked upon Him, had heard Him on many occasions; and many in the countryside were in health because of His healing. Therefore " there was much murmuring among the multitudes concerning Him; some said, He is a good Man; others said, Not so, but He leadeth the multitude astray." He went up into the midst of that confusion and that questioning, and that curious interest; and " no man spake openly of Him for fear of the Jews." The atmosphere is revealed in that statement. The growing and bitter hostility of all authority was so evident, that if people talked about Him they did it under their breath.

So we come to the second movement, and we see Him in connection with the rulers.

" When it was now in the midst of the feast Jesus went up into the Temple."

That would be about the fourth day. Three days had run their course. How long He was there before, we cannot tell; but now He went openly into the Temple, and began to teach. He knew the hostility. Had He not told His brethren so; but He went up. There was something to be said at that feast. One of His greatest utterances must be spoken there and then. There is no account given here of the early stages of His teaching; but what John does record, is the effect produced upon those people by His teaching. The Temple in Jerusalem was the home and centre of all the learning of the national life. Of His teaching there we are told, " The Jews therefore marvelled." Marvelled! For the time being any outburst of hostility was suppressed. They said, " How knoweth this Man letters, having never learned ? "

Once again, they were failing of the highest. They were

not impressed with the spiritual note, or the ethical intention. They would have made Him King because He had fed them. When He talked about bread from heaven to eat, they challenged Him, and said it was absurd, because they were carnal. Now again they were impressed, not by any high spiritual and moral significance in what He said. What dip impress them? That He had the " letters," the *grammata*. " How hath this Man the letters never having learned? " What impressed them was the intellectual accent, and knowledge of Jesus. That is the meaning of " the *grammata*, the letters." We speak to-day of a man as being a man of letters.

Yet, while their marvel reveals their failure, it is significant that these people, not in provincial Nazareth, but in the centre of culture heard, not a Man with a Galilean accent, but a Man of intellectual and cultured speech. He stood there among men who talked the language of learning, and were learned men; they stood and listened to Him, and said, He has our accent. How did He get it?

It was a remarkable admission, but a revelation of their failure. Not the spiritual emphasis, not the moral intention, but the learned accent impressed them. It is always a revelation of disastrous failure when people are impressed with a learned accent, and miss the spiritual intention and moral value. They had missed it.

Yet thank God, they said it; because it reveals this among other things, that our Lord had the accent of the learned. It is a great mistake to suppose that Jesus made no arresting appeal to any except the illiterate. He did, and the literati were caught by the language, and the intelligentsia by the accent of scholarship. It is as though a lad from the country who might be expected to have the accent of the provinces, should arrive in the University, and begin to speak in the language of the schools. I can almost hear them. Really, this is most remarkable. This young fellow never went to the Varsity, but he seems to have the accent of the school-men. That is exactly what they said about Jesus.

What then was His answer to their " How? "

" My teaching is not Mine, but His that sent Me." That is the first time in the records that He distinctly declared that whatever He said, was directly from God. He repeated it often afterwards.

Observe carefully that He referred to His " teaching," not His accent. They were captured by the accent of the learned. It was as though He said to them ; Do not waste your time with the accent. Get hold of the teaching. My teaching is not Mine ; it is His that sent Me. I am the Mouth-piece of God, and if you want to prove it, there is one way, said Jesus.

" He that willeth to do God's will, he shall know of the teaching, whether it be from God, or whether I speak from Myself." This is a passage of which we have often made wrong use. It is said to mean that if we will to do God's will we shall know what God's will is. But that is not the statement. It is rather that if we will to do God's will, we shall know whether His teaching is God's or not. The attitude of soul for the detection of final authority, is that of willing to do God's will. When men are wholly, completely consecrated to the will of God, and want to do that above everything else, then they find out that Christ's teaching is Divine, that it is the teaching of God.

John vii. 25-36.

Our reading began with the words, " Some therefore of them of Jerusalem said." The " therefore " marks continuity, and shows that what we have read, and are now to consider, is intimately related with that which has immediately preceded it. Let us remember that here in chapter seven we begin John's account of the final period in the ministry of our Lord. Chronologically we are just beyond Cæsarea Philippi, and the confession of Peter. The Lord had now told His disciples for the first time that He was going to the Cross ; and all recorded from now on, is in the atmosphere of the Cross.

I

John's " therefore " makes us enquire, Wherefore ? What
is the reference ? Chapter seven is wholly occupied with
the visit of Jesus to Jerusalem in connection with the Feast
of Tabernacles.   He had very largely abandoned Judæa,
because Judæa had proved its hostility to Him.   We were
told, at the beginning of the chapter, that He walked in
Galilee, for He did not desire to walk in Judæa, because the
Jews sought to kill Him. But now we find that for a time, a
comparatively brief one, He went up again to Jerusalem.
The account of that visit runs on to the end of chapter ten.
We have had the account, in the first movement, of His
presence and teaching at the feast, and the problem created
by that teaching in the midst of the rulers, so that they
marvelled and said, " Whence hath this Man letters, having
never learned ? " We have considered how He answered
them, by telling them that His teaching was not His own,
that what He was saying He had received directly from
God.   That explains the " therefore " which introduces the
present section.

To summarize the section.   The inactivity of the hostile
rulers raised discussion among some of the citizens.   Having
recorded the story of Jesus and His brethren, and the rulers
in connection with the feast, John now gives the account of
Jesus and the citizens, and the discussion that resulted.

Now let us examine this story of discussion, ending as it
did in a futile attempt to arrest Him. We are in the atmosphere of definite and fierce hostility ; and the story opens
by telling us, " Some therefore of them of Jerusalem said, Is
not this He Whom they seek to kill ? And lo, He speaketh
openly, and they say nothing unto Him." The words, " Some
. . . of them of Jerusalem " refers to citizens rather than the
rulers. They were confronted with something that puzzled
them.   These citizens evidently knew the determination of
the rulers to put Him to death.   They knew more than the
Galileans did, who did not measure or understand the hostility
of the rulers. They said, Is not this the Man they are seeking
to kill ? The thing that perplexed them was the fact of His

open speech; and that these hostile rulers were doing
nothing. They could not understand it. What had happened
to the rulers? Why this apparent change of attitude? Was
not this the Man they wanted to arrest and put to death?
Yet here He was, standing in the midst of the multitudes,
preaching and teaching openly; and the rulers were doing
nothing. It was a perplexing situation. If we put ourselves
in their place, we shall understand their perplexity. What
had happened to the rulers? There was the Object of their
bitter hostility, right in the midst of the feast, and in the
midst of the crowds in the open courts of the Temple, teaching
the multitudes, and the rulers were doing nothing. His
brethren had advised Him to go up to Jerusalem, and show
Himself openly, to manifest Himself to the world. He had
said, My season is not come. He had dismissed their suggestion. Nevertheless He was now there. We are not told
that He was working any miracles, but teaching; and the
rulers were laying no hands on Him. It was a perplexing
situation to the citizens. We know why the rulers lay no
hand on Him. I do not think they knew themselves. The
reason is declared presently, but we will postpone the reading
of it until we reach it.

Then these citizens discussed the situation. I have no
doubt we get the discussion in brief, but it is very clear.

They made a suggestion to account for the inactivity of the
rulers; " Can it be that the rulers indeed know that this is
the Christ? " The verb *to know* there means to acquire
knowledge, and we get nearer the real meaning of what they
suggested, if we read, Have they found out after all that this
is the Christ? These citizens were not affirming that He was
the Christ, but were trying to account for this sudden strange
inactivity of the rulers, when Jesus had put Himself in their
power by coming and standing in Temple courts and teaching
openly. They say, What has happened? Can it be that
they have found out that He is the Christ?

But they at once dismissed their own suggestion. " Howbeit we know this Man whence He is; but when the Christ

[131]

cometh, no one knoweth whence He is." Two statements,
first that they knew Him ; secondly that when the Christ
came, none would know whence He came. The second was
the current opinion at the time. It was being taught by the
rabbis that the Christ would suddenly appear, and no one
would know whence He came, an opinion probably based upon
a sentence in Isaiah, which, it may be, they misinterpreted,
" Who shall declare His generation." It was the popular
view at the time that no one would know whence He came.
That was their conviction, and so they said, We know all
about Him ; we know whence He came ; and the fact that
we know whence He came proves He cannot be Messiah.
So that cannot be the reason for the inactivity of the rulers,
for they must know, as we citizens do, whence He is. So
their own suggestion had to be dismissed.

In the midst of the discussion our Lord intervened. He
knew what they were saying ; He knew their perplexity.
" Jesus therefore cried in the Temple." This word " cried "
is a very strong word, showing that what was now said was
not said quietly, but under the stress of great emotion.
Remember all that had preceded this. He had come up to
the feast, and had been teaching. He had claimed that the
authority for His teaching was that it was not His own, it
was the teaching of God. Then this discussion had broken
out about the impotence of the rulers. Then " Jesus cried."
It was a great outburst of emotion. One writer has said
that writing long years after, as John assuredly did, he could
still hear the protesting accents of Jesus. It was not a quiet
statement this. He " cried in the Temple."

Now let us listen to what He said. I wonder if we know
what He meant. He said, " Ye both know Me, and know
whence I am." Let us halt with that. Did He mean that to
be taken literally ? Was He admitting they were correct
when they said, " We know this Man whence He is " ? Or
was it a statement characterized by irony ? You know Me ;
and you know Me whence I am ! Or was it said in the accents
of scorn for them, and as a rebuke of their suppressed con-

viction concerning Him ? Perhaps it is better to leave that
question an open one. I am not going to answer my questions
save to say that perhaps the two elements merge in what
He said.

But He had not done. " And I am not come of Myself,
but He that sent Me is true, Whom ye know not." They
said, We know all about Him. He cannot be the Messiah.
He said, You know Me ; is that your claim ? Well, listen
again, what I have been telling you before, I am not come of
Myself—I am sent.

And then this final statement, " Whom ye know not."
The One Who sent Me, " ye know not." It is as though our
Lord said to these men, whether they knew Him or not,
whether their boast was an empty one or not, whether they
were suppressing a conviction and certainty or not ; the one
sure thing was that they did not know God. On the other
hand He did, " I know Him ; because I am from Him."

" They sought therefore to take Him." Mark these " there-
fores." " Therefore," why ? Because of the claim He was
making. All through this Gospel of John there is the revelation of the fact that the deepest reason of hostility to Him
was, as they supposed, His blasphemy. It began in chapter
five, when He said, " My Father worketh even until now, and
I work." They then had said, He makes Himself equal with
God. Here again for the same reason, they sought to take
Him.

Then we come to the real reason for the inactivity of the
rulers. " No man laid his hand on Him." Why not ? " His
hour was not yet come." That revealing sentence at once
sets the Lord before us in the deepest truth concerning
Himself, His presence, and His mission. That is why they
could not lay hands on Him. His hour was not yet come.
The rulers of the people would have killed Him, and the
citizens were inclined to arrest Him, and bring Him before
the Sanhedrim, and put an end to His supposed blasphemy ;
but they could not lay a hand on Him. Surrounded by the
protecting power of God, they could not lift a hand to touch

Him. If we study this story of the life of Jesus, and try to account for it on the ground of that which is purely natural, we constantly break down. Why did they not lay hands on Him? There He was, an unarmed citizen, just a Galilean peasant; and there were the men of authority and power, hostile, wanting to kill Him, but they laid no hands on Him.

Then follows the statement: "But of the multitude many believed on Him." Two things are seen operating. He was winning His way with some, "They believed *on* Him." Such talked in His defence, "When the Christ shall come,—when the fact materializes,—will He do more signs than those which this Man hath done?" That reveals a popular reaction in favour of Him. Then the Pharisees heard the multitude "murmuring these things concerning Him." Therefore they would act. The expression "chief priests" refers not merely to Annas and Caiaphas, but to the whole priestly caste, as banded together. It had become a political party. "The chief priests and the Pharisees sent officers to take Him." They were determined to lay hands on Him, determined to stop this kind of thing, determined to put an end to the movement in His favour that was ever and anon manifesting itself. They would act officially. They sent officers. They could not do so except under the authority of the Sanhedrim. That authority gained, they sent officers to take Him. That is all so far. We will finish that in our next study.

"Jesus therefore said." Once more a revealing "therefore." These men were sent, He knew, He saw them come. We can visualize the crowds all about Him. The strange conflict and discussion, ebbing and flowing for and against Him. He saw these officers arrive, and knew the purpose of their coming. Therefore He spoke. Among all the things recorded as having fallen from the lips of Jesus, none, when rightly apprehended, are more startling and arresting than these. "Yet a little while am I with you, and I go unto Him that sent Me. Ye shall seek Me, and shall not find Me; and where I am, ye cannot come."

The significance of those few sentences is not discovered

until among other things, we watch the tenses. He said,
" Yet a little while am I with you." Present tense. I am
here, and I am going to stay here a little while ; and then
I am going back to Him that sent Me. I am here, as I have
told you, sent ; not on My own authority, sent. Presently
I am going back. He did not tell them when. He did not
tell them how. He simply said in effect to them, I am here
in a programme, a Divinely arranged programme. I am here,
sent, and I am remaining a little while ; and then I am
going back. You shall seek Me ; future tense. Then finally,
the present tense, " and where I am, ye cannot come." Not
where I am going, ye cannot come ; but, " Where I *am*, ye
cannot come."

There He stood. The officers had come to arrest Him, and
He talked in language such as we can find on the lips of none
other man in all human history. He talked in a language in
which there merged all tenses. He talked with cosmic consciousness. He talked as One utterly disdainful of the
hostility directed against Him. It is as though He had said,
I know what you are here for. I know you have been sent,
you have been seeking Me. Therefore, hear Me. I am
staying a little while, and then I am going back to the One
Who sent Me. I am here because I am sent ; and I am here
until that is accomplished for which I have been sent. Then
I am going back. Mark the quiet august majesty of it.
Again ; presently you will seek Me and you will not find Me ;
I shall not be here presently. I am going back to the One
Who sent Me. I am here now, but where I am, you cannot
come. You cannot arrest Me. You cannot lay hands on Me,
until the time in the economy of God arrives, and that will
be when that is done for which I am here. I am here yet a
little while, and then I am going back to Him Who sent Me,
and in the mean time you are powerless. Ye cannot come
where I am.

And they did not come, and they did not arrest Him. There
is something of sanctified and glorious humour in the situation.
They were sent to arrest Him, the representatives of authority.

They went, and when they arrived, they heard Him talking.
Then they went back empty-handed.   When they arrived,
their masters said, Where is He? and they made that
significant answer, " Never man so spake." We were sent to
arrest Him, but He arrested us.   We were sent to lay hands
on Him ; He laid no hands on us, but He paralyzed us by
the majesty of His speech.   " Never man so spake."

Keep all this in its setting.   It was the last period of His
ministry ; hostility was becoming more and more marked ;
difficulties were crowding upon Him ; challenges were
constantly offered to Him concerning His Person, concerning
His purpose, concerning His teaching, concerning Himself.
The conflict round Him thickened.   The supreme revelation,
while we are made conscious of the conflict and the difficulties,
is that of the quiet, calm dignity of " the Word made flesh."
His language was that of eternal consciousness, governing
temporal conditions.   Sent of God, and therefore all the ages
in harmony with the span of His earthly life.   The three and
a half years of ministry linked with eternity.   No blundering
man is this, no earthly politician, manipulating events in
order to produce results ; but One Who says, I am sent ;
I will be here a little longer ; presently you won't find Me.
In the meantime, where I am, ye cannot come.   Eternal
consciousness governing temporal conditions ; and therefore,
cosmic procedure amid chaotic conditions.   Chaos everywhere, break-up everywhere ; and yet we hear Him speak,
and we find the speech of One Who is no victim, no child of
circumstances ; but the Son of God, the *Logos* incarnate, and
all the majesty of the eternities, and the authority of God
merge in His attitudes and in His speech.

John vii. 37–viii. 1.

In this paragraph we have the account of the last things
in connection with the feast of Tabernacles.   Everything

preceding, in this chapter, has been preliminary, and leading to this. Here we have recorded the great call of Jesus, fittingly uttered at this feast.

The relation of our Lord to the great feasts is a subject of interest. Here we see Him at the feast of Tabernacles, with all its historic associations, virtually showing how in and through Him, all that the feast had typified, was being fulfilled. At the Cross, we see Him fulfilling the significance of Passover. Luke put it very clearly about Pentecost, when he said, " The Day of Pentecost was now being fulfilled."

John tells us that this was the last day ; and the last day of the feast was the eighth. The feast proper lasted seven days, but to the seven—there was added an eighth ; and by Levitical law, that day was always observed as a Sabbath. We are familiar with the facts of the ritual of the feast as it was then observed. A great deal had been added to the Mosaic requirements in the ritual of the Temple at the time. A recognition of this will help us in considering the call of Jesus.

Some Jewish writers tell us that during the observance of the feast for seven days, on each day water was carried in golden vessels from the Pool of Siloam, and poured out in the presence of assembled worshippers in the Temple. Other Jewish writers tell us that for seven days there was a procession of the priests who went with empty vessels, either to Siloam's Pool, or outside the city to the brook Kidron, filled their vessels with water, and came back, chanting parts of the Great Hallel, then pouring out the water within the Temple courts. They tell us moreover that the symbolism related to two facts, one, that God had supplied their need with water in the wilderness, a physical provision ; the other, that promises had been made, as in Ezekiel, and more briefly in Joel, and in Zechariah ; that there should come a day when rivers of water should revivify the desert lands, a spiritual significance. This observance continued for seven days. On the last day there was no procession of the priests, no carrying of the golden vessels of water ; and the omission was as significant as the observance had been. The omission was to show, first that now there was no need for the supernatural supply of water, because they were no longer in the wilderness, but in the land ; and secondly, that the great promises of spiritual refreshment had not yet been fulfilled.

That is the background ; and the moment we recognize it, we see that for those listening multitudes, especially such as appreciated the value of their own ritual, there was something very significant in the fact that Jesus stood that day, the day when they were no longer carrying the waters, and cried, " If any man thirst, let him come unto Me, and drink. He that believeth on Me, as the Scripture hath said, out of his inner life shall flow the rivers of living water."

John says, " Jesus stood and cried." We are arrested by that word " stood," because the attitude of the teacher was never that of standing. The teacher always sat. But on this occasion it is distinctly and emphatically stated that He stood ; which means that He was taking the position of a Herald, with a great proclamation to make.

Again we are arrested by the word John uses here, when he says not that Jesus stood and said, but that " Jesus stood and *cried*." We came across that word in our previous study, in verse twenty-eight. There we read that " Jesus therefore cried in the Temple, teaching and saying." The verb is one that shows He spoke with strong emotion. In each case it was a great outburst. A little while before, it was an outburst of protest ; now it was an outburst, not of protest, but of invitation. In each case a great emotional cry passed the lips of Jesus. He stood as a Herald, and He cried. What He said, and the effects produced, are recorded in this paragraph.

After the record of what Jesus said, John, in verse thirty-nine, has given us an interpretation. " This spake He of the Spirit, which they that believed on Him were to receive ; for the Spirit was not yet,"—and our translators have supplied a word—" given." The text says, " The Spirit was not yet." Of course that cannot mean that the Spirit was not yet in existence, nor that the Spirit had not previously been active. The sense cannot be interpreted better than by the word " given." Let us consider this interpretation, before considering the call in itself.

" This spake He of the Spirit," Who " was not yet given ; because Jesus was not yet glorified." We have to remember that John was writing this long years after ; and, from his knowledge of all that transpired subsequently. Looking back, he understood what Jesus had meant that day. I wonder if John understood at the time. I very much doubt it. In an earlier stage in his story he recorded something Jesus said, " Destroy this temple, and in three days I will raise it up " ; and then said that the disciples understood it *after He was risen from the dead*. So here, I have no doubt he was looking back, and looking back, in the light of the things that had transpired, from the hour in which he heard his Lord utter this great proclamation, he said, He spake of the Spirit, which was not then yet given.

These words reveal the Lord's consciousness of the persistent lack that characterized those among whom His ministry was exercised. We have seen it all the way through. We have seen the people listening to Jesus from a material standpoint only, always seeming to miss the spiritual. After the feeding of the five thousand, John records how He rebuked them for that very thing. When He spoke of His own flesh as meat for the world, He told them the flesh profited nothing ; the Spirit was the supreme thing. Here was a recognition of that persistent lack. From the hour when He said to Nicodemus a man must be born anew, born of the Spirit ; all the way through we have seen materialized thinking, and materialized living. " The Spirit not yet." " Not yet " was an evident reference to something new that took place afterwards ; an evident reference to Pentecost, and the coming of the Holy Spirit then. Jesus was thinking of that, and speaking in terms which revealed that fulfilment would come by the coming of the Holy Spirit, in that new way.

Then mark the significance of this. John tells us why the Spirit was not yet given in that new way. " Jesus was not yet glorified." And again John, looking back, was writing as the result of what he had learned. On the last page in John concerning the public ministry of Jesus, in chapter twelve, we have the story of the coming of the Greeks, in connection with which Jesus said ; " The hour is come, that the Son of man should be glorified. Verily, verily, I say unto you, Except a grain of wheat fall into the earth and die, it abideth by itself alone ; but if it die, it beareth much fruit." " The hour is come when the Son of God should be glorified." He was referring to His Cross. Here John referred to the same thing, and in the same way, in terms of victory, of glory. Jesus was not then glorified. He had not passed to His Cross, and His passion baptism, and to His resurrection ; and therefore " the Spirit was not yet." But though the Spirit was not yet given, because Jesus was not yet glorified, nevertheless He uttered this great call, the full significance of which could only come by the way of His Cross, and by the way of that which resulted from the Cross, the coming in a new manner, of the Holy Spirit.

Now we listen to the voice of Jesus. He said two things, quite separate from each other, but for ever joined to each other. First, " If any man thirst, let him come unto Me, and drink " ; a most amazing thing. Notice carefully. " If any man "—mark the universality of it. " Thirst," mark the absence of anything in the nature of specializing. Whatever the thirst may be, whether it be spiritual, a passion for purity and power ; or whether it be in the region of the affectional nature ; He challenges the agony of humanity, the clamant cry of the race, thirsting, thirsting. " If any man thirst," whatever his thirst may be, " let him come to Me, and drink," He challenged universal thirst, and declared that He was able to quench it, whatever it might be. Now, in that first saying, there is only room for two people. Who are they ? A thirsty soul and Jesus. " If any man "—He is individualizing. The crowds were all round about Him. He broke the crowds up into their component parts, and separated every man from every other man. Any man, individually, to Him.

Two people can get into that first word, only two. Who are they? Jesus and me. Let each say that for himself or herself. What am I thirsty for? What is the clamant cry in the centre of my life? Whatever it is, Christ is still saying, " Come to Me, and drink." He claimed, and He claims, to be able to quench all human thirst.

The next saying was not purely personal. It was entirely relative, but it is linked with the personal. " He that believeth on Me "—that is the man who hears My call and obeys it, the man that comes to Me with his thirst that it may be quenched, " he that believeth on Me, as the Scripture hath said, out of his inner life shall flow the rivers." How many people are in that verse? You never know. Supposing I hear that call and obey it; my thirst is quenched, then what? Out of me the rivers flow, and how far they will flow I shall never know, how many people's thirst will be quenched from the rivers flowing out of my life, because I am satisfied with Jesus, no one will ever know. " He that believeth on Me, as the Scripture hath said, out of his life shall flow the rivers "; all the rivers, described by Ezekiel, that come by the way of the altar, and underneath the threshold, and spread to the Arabah, the desert land; and everywhere they come, there is life.

Mark the inter-relationship between these two sayings. I never can get into the second part of that verse, save through the first part. As long as I am a thirsty soul, I can supply no rivers that quench the thirst of other souls. In one of our great hymns there are two lines, which I never sing without thinking of this call of Jesus,

> " Thou, O Christ, art all I want."

That is the language of the man who has heard His call, and has gone to Him for the quenching of his thirst. What is the next line?

> " More than all in Thee, I find."

That is the overflowing life. There can be no overflowing life, until the life is filled and satisfied.

In passing, do not forget that group of men standing there, listening to Jesus, sent by the high priests to arrest Him. They heard Him speak those things of stupendous significance. A little while ago they had heard Him say, Where I am, you cannot come. You cannot touch Me ; you cannot lay hands on Me. I am here now. I am going back when the programme is done, to Him that sent Me ; and until that programme is done, you cannot touch Me. They heard that ; and then they heard this. They were listening, and they listened to words more wonderful than human ears had ever heard uttered before. All the suggestiveness of the past, claimed by One as being fulfilled in Himself.

And so we pass to consider the immediate results. What happened ? There was division. Christ has always been divisive, and will be until, in the process of time, and in the fulfilment of the Divine economy, He shall have gathered all wheat into His garner, and flung out all chaff to be burned. " Some . . . said, This is of a truth the prophet." We have come across that reference two or three times, " The Prophet." Undoubtedly the reference was to Moses' prediction in Deuteronomy, that God would send them a prophet like unto himself. They did not for a single moment seem to think of this as a Messianic promise. They believed a prophet was coming, and they said, This is He. That thought had emerged when they had talked about manna, so now, when He talks about water. Had not Moses produced water supernaturally in the wilderness ? Yes, they said, This is undoubtedly the prophet. Others said, This is the Christ. Then " Some of them said, What, doth the Christ come out of Galilee ? " These people had been saying, We know all about Him, whence He is ; and a little earlier they had said, We know His father and mother ; and on this very day they had declared they knew whence He was, and they still thought that they did. But how ignorant they were still, even as to the actual facts of the case. Out of Galilee, they said ; we know perfectly well the Messiah is coming from Bethlehem, the city of David. That was where He had come from. So, not only were they at fault, in that they had no recognition of the spiritual and profound fact of His personality, they were also ignorant of the local facts. Finally, some were so hostile that they would fain have laid hands on Him, and taken Him before the Sanhedrim.

Why would they have taken Him to the Sanhedrim? What inspired that section of the crowd that would like to have arrested Him, and handed Him over to His enemies? They had caught the tremendous significance of what He had said about being able to quench human thirst, and His claim that if men believed on Him, through them should flow the rivers. They thought it was blasphemy. We have seen that before. It began in chapter five, when He made Himself equal with God, and again and again they understood His claim, but rejected it. They were quite right in their understanding of the claims He was making, but they did not accept them; therefore they would arrest Him. So after that great proclamation we see that divided crowd.

Now what followed? The return of the officers without Him. These were orderlies from the Temple, who were under the command of the Sanhedrim. When it is said that the priests and the Pharisees sent to take Him, it is a way of declaring that an official decision had been arrived at to arrest Him. These orderlies would not have proceeded at the command of any one single ruler, and the Sanhedrim was still sitting, waiting for the officers to bring Jesus back. All the attitudes of high priests and scribes and elders (to name the constituent parts of the Sanhedrim) in connection with Jesus were illegal. The Sanhedrim never met on the Sabbath day, but they met that day. It was a Sabbath, it was the eighth day. All the sanctity of the Sabbath was round about it, and yet their hostility permitted them to break the law. When these orderlies went back without Him, they challenged them; " Why did ye not bring Him? " Their answer stands on record, another of those incidental things which are sublime, " Never man so spake." What a curious reason to give for disobedience. I hardly like to suggest a similitude, but supposing, that for any reason, the officers of the Government were sent to arrest a man in Hyde Park, and they came back presently without him; and the authorities said, Where is he? and they said, Never man spoke like that. It is a most amazing thing. They were sent to arrest Him. They could not do it; they could not lay hands on Him. Why have you not brought Him? The only answer is, Never Man spoke like that. We could not stretch a hand out to touch Him, and the reason was we heard Him talk. They may have heard a great deal more than is recorded in those few sentences, but they were enough. They heard Him speak in the language of supreme disdain in the presence of hostility manifested by the rulers. Then they had heard Him utter those tremendous words, challenging the thirst of humanity, and declaring that if men would believe on Him, out of their lives should flow rivers of water and blessing. They went back, and said, No, we did not arrest Him; He arrested us. We laid no hands on Him, but He laid on us the superlative spell of His speech. We heard Him say such things as we never heard before. I am not going to suggest that they meant this; but whether they meant it or not, this is the full significance of what they said. They said, " Never Man so spake." They were quite right. It was not the voice of a man merely; it was the voice of God. That is what He had said, when the rulers said, " Whence hath this Man these letters," " My doctrine is not Mine, but His that sent Me." Here it was ratified in the confession of a group of men, not perhaps apprehending the fulness of what they said; but saying honestly what they felt at the moment, " Never man so spake." We may put the emphasis where perhaps they never put it—" Never *man* so spake." No mere man can challenge all humanity, and declare his ability to quench its thirst; no mere man could say that by confidence in him, rivers shall flow from those reposing such confidence, for the blessing of others. That was the speech of God.

The story ends with the account of the anger of the rulers, and their scorn, and their satire, Are you also deceived?

And then that word, so singularly human, " Hath any of the rulers believed on Him, or of the Pharisees ? " Has any notable person taken up this matter ? The question of false pride. And finally the contempt for the crowd. Remember these were the spiritual and moral and civil rulers, whose chief concern ought to have been the welfare of the people. Listen, " But this multitude which knoweth not the law are accursed." We see the type of those who were in opposition to Christ.

But there was one voice raised in defence. Nicodemus, being one of them, which means he was a member of the Sanhedrim, raised his voice on behalf of Jesus on the lines of strict justice. Then again the contempt expressed itself, " Art thou also of Galilee ? Search and see that out of Galilee ariseth no prophet." That is all. It is a story of strange tumult.

How does it end ? There is no question whatever that the fifty-third verse of chapter seven, and verse one of chapter eight should be kept together. " They went, *they* went every man unto his own house ; but Jesus went to the mount of Olives." That is all I know. If I may be allowed the figure of speech, there the curtain drops.

" They went every man to his own house." There may be so much in that. They had houses to go to, and they went. Jesus—" Foxes have holes, and the birds of the air have nests ; but the Son of man hath not where to lay His head." He " went unto the mount of Olives." They scattered, that promiscuous crowd, to their own homes, back to the quietness and the comfort, oh, it may be to the disturbance created by conscience, I do not know. Jesus went to the mount of Olives ; and He went into a greater peace than they, a greater quietness than they. He went, as His custom was, unquestionably to the peace and the strength of communion with God.

John viii. 2–30.

THIS section begins with a paragraph (verses two to eleven) often described as a doubtful paragraph ; and there is reason for such description. In the King James Version there is nothing to suggest that there is any question about it. When the English revisers did their work, and when the American revisers did theirs, the two companies were in agreement that there is a doubt as to whether this story came from the pen of John. Consequently those who use the Revised Version will find the paragraph, beginning with the fifty-third verse of the seventh chapter, and running through the eleventh verse of chapter eight, put within brackets. That is so in the English, and American Revisions. If we consult the Greek Texts, we find that Westcott and Hort have lifted the paragraph out completely, and inserted it as an addendum at the end of the book. Nestlé's Text has restored it to its place, but has put it in brackets.

It is very doubtful as to whether John wrote it. I am not going to be over-dogmatic, but personally I do not think he did. There are many internal evidences, that it was not from his pen. In some old manuscripts, the paragraph is found in the Gospel of Luke. Possibly it was added by the hand of that remarkable extra-illustrator, Papias.

Evidently, however, all those who have examined it, and who are not sure of authorship, feel that there is something about it which makes them feel that they cannot leave it out. Westcott and Hort were convinced that it ought not to be where it is ; so they put it in at the end of the book, but they put it in. Added probably by some other pen, I still believe it to be in strict chronological sequence. I propose therefore to treat it as authentic, and in proper sequence historically.

We have then in this section three matters ; the incident recorded in verses two to eleven ; then in one verse (verse twelve), the great claim of Jesus, which in the sequence of John, is the second of the great " I am's " ; and then following, from verse thirteen to the end, we are again in the atmosphere of opposition, and questioning, and discussion.

This incident is one of the most fascinating and beautiful, in some ways, in all the account of the ministry of our Lord.

It is very startling. It is very revealing also, of the attitude of His enemies towards Him, and principally of Himself. The thing occurred, we are told, in the early morning ; " And early in the morning He came again into the Temple." It follows quite naturally the story of the preceding chapter, that of the feast of Tabernacles, the last day of the feast, the eighth, when He had uttered His great call, challenging human thirst. He had spent the night in the mount of Olives. Every man had gone to his own house ; Jesus had gone to the mount of Olives ; and early in the morning He came, the day after the feast. The dispersing crowds would characterize that morning ; with many still lingering. If we glance on for a moment to verse twenty, we find that " He spake in the treasury." That refers to the courts of the women, where the treasury was situated.

When on the previous day He had made His great call, " If any man thirst," He had *stood*, which marked a distinct difference in His attitude for the moment. He stood as a Herald. Now He went back and resumed the attitude of the Teacher, He sat down. When He stood, and uttered that call, He was not teaching, but making a proclamation. Now, going back, He again assumed the position of the Teacher. The crowds gathered round Him. As they listened to Him, there was a stir, a movement in the crowd, and there came into the midst certain scribes and Pharisees, bringing a woman. It is impossible to read the story without realizing the brutal indelicacy of their action. Whatever this woman had done, and however guilty she was, legally they had no right to drag her into the public gaze. The Sanhedrim had its sittings in the very next part of the Temple to where Jesus was teaching. Probably they intended to take her there presently ; but they had no right to drag her into publicity. With the same brutal indelicacy they told her story ; as they said she had been " taken in the very act." It was brutal, but I shall always be glad they said it, because it leaves no doubt whatever about this woman's guilt. It was not a question of hearsay.

We can visualize that scene in the early morning, Jesus sitting as a Teacher, the people gathered round about Him, and this interruption of rulers, religious and moral rulers, custodians of morality, hounding in a woman, and laying bare her sin to the crowd.

Then they raised their question. Moses commands that such should be stoned. What sayest Thou ? John is careful to tell us their motive in saying this. " This they said, tempting Him, that they might have whereof to accuse Him." They were trying to put Him in an awkward place, on the horns of a dilemma. Roman law said that life must not be taken except with Roman authority. Moses said she was to be stoned. What would He say about this ? If He said she was to go free, He would be contradicting the Mosaic law. If He said she was to be stoned, He would be involving Himself with the Roman authorities.

Then follows the matchless story. What did He do ? He stooped down and wrote. No, I cannot tell you what He wrote. I have often wondered, and read the legends, and they are all suggestive. What He wrote we do not know, but the attitude was everything. It was the attitude of attention to something else, and refusal to satisfy His questioners. It was the attitude of dismissal.

But they would not let Him alone. They were determined to have an answer ; and so John says that " He lifted up Himself, and said, Whosoever among you is sinless." This is the only place in the New Testament where this particular word occurs. It is not merely, Whosoever among you never sinned. It is far more than that. It means literally, sinless. " Let him first cast a stone at her."

In these words He did not answer their enquiry in the realm of comparison between Moses and His own opinion. It is as though He had said, I am not discussing Moses with you. If that is the law of Moses, let it stand as a law ; but if I do not discuss the law or the sentence, I am here to appoint the executioners. In that saying our Lord revealed for all time this principle, that sinlessness is the only qualification for punishing. That sentence put me out of the stone-throwing business for the rest of my life ! " He that is without sin among you, let him first cast a stone at her."

Then He stooped down and wrote again. Look at that crowd going out. That is one of the most gloriously humorous things on record. Every last man of them went, and it is interesting that John says they went out one by one, from the eldest to the youngest. I wonder what that means. Were they still standing on the precedence of the elder over the younger ? I prefer to think that the oldest man went first, because he had most sense. Be that as it may, He cleared them all out. Exit the executioners.

Then we come to the supreme wonder and glory of the story. Jesus was left alone, with the woman in the midst. Now what do we see ? Incarnate Purity standing confronting the saddest thing in all human life, convicted impurity. There is no mistake about the sin. What then do we see ? According to His own declared principles, He was the only One Who had any right to cast a stone at that woman ; He was without sin. If we did not know the story so well, and we were hearing it for the first time, we should almost stop with bated breath, and say, what did He do ?

First of all He called her by the same name which He used for His Mother, at Cana, and on His Cross, " Woman." Whenever that word fell from the lips of Jesus, it was a word of infinite tenderness. Oh marvel of marvels, Woman ! That crowd that had gone would have described her by a harsher word ; they would have used the term harlot, or prostitute, or something worse. He said, " Woman " ! Then He said, " Where are they ? did no man condemn thee ? " Then, the only word recorded as falling from her lips, was uttered. We do not know her name. Have you ever noticed every such woman you meet in the course of Jesus' ministry remains anonymous? Mary of Magdala was not a sinning woman in this sense, in spite of the stupid blunder of all the years. All these are anonymous. Their names are never recorded. I do not think they will ever be known, because they will

have new names in that land Beyond. The only thing she
is reported as saying is, " No man, Lord."

If we had looked at the woman when she was being brought
in, and then if we had looked at her when she said, " No
man, Lord," we should have seen a great change in her face.
I know how she looked when they took her in. She was
rebellious, she was defiant, she was angry. That method of
handling that sort of woman always produces that result.
But when she looked into the eyes for a moment of another
kind of Man, a Man Who dismissed her accusers, I tell you
her eyes were losing the defiant look, and becoming tear-
dimmed ; and I think there was a quiver in her voice as she
said, " No man, Lord."

Then came the amazing, the astounding words, " Neither
do I condemn thee."

I do not think that the full meaning of what He said is
found in what I now suggest, but I feel sure it was involved
in it. I think we may put the emphasis on the last word.
" Neither do I condemn *thee*." He was not condoning her
sin ; but among other things, He meant this : These men
say you were caught in the act, woman ; if so, where is the
man ? Yes, Mr. Kipling, " the sins we do by two and two,
we must answer for one by one " ; but we have no right to
put all the blame on the one. " Neither do I condemn *thee*."

But He meant more than that. If we turn to Romans
eight, we find out what He meant. " There is therefore now
no condemnation to them that are in Christ Jesus." He
put Himself and His redeeming and atoning love and passion
between her and her sin. The Lamb was " slain from the
foundation of the world." " Neither do I condemn thee ; go
thy way ; from henceforth sin no more," or rather, continue
no longer in sin.

The incident was over. " Again therefore Jesus spoke unto
them, saying." There are those who link that " therefore "
with verse fifty-two in chapter seven. I link it with this
story. Then He uttered His claim. " I am the Light of the
world," that was personal. " He that followeth Me shall

not walk in the darkness, but shall have the light of life,"
that was relative.

The personal was inclusive. " I am the Light of the cosmos." The word is used in differing ways. We read that
" God so loved the *cosmos*, that He gave His only begotten
Son " ; and then " He that loveth the *cosmos*, the love of
the Father is not in him." Strange apparent contradiction ;
but we know the difference in the use of the word in these
and other cases. When Jesus said, " I am the Light of the
world," the claim was superlative and inclusive.

But He had not finished. " He that followeth Me shall not
walk in the darkness " : and that is not all : " He shall
have the light of life." First the personal, " He that followeth
Me shall not walk in the darkness " ; secondly, the relative,
" he shall have the light of life " ; which means not merely
that he shall walk in light and not in darkness, but he shall
be a centre of light ; the light proceeding from him. Thus
we have the same two ideas found in His call at the feast of
Tabernacles. If any man thirst, let him come to Me and drink.
He that believeth on Me, out of his inner life shall flow the
rivers. Now as to the Light of the world. He that followeth
Me shall not walk in darkness ; he shall have the light of
life, and so light shall shine forth from him.

If this really did happen immediately after the feast of
Tabernacles, notice that all this was said in the treasury. That
refers to the women's court, where stood the golden chests.
That is where Jesus was when later He saw the widow casting
in her mite. During the feast, the golden chests were
illuminated. Some Jewish interpreters say they were
illuminated every day during the feast. Now the feast was
over, the lights were out ; and He Who had stood and claimed
the fulfilment of the prophecy of the rivers, now stood and
said, " I am the Light of the world. He that followeth Me
shall not walk in the darkness, but he shall have the light
of life."

Discussion began immediately. The Pharisees said to Him,
" Thou bearest witness of Thyself ; Thy witness is not

true." Let us glance back to chapter five and verse thirty-one. There, in the story of the derelict, Christ said, " If I bear witness of Myself, My witness is not true." These men were quoting Him. They were quoting Himself against Himself. Now when He said, " I am the Light of the world " they quoted Himself, endeavouring to show His inconsistency. But He cannot be trapped. What He said was true. The consistency of Eternity explains the apparent inconsistencies of time.

How did He answer them ? He declared that even if He bare witness of Himself, whatever He said was based on certain knowledge. I know Whom I am, I know whence I am, I know whither I go. He was not speculating in anything He said. They judged after the flesh. He judged no man. But if He did, He was not speaking alone. He and the Father were united ; They judged together. They did not know. They were flesh-bound, blinded with the dust of material thinking.

Then using one of their own laws, He declared that in the mouth of two witnesses, truth was established. Here then were the two. He and the Father were never separated.

Then came the bitter thrust, " Where is Thy Father ? " They were mocking Him. For the moment they would not question the claim that He was one with the Father. It is as though they said, Supposing God is Your Father, then produce Him. You say He is witnessing with You, how do we know He is witnessing with You ? We still only have Your own words. Where is Your Father ? In hostility, they were in exactly the same attitude as Philip was in friendship, a little later on, when he said to Jesus, " Show us the Father, and it sufficeth us." Jesus gave in effect the very answer He gave to Philip. He said, " If ye knew Me, ye would know My Father also." If you knew My Father, you would know Me.

At that point in his narrative John says, " These words spake He in the treasury, and no man took Him ; because His hour was not yet come." He was held secure from all hostility until His hour came.

Then He continued, and He said, " I go away, and ye shall seek Me, and shall die in your sin ; whither I go, ye cannot come." Those were words of condemnation. Again the Jews were perplexed. They said, " Will He kill Himself, that He saith, Whither I go, ye cannot come ? " He replied in the same tone of severity as He said, " Ye are from beneath, I am from above ; ye are of this world, I am not of this world." Their whole outlook was fleshly, and therefore of Satan. He was not from beneath ; but from above. All His vision, and His passion were centred and rooted in the things of heaven.

Then they in anger flung at Him the question, " Who art Thou ? " He replied in effect, Who am I ? I am the same that I have claimed to be from the beginning. And then, When you have lifted up the Son of man, you will know ! That is what He had said to His Mother, " Mine hour is not come " ; and to His brethren, " My time is not yet come." All through He is seen with His eyes upon the Cross. When you have lifted Me up you will know. There is no other way of knowing. There is no other way for the opening of eyes spiritually blind, than the way I go.

Then He made His final claim in this discussion. " He that sent Me is with Me ; He hath not left Me alone ; for I do always the things that are pleasing to Him."

That claim is linked with the statement immediately preceding it. When you have lifted up the Son of Man you will know. In these words we catch the accents of the everlasting mercy. He had spoken to them in anger. He had had to tell them the truth. They were from beneath ; and all their attitude was mastered by hell. But He was in the world under the mastery of high heaven. One day, He told them, the revelation would come to them. When they had lifted up the Son of man, they would understand. " I do always the things that please My Father " ; and within those are the things to which I refer, the lifting up of the Son of man. So in the midst of all the bitterness of opposition, and the sternness of rebuke, there was the vibrant tenderness of the everlasting mercy.

The last sentence is, " Many believed on Him." There was, for a moment, a reaction in His favour ; but it was not worth much, as we shall see presently.

John viii. 31–59.

ONCE more the word " therefore " in verse thirty-one marks continuity. Following His claim, " I am the Light of the world," there had been discussion, and that discussion had resulted in some reaction in His favour. This paragraph shows how superficial that reaction was, as it records the way in which our Lord dealt with the Jews who believed on Him.

" Jesus therefore said to those Jews which had believed Him, If ye abide in My word, then are ye truly My disciples." The paragraph ends with the statement, " They took up stones therefore to cast at Him." All the way through He was dealing with that section of the crowd that had felt this reaction in His favour. As we follow through, I repeat, we discover how little worth while that reaction was. We see Him all the way now, proceeding with great majesty and supreme dignity, and becoming more and more lonely, isolated ; until at the end the isolation was complete, no one was with Him.

This section may be set out in a sevenfold sequence of statement and reply. In that way let us follow the story.

The first section is found in verses thirty-one to thirty-three.

" Jesus therefore said to those Jews which had believed Him, If ye abide in My word, then are ye truly My disciples ; and ye shall know the truth, and the truth shall make you free."

That is the first movement. Our Lord thus gave these Jews, attracted to Him, clear, if brief instructions as to discipleship. The one necessity was not the emotional attraction of which they had been conscious, but that of abiding. " If ye abide in My word, then are ye truly My

disciples." Not the inclination towards Him, which produced admiration ; but such complete subjection, that they
would abide. He also declared what the results of such abiding
would be : " Ye shall know the truth, and the truth shall
make you free " ; knowledge and complete emancipation.

They immediately objected to His suggestion of possible
freedom, claiming that they were already free. They said,

" We be Abraham's seed, and have never yet been in
bondage to any man ; how sayest Thou, Ye shall be made
free ? "

It was a remarkable answer, an answer in some senses,
justified. What did they mean when they said they never
had been in bondage to any man ? They had been in bondage.
They had been in bondage in Egypt. They had been in
bondage in Babylon. They had been in bondage to Syria.
They were then under Roman bondage, and yet they said
this. Now, as a matter of fact, they never had been subdued ;
neither Egypt, nor Babylon, nor Syria, nor Rome, none had
ever broken the spirit of the Jew. So far they were quite
right ; and our Lord in replying to them did not deny what
they said, from the standpoint of their own view.

The next section is found in verse thirty-four to the
beginning of verse thirty-nine.

" Jesus answered them, Verily, verily, I say unto you,
Every one that committeth sin is the bondservant of sin. And
the bondservant abideth not in the house for ever ; the son
abideth for ever. If therefore the Son shall make you free,
ye shall be free indeed. I know that ye are Abraham's seed ;
yet ye seek to kill Me, because My word hath not free course
in you. I speak the things which I have seen with My Father ;
and ye also do the things which ye heard from your father."

" They answered and said unto Him, Our father is
Abraham."

Thus in answering their claim to freedom, He did not debate
the subject with them. He acknowledged it in a certain way.
He admitted that there was a sense in which their spirit
had never been broken, they had never been subjugated,

they had never bent the neck to any outside national power. But He immediately lifted the whole consideration to the realm of the ethical, and showed them He was not talking in the realm of the material at all. These people were thinking all the time on the level of the material, thinking of the flesh all the time. Whether of the Messiah, or of the Kingdom of God, they were thinking in the terms of the earth ; and our Lord was ever calling them to lift their thinking on to the higher level, the spiritual level, the level of righteousness, and the level of the ethical. He said to them in effect : You never have been subdued by any outside nation, but you have been, and are the slaves of sin, the bond-servants of sin. Then He told them that those who are the slaves of sin are excluded from the house, the house standing there for the whole economy of God. The writer of the letter to the Hebrews dealing with the Son, and the servant, uses the word house, in that way. Now, said Jesus, the bond-slave of sin is excluded from the house ; but the Son abides, and he whom the Son sets free, also abides. He said they were Abraham's seed after the flesh, but they were rejecting the Son. He spoke from the Father. They were acting from their father, in such a way as to deny the claim they were making of relationship to Abraham. Never subdued by material forces, but so mastered by sin that they had lost their contact with God, and were unable to understand when the Son spoke from the Father to them.

Then they answered, still boasting in the flesh. When He told them that they were of their father ; they said, " Our father is Abraham."

The next section is in verses thirty-nine to forty-one.

" Jesus saith unto them, If ye were Abraham's children, ye would do the works of Abraham. But now ye seek to kill Me, a Man that hath told you the truth, which I heard from God ; this did not Abraham. Ye do the works of your father.

" They said unto Him, We were not born of fornication ; we have one Father, even God."

Our Lord had admitted that they were the seed of Abraham ; that is a fleshly matter ; but now declared they were not the children of Abraham ; that is a matter of the spirit. In the ninth chapter of the letter to the Romans, at verse six we read, " They are not all Israel, which are of Israel ; neither, because they are Abraham's seed, are they all children." There we have in apostolic writing the reaffirmation of the truth that our Lord was then declaring, the truth that Israel after the flesh, has never realized ; and the truth that a great many Christian people do not seem to have realized. There are multitudes of Christian people to-day who are thinking still of Israel after the flesh. Relationship after the flesh is of no value unless there is the relationship of the spirit. Spiritual relation is proven by works. Our Lord declared that they were proving their relationship by the works they were doing.

It is quite evident that those listening to Him caught the significance of what He was doing. They recognized that He was insisting upon it that the one thing of supreme importance was the spiritual, and not the material ; that spiritual relationships may exist, even when fleshly relationship is absent. And so, professing to accept His intention, they denied His suggestion. They said, We are not born of fornication ; our Father is God. Thus they attempted to affirm the spiritual relationship. He was denying the value of their fleshly relationship to Abraham, unless there was spiritual relationship with Abraham. Unless the works they did, demonstrated the fact that they bore the same relationship to God which Abraham bore, and demonstrated by his works, their fleshly relationship was of no value at all. They replied by affirmation. We are the children of God, we were not born of fornication. Thus they ignored what He was insisting upon as the spiritual and ethical being supreme.

The next section begins at verse forty-two and runs through verse forty-eight. It is characterized by dread solemnity.

" Jesus said unto them, If God were your Father, ye would

love Me ; for I came forth and am come from God ; neither have I come of Myself, but He sent Me. Why do ye not understand My speech ? Even because ye cannot hear My word. Ye are of your father the devil, and the lusts of your father it is your will to do. He was a murderer from the beginning, and stood not in the truth, because there is no truth in him. When he speaketh a lie, he speaketh of his own ; for he is a liar, and the father thereof. But because I say the truth, ye believe Me not. Which of you convicteth Me of sin ? If I say truth, why do ye not believe Me ? He that is of God heareth the words of God ; for this cause ye hear them not, because ye are not of God."

The clarity of this answer of Jesus leaves no room for doubt about these matters. First, mark His claim ; " If God were your Father, ye would love Me." Presently when Philip said, " Show us the Father," He replied, " Have I been so long time with you, and dost thou not know Me, Philip ? He that hath seen Me hath seen the Father." Imagine anyone else saying a thing like this, If you knew God you would love Me. That is what He said to them with perfect clearness. Then He told them what lay at the back of that deafness and dulness, their blindness and denseness ; they were of their father the devil ; their spiritual relationship was a relationship with hell.

Then, in this passage, our Lord, in the most remarkable way defined the devil. He said two things about him. He is a murderer, and he is a liar. That covers all the ground. He is a murderer from the beginning. He is a liar from the beginning. Once more we go back to the beginning of the Gospel. John, looking back upon Jesus said, " We beheld His glory . . . full of grace and truth." Satan is a murderer and a liar, the exact antitheses of grace and truth. In other words, all that God is, Satan is not. God is grace. The devil is a murderer. God is truth. The devil is a liar. Thus our Lord showed that relationship is proved by action. If they had been of God, they would have discovered grace, and responded to it ; and truth, and loved it ; but they were

[158]

seeking to kill Him. Hate was in their heart, and they were false. That demonstrated their relationship. They were of their father the devil.

Thus He had once more insisted upon it that the ethical is the proof of the spiritual. Their evil deeds demonstrated their relationship to Satan. Real spiritual relationship with God will always bring forth works like the works of God.

" The Jews answered and said unto Him, Say we not well that Thou art a Samaritan, and hast a demon."

Now they were getting angry. They felt the impact of the terrible things He had said to them ; and now they charged Him with being a Samaritan. In their view the Samaritan was opposed absolutely to the Jew. " The Jews have no dealing with the Samaritans." To the Jew the Samaritan was the incarnation of opposition to his position and race and nation ; and they said Jesus was a Samaritan ; and moreover, that He was demented.

So to the next section, verses forty-nine to fifty-three.

" Jesus answered, I have not a demon ; but I honour My Father, and ye dishonour Me. But I seek not Mine own glory ; there is One that seeketh and judgeth. Verily, verily, I say unto you, If a man keep My word, he shall never see death. The Jews said unto Him, Now we know that Thou hast a demon. Abraham is dead, and the prophets ; and Thou sayest, If a man keep My word, he shall never taste of death. Art Thou greater than our father, Abraham, which is dead ? and the prophets are dead ? Whom makest Thou Thyself ? "

Our Lord first denied quite simply, and in dignified language, what they had said, " I have not a demon." Then again explained Himself as He said, " I honour My Father, . . . I seek not My own glory " ; and then that superlative utterance, " If a man keep My word, he shall never see death."

They could only interpret on the ground of the physical. Never see death ? What did our Lord mean ? Presently we shall hear Him say to Martha, " He that believeth on Me, though he die, yet shall he live ; and whosoever liveth and believeth on Me shall never die." Both on this occasion and on that He was speaking in the realm of the spiritual. He did not mean that men would never die physically. He now declared that the man who keeps His word is placed beyond the possibility of any destructive influence bearing in and breaking down his essential life; he shall never see death. They could not rise to this height, and so they said, Now we know Thou hast a demon. Abraham is dead, and the prophets are dead; Whom makest Thou Thyself?

Now verses fifty-four to fifty-seven.

" Jesus answered, If I glorify Myself, My glory is nothing; it is My Father that glorifieth Me; of Whom ye say, that He is your God; and ye have not known Him; but I know Him; and if I should say, I know Him not, I shall be like unto you, a liar; but I know Him, and keep His word. Your father Abraham rejoiced to see My day; and he saw it, and was glad.

The Jews therefore said unto Him, Thou art not yet fifty years, and hast Thou seen Abraham? "

Again, if familiarity with the Scriptures has not blunted us, we listen with amazement to the things He said. They said, "Whom makest Thou Thyself?" He immediately answered in effect, I am not making Myself anything; I do not glorify Myself at all. My Father glorifies Me. Then He added the thing that for a moment stunned them, and called forth their mocking laughter. " Your father Abraham rejoiced to see My day; and he saw it, and was glad." What did He mean? It is rather interesting, the interpretations that have been suggested. Someone said that He must have meant that Abraham was still living in the spirit world, and so was watching Him even then. Was He not rather speaking out of that eternal consciousness which He so constantly manifested? Was He not rather saying; My day did not begin when I was born into your world. My day stretches back, and includes all the past. Your father Abraham rejoiced to see My day.

I believe, however, that there was historical application in the words. I have long been convinced that the appearance of Melchisedek was one of the Christophanies of the Old Testament. He is described as " King of righteousness, King of peace." He met Abraham returning from the slaughter of the kings, and He blessed him ; and the less is blessed of the greater. Historically Abraham stood face to face with Christ, in my conviction, when Melchisedek met him.

Then we hear the ribald mockery of the Jews,

" Thou art not yet fifty years old, and hast Thou seen Abraham ? "
I never read that without thinking that it was a possible revelation of how old Jesus looked. Yet He was only three and thirty. I think if I were an artist, and ever attempted to paint the face of Jesus, I would not paint too young a face at that time ! I think the years so full of sorrow and travail had told upon Him.

This brings us to the final section, verses fifty-eight and fifty-nine. Here we come to the third great sign of this Gospel in the realm of words. First, " I am the Bread of life." Then, " I am the Light of the world." Now—and I pray you notice that our Lord introduced this statement with the formula which He employed when He would rearrest attention, and emphasize the importance of what He was about to say. " Verily, verily, I say unto you, Before Abraham was born, I am." That is a supreme claim to Deity ; perhaps the most simple and sublime of all the things He said with that great formula of old, the great " I AM." " Before Abraham was born, I am." Not, I was. That would simply mark priority, the priority of existence. But the " I am " claims the eternity of existence, antedating the whole of the Hebrew economy, existing in eternal Being. These are the words of the most impudent blasphemer that ever spoke, or the words of God incarnate.

Then what ? " They took up stones therefore to cast at Him." Mark the " therefore." Because of that, because of what He had now said, because of His blasphemy. That

L [161]

was the deepest reason of hostility, that He was blaspheming. They were quite right, if the things He said were not true. " They took up stones therefore to cast at Him."

Then mark the quiet majesty of the final statement. " Jesus hid Himself, and went out of the Temple."

That was a wonderful day, taken from beginning to end, What a marvellous revelation of the Lord this chapter affords. It is a chapter of conflict, definite hostility, unbelief ; blindness to spiritual things ; deadness as to moral sense ; but we see the Word here in action, and we hear Him in speech, and watching the process, we find the reason of the action, and the inspiration of the speech.

How do we see Him in action ? In dealing with that woman. How do we hear Him in speech ? Saying, " I am the Light of the world " ; " Before Abraham was born, I am." How are we to account for it ? What was the secret of it all ? Again we listen, and from the things He said, we have the explanation of everything. " I am not alone," " I and My Father," " I am from above."

I think we may end with John's word, " And we beheld His glory—full of grace and full of truth."

John ix. 1–38.

THIS paragraph opens with the words, " And as He passed by." The time note is quite indefinite. This incident may have occurred immediately our Lord left the Temple on the occasion, the record of which is in the previous chapter ; but more likely somewhat later, for then we are told that He hid Himself.

The whole story begins at verse one in chapter nine, and ends at verse twenty-one in chapter ten. Our present consideration takes us as far as the thirty-eighth verse of chapter nine.

The whole story moves in the same atmosphere in which

we have been following our Lord, specially in these more recent studies in connection with the feast of Tabernacles. It is that of organized religion in opposition to Jesus, and of Jesus in opposition to organized religion.

This is the story of the seventh great sign in John's selection. the penultimate sign, the eighth and last being that of the raising of Lazarus.

This sign led to an action on the part of Jesus of distinct rupture with organized religion, as it was opposed to Him, and His setting up of a new economy. This was distinctly a dividing line, a crisis. He did something here which He had never done before.

The paragraph has four movements. The record of the sign, in verses one to seven ; the discussion following it, in verses eight to twenty-three ; the excommunication of the man by organized religion, in verses twenty-four to thirty-four ; and finally the consequent action of Jesus, in verses thirty-five to thirty-eight.

The sign itself. " And as He passed by." That is no uncommon statement. Our Lord was always doing things apparently incidentally. He found His opportunities everywhere. " He saw a man blind from birth." John surely was intentionally superlative in his selection of these " powers," which were also therefore " wonders," but which he never called " powers " or " wonders," but always " signs." This is the only case on record of our Lord's dealing with congenital disease. There may have been many others ; but this is the only one recorded. This man was born blind ; he had never looked on the shimmer of Galilee, had never seen the flowers decking the sod. This the disciples recognized when they said, " Who did sin, this man, or his parents, that he should be born blind ? " It was a superlative case. John significantly says that " He saw a man," and " His disciples asked Him." Quite evidently they saw the eyes of Jesus resting on this man ; and immediately they asked the question. In all probability they had often seen the man, because he was gaining his living by receiving alms.

He was living on charity. The eyes of Christ resting on the man, attracted the disciples. Immediately they asked a question, and stated a problem.

What then was their problem ? The problem of a man born blind, suffering disability. Their philosophy of life was that all disability was the result of sin, and when they looked at that man, a problem was created. They said, " Rabbi, who did sin . . . that this man should be born blind ? "
They illustrated their enquiry by making two suggestions, the only two which occurred to them. They said, " Who did sin, this man, or his parents, that he should be born blind ? " It was a startling question. It would seem as though they had some belief in the pre-existence of the soul. " Who did sin ? " Had this man sinned before he was born into this world ? That was one suggestion. Was this disability the result of his own action in some previous existence ? Or was his blindness the result of the sin of his parents ?

The answer of Jesus is arresting. He said, " Neither did this man sin, nor his parents." Thus He dismissed their two suggestions. What did Jesus say about the pre-existence of the soul ? Nothing. He ignored the suggestion ; " Neither did this man sin, nor his parents." Therefore no argument, either way, can be based upon this story.

How then did He reply to their enquiry ? Let us look at the passage as it appears in our versions, from the standpoint of punctuation.

" Jesus answered, Neither did this man sin, nor his parents ; but that the works of God should be made manifest in him. We must work the works of Him that sent Me, while it is day."

If that punctuation is to be accepted, then Jesus meant that this man was not born blind because of his own sin or his parents', but in order to give God an opportunity to show what He could do with a blind man. I absolutely refuse to accept that interpretation.

Some years ago when I was facing that paragraph, and feeling that the thing suggested by that reading was absolutely foreign to the truth about God, I ventured to repunctuate it. Let us read it as thus changed.

> "Neither did this man sin, nor his parents. But that the works of God should be made manifest in him, we must work the works of Him that sent Me, while it is day."

I sent this form of punctuation to an eminent Greek scholar, and I asked him to express an opinion. Let me read his reply, a reply characterized by proper caution, and yet revealing a very clear principle.

> "He would be an exceedingly bold scholar who would undertake to prove the punctuation should be one way or the other on the mere ground of the Greek itself. It seems as if the question would have finally to be decided on doctrinal grounds, for it is plain that the difference in punctuation of the verse would change the meaning altogether. If one reading would be more in spirit with the tenor of Christ's teachings, as seems quite probable, that would be quite naturally preferable."

That settled it for me. What Jesus said was, I am not here to answer that kind of question. It may be perfectly justifiable. I am not here to explain the mystery of evil. I am not here to solve these problems. I am here to remove the cause of them. "We must work the works of Him that sent Me while it is day."

Involved in that answer is a revelation that blindness from birth is not the will of God for any man. But the mission of Christ was not that of solving the problem, but that of removing the disability which created the problem.

Then the act. He made clay with spittle, and anointed the eyes of the man, and told him to go and wash. This was an occasion when He made use of means. The particular value of the means I do not pretend to know. We do know that spittle was looked upon at the time as being remedial. Whether our Lord was accommodating His method for the sake of those around Him at the time, I cannot say. Sometimes He removed disability without any means. At other times He used means. That illuminates the whole region in which we discuss healing. Without means, or with means ; it is always God Who heals. He did not explain. After the anointing he was to go and wash. He obeyed, and came back seeing.

Now immediately discussion arose. First of all we have the question among his neighbours. Evidently he went back to his own neighbourhood, and they were amazed, and their amazement created uncertainty as to the identity of the man. As we pass over the ground, let us watch the man, growing in apprehension. His first answer was perfectly simple and convincing. They said " It is he," but some said, " No, but he is like him " ; and he settled the whole thing when he said, " I am he." I am indeed the man who sat and begged, and made my living on charity. I am looking at you. I have seen trees to-day for the first time. He told them how it was done. We see how little he knew ; " A man called Jesus." He knew that much, and that was his first witness.

Then they took him before the religious authorities, and at once we see the reason. This thing had been done on the Sabbath day. This question of the Sabbath persists all through. It began in chapter five, when Jesus had caused a man to carry his mattress on the Sabbath day. Their hostility was stirred, because they saw a man carrying his mattress on the Sabbath day, and failed to see the man who carried it, who had been a derelict for thirty-eight years, and was no longer a derelict. Here we have the same thing. A man born blind, his eyes were open, he was looking at them ; but failing to see him, they were concerned with the method. This Man made clay on the Sabbath day. In the Traditions of the rulers one thing specifically forbidden was to make clay on the Sabbath day. That is what Jesus had done. That is all they saw. The man had his eyes open. They could not see that. They saw the violation of the Sabbath.

Arraigned before the Pharisees, this man came to the second stage in his development. They said, " What sayest thou of Him ? " He replied, " He is a prophet." Thus the apprehension of the thing that had happened to him was getting hold of the man himself. When they badgered him, he came to the conviction that the Man named Jesus must be a prophet.

Then perplexed, the rulers called the parents. The story of the parents may be dismissed very briefly. It is quite natural. They knew perfectly well, as John tells us, that it had been decided by the authorities, that anyone who claimed that Jesus was Messiah should be excommunicated, put out of the synagogue. The terror of that was upon them. They nevertheless corroborated the fact of the wonder wrought. Two things they were certain about. One was that he was their son. The second was that he had been blind, and now saw. They were not prepared to say how. They referred the authorities back to the boy, " He is of age, ask him."

Then came the re-arraignment of the man. First they laid on him the charge, " Give glory to God, we know that this man is a sinner." Here if we want to understand the answer of the man, we must put ourselves imaginatively into his place. He had never seen his mother's face till that day. Some Man named Jesus had put clay on his eyes, and sent him to Siloam to wash, and he went and washed, and he saw for the first time. And now these men in authority solemnly charged him, " Give glory to God ; we know that this man is a sinner." His first answer was a restatement of the fact, and a refusal to discuss the question raised as to whether Jesus was a sinner. " Whether He be a sinner, I know not ; one thing I know, that, whereas I was blind, now I see."

That body of religious rulers could not get beyond that. The fact was attested by the man himself, and by his parents.

What did they then do ? They went back to the old position, and said, How did He do it ? Again they turned from the fact clearly established, which ought to have arrested them, and settled for ever their attitude towards Jesus. But no, they went back, and wanted to hear again how, because in the *how* lay their cause of complaint, that He had broken Sabbath.

Then the man became satirical, and out of patience with these rulers. He was gaining ground. He said, I have told you. Would you like to hear it again? Then came that thrust. I wonder from what part of his soul it came. " Would ye also become His disciples ? " Why that " also " ? This man was finding that he could not get away from the Man Who had opened his eyes, that whatever else was going to happen, something was happening as to his relation with the One Who had given him his sight. " Would ye *also* become His disciples ? "

Then they were angry, " they reviled him " ; they claimed to be the disciples of Moses, and repudiated Jesus.

This reviling carried the man further. He went beyond something he had said a moment or two before, " Whether He be a sinner, I know not." He began to think aloud, thought it out for himself. Sinner ! Did I say I did not know ? " If this Man were not from God, He could do nothing." The man is growing in apprehension.

Then they excommunicated him, they cast him out. Personally I am convinced that that meant literal excommunication. There are those who think that it meant they put him out of the synagogue. John had carefully said, " The Jews had agreed already, that if any man should confess Him to be the Christ, he should be put out ot the synagogue." The putting out there, means excommunication in the full sense. So they cut that man off. From that time he had no right to cross the threshold of temple or synagogue. From that moment he was cut off from all the privileges of his religion, excluded from the society of devout and decent souls. It was no light matter. Organized religion had excommunicated a man, excommunicated him because having received this great gift of sight, he had grown in his testimony and his understanding and his conviction concerning the Man Who had done it, along a line so severely logical that one can hardly understand how any man could fail to follow him. He had come to that position of certainty that the One Who did the thing was of God. On that basis they excommunicated him.

So we come to the action of Jesus. "Jesus heard that they had cast him out," and Jesus found him. Let us attempt to visualize this thing in its completeness, not merely as the historic and incidental, but from the standpoint of the economy of God. On the one hand we see the great economy of the past; the stately and wondrous economy, the Divinely arranged and appointed economy, stretching away back to Moses, and coming down through the centuries, with all the rites and ceremonials Divinely appointed. At this moment it was moribund, decadent, dead. No breath of spiritual life was in it. This moribund and decadent and dead organization of religion had excommunicated one man, a blind beggar as he was, but who was now a seeing man. Then Jesus found him. Thus I see something happening, in which there is a rupture between the Divinely arranged religion that fails, and the economy of God that never fails. Jesus found him, and finding him He said to him, "Dost thou believe on the Son of God?" At this point a question arises. Did He say "Son of God," or "Son of man"? Some of the old manuscripts read one way, and some another; and there has been much discussion as to which is correct. It reads here in verse thirty-five in the Revised, "Dost thou believe on the Son of God?" and in the margin, "Many ancient authorities read, Son of man." I do not find myself able to make any dogmatic assertion, but personally I do not think He said, "Son of God"; I think He said, "Son of man." That was His name for Himself. It was the name that linked Him with humanity, but He ever employed it in such connections as reveal His relationship with something infinitely profounder. He used a name that marked a position, a relationship, a name that in some senses was an interpretation of personality; " Dost thou believe on the Son of man, or Son of God ? " as the case may be. The man replied " And who is He, Lord, that I may believe on Him ? " Now mark the claim, positive, and unequivocal, " Thou hast both seen Him, and He it is that speaketh with thee." Then all the doubts vanished, and whichever title was used, He had gained the soul of the man, and he said, " Lord, I believe. And he worshipped Him."

It has been said that the word " worshipped " here may mean simply the rendering of homage to a creature. That is entirely gratuitous and false. That word is very rare. It only occurs in chapter four, here, and again in chapter twelve ; and it is only used of the attitude of the soul in the presence of God.

Observe the ascending scale in this man's consciousness of Jesus. " A man called Jesus " ; " He is a prophet " ; " If this Man were not from God, He could do nothing " ; " Lord, I believe. And he worshipped Him."

Thus the scene ends with Jesus receiving the worship of a man. An excommunicated man, a man put out of the synagogue, is received into relationship with God, in the act of his submission and his worship.

There is tremendous significance in the incident. The whole system of Judaism as it then was, is seen blind, so blind that it does not discover the value of the wonder wrought, or understand it as a sign ; blinded by its loyalty to technicalities and traditions and minutiae, which only blast the soul, apart from life. That system put this man out. Then we see two people ; the Word incarnate, the only begotten Son of the Father, full of grace and truth, and this excommunicated man. Jesus receiving this man's worship. In that moment the new economy was born.

What happened that day was not, in the last analysis, that organized religion excommunicated a man. It was that a man in fellowship with Jesus, excommunicated organized religion.

Immediately upon that, our Lord proceeded to interpret

what He had done, and we have the next two great signs in the realm of words, " I am the Door," " I am the Good Shepherd." To this we pass in our next study.

John ix. 39—x. 21.

THE paragraph opens with the words, " And Jesus said," following closely upon the record of the act of worship rendered to our Lord by the man whose eyes had been opened, and contains His teaching resulting therefrom.

In the course of this teaching we have two of the signs in the realm of words, two of the " I am's " of Jesus, " I am the Door," and " I am the Good Shepherd " ; and it is important that we should see the significance of the things said in the light of the things done. Bishop Westcott very beautifully says,

" The separation between the old and the new was now consummated, when the rejected of the Jews sank prostrate at the feet of the Son of man."

In the paragraph there are two movements ; first a general statement from the lips of our Lord in verses thirty-nine to forty-one in chapter nine ; and then a particular application of that statement in the first twenty-one verses of chapter ten.

In the presence of the man, excommunicated by organized religion, and received by Himself, He said :

" For judgment came I into this world, that they which see not may see ; and that they which see may become blind."

When talking to Nicodemus He had said that He was not sent to judge the world (iii. 17) ; in His teaching He had said " I judge no man " (viii. 15) ; yet now He declared He came for judgment. There is no contradiction whatever between the two statements. The word He employed here, *krima*, not *krisis*, describes a result, rather than an action.

[171]

He had not come to act in judgment, but His coming did create a crisis.

The nature of that judgment He then explained ; " That they which see not may see ; and that they which see may become blind." " Those who see not, may see." " Those who see not," are those who are conscious of blindness. He had come that such might have sight. There was the blind man. He knew he was blind ; and he had received his sight. That was a physical fact, and our Lord here employed the physical to illustrate the spiritual. In the case of that man the physical wonder had been coincident with the spiritual. He had been spiritually blind, but he had come to a clear vision. At the beginning he had said, " A man named Jesus " ; then he had said, " He is a prophet " ; later he had declared that He must be " a man from God " ; and finally he had worshipped Him. The man born blind was conscious of his blindness, and had received his sight. On the other hand, those who saw, that is those who claimed to see, claimed to know, these critics round about our Lord, were unconscious of their blindness ; and Christ said His coming, in their case, did but seal their blindness.

The same principle is found in other parts of our Lord's teaching. In Matthew eleven we have that remarkable ejaculation of Jesus in the midst of difficult conditions when He said,

" I thank Thee, O Father, Lord of heaven and earth, that Thou didst hide these things from the wise and understanding,"—

that is, the clever people that think they see,—

" and didst reveal them to babes."

The Pharisees immediately raised a protest. " Those of the Pharisees which were with Him." That is an arresting phrase. It may refer to those who had professed to believe in Him, or it may merely mean those who were near Him at the time. If the former, they were still claiming to have received Him and accepted His teaching ; and so protesting against the suggestion. His reply shows that their belief had no value. It may be that the reference is to those who were with Him at the moment. In either case it was a question of protest. " Are we also blind ? " Whoever these Pharisees were, it is evident that they had caught the spiritual significance of what He was saying.

His answer to them is revealing. " If ye were blind, ye would have no sin." He virtually charged them with wilful rejection. If you were really blind, if you really had not apprehended the things I have been saying, and the teaching I have been giving, you would have no sin; " but now ye say, We see ; your sin remaineth." I cannot read that without realizing that these Pharisees whomsoever they may have been, had seen clearly the spiritual significance of His teaching. If you were blind, you would have no sin ; but because you have apprehended, and are still rejecting the thing you have seen, " your sin remaineth."

Having made this general statement, and replied to the enquiry of protest, He went straight on, and again employing that re-arresting formula of speech, " Verily, verily," He gave a particular application and interpretation of what He had said in His general statement.

He first gave them a parable. " This parable spake Jesus unto them " (verse six). The picture is peculiarly Eastern, and we must grasp the Eastern significance if we are to follow the personal claim and application which our Lord made. The picture is that of the shepherd and the fold and the flock. Those were figures of speech in constant use. The shepherd always represented kingship, full and final authority. It was Homer who said, " All kings are shepherds of the people." That saying embodies the Eastern idea. The shepherd is the king, the king is the shepherd ; and his authority is based upon his care for the sheep.

The fold represented the whole system of the Kingdom over which the Shepherd reigned. The flock referred to all those over whom He reigned. That is the picture which Jesus employed in illustration of the new order He had come to establish.

[173]

Then He said, " I am the Door." The door is the way by which the sheep enter the fold. They had cast that man out of one fold. Jesus took him into another. The door stands for the way of entrance, and the shepherd represents the authority over all who enter by the door.

By authority they had excluded a man. By authority Christ received him. This interprets the value of the two-fold claim He now made. He said, " I am the Door," I am the Way into the true order of life. In that connection He said, " All that came before Me are thieves and robbers." That has caused a good deal of trouble to some people. Was He calling John the Baptist, and the prophets, and Moses thieves and robbers ? Obviously not. He was referring to all who had made that claim, any false christs who had appeared, any who were claiming to have the right to admit men into the final order of life.

Thus He stood at the parting of the ways, saying, " I am the Door," thus making an emphatic claim, that through Him, and through Him alone, men should enter into the final order, in which there is perfect liberty. They "shall go in and out." Moreover, there is perfect sustenance. They " shall find pasture." These were poetic and glorious references to the breadth and beauty and beneficence of the new order which He had come to establish. Mark the universality of intention ; If any man, *any* man, enter by this way, come to Me, he shall find his way into this true order.

And so we come to the fifth " I am," " I am the Shepherd, the Good." That is to put it in the Greek form. I like to keep the Greek idiom, because it suggests a contrast. " I am the Shepherd, the Good." " All that came before Me were thieves and robbers. . . . The thief cometh not, but that he may steal and kill and destroy." In contrast, " I am the Shepherd, the Good." Then He interpreted the goodness. He revealed why He is " the Good." " The good Shepherd layeth down His life for the sheep." That is, the Good Shepherd dies for the sheep. Presently He repeated the statement, but with a different application, as He said,

"I lay down My life for the sheep." This means more than death; it declares that the life laid down is placed at the disposal of the sheep. First, I lay down My life for them, that is on their behalf. Secondly, I lay down My life for them, that is that they may possess it. He died in conflict with the wolf; and then through that dying He released His life, that the sheep might share it, and by sharing, possess that which would make them also more than conquerors over the destroying wolf. In that connection He revealed the scope of His purpose. "Other sheep I have, which are not of this fold; them also I must bring, and they shall hear My voice, and they shall become one flock, one shepherd." That was the larger outlook. In chapter eleven we shall find the same idea in a most arresting and remarkable comment from the pen of John. Caiaphas was talking to the rulers about Jesus, and said among other things, "It is expedient for you that one man should die for the people, and that the whole nation perish not." That was the language of devilish and damnable policy. Right there John writes this remarkable thing. "Now this he said not of himself; but being high priest that year, he prophesied that Jesus should die for the nation; and not for the nation only, but that He might also gather together into one the children of God that are scattered abroad." Which means that Caiaphas said more, and better, than he knew. While he uttered the language of political expediency, he declared a profound truth. "Other sheep I have, which are not of this fold." "He should die, . . . that He might gather together into one the children of God that are scattered abroad."

In connection with this interpretation of the Good Shepherd He made claims which are superhuman, and reveal the perfect fellowship existing between Himself and His Father. This fact of fellowship is expressed in the words: "Therefore doth the Father love Me, because I lay down My life that I may take it again." Then followed words which are superhuman. "No one taketh it away from Me, but I lay it down of Myself." Nothing He ever said was more stupendous

than that. " No one taketh My life away from Me." But
they did, didn't they ? Never. All they did was to destroy
His body, as He said they would. They never touched His
deepest life. But that deepest life was laid down. There,
is at once the mystery, and the heart of the atonement.
The dying for the sheep was voluntary on His part, not
compelled even by human malice. " No one taketh it away
from Me. I lay it down of Myself." That is the only point
in all the process of this Gospel that Jesus claimed to do
anything of Himself. But what follows reveals that in this
also He was acting with His Father. " I have authority
to lay it down, and I have authority to take it again." What
authority ? " This commandment received I from My
Father." So there is no contradiction. He was acting of
Himself in dying, in order to the impartation of life to the
flock ; but the authority for the action was received directly
from His Father.

This discourse of Jesus produced division, sharp and
bitter. Some of them were so angry, that they said, Why
do you listen to Him, He has a demon and is mad. Others
were conscious of something other, and said, No demon-
possessed man speaks like that ; no demon-possessed man
opened the eyes of the blind.

The whole story is revealing. We have seen a man excommunicated by the old order, the Divinely created order.
The economy of the past was an economy from God. But
that which is Divinely created, if it loses the Divine breath,
God rejects. His own arrangements, when rendered null
and void, He sweeps away. " He taketh away the first,
that He may establish the second." Why ? Because the
first has failed, and can make nothing perfect.

Here was the point in the ministry of Jesus, where, by an
action, He opened the door of the new economy, and assumed
authority over it. That poor blind beggar was barren of
spiritual apprehension, Jesus opened his eyes, and by that
act in the physical, led him processionally to the recognition
of Who the Man was that had done it, so that he rendered

worship to Him. He received that worship, and by that act opened the door of the new economy. The man now entered the new order through the Door ; and from that moment he was under the true authority, the authority of the Shepherd Himself.

These two " I am's," the Door and the Good Shepherd, are interlocked in a wonderful way in the light of Eastern life. It was once my privilege to cross the Atlantic with Sir George Adam Smith. I shall never forget the fascination of that voyage, as he talked of those Eastern lands he knew so well. One story he told me was this. He was one day travelling with a guide, and came across a shepherd and his sheep. He fell into conversation with him. The man showed him the fold into which the sheep were led at night. It consisted of four walls, with a way in. Sir George said to him, " That is where they go at night ? " " Yes," said the shepherd, " and when they are in there, they are perfectly safe." " But there is no door," said Sir George. " I am the door," said the shepherd. He was not a Christian man, he was not speaking in the language of the New Testament. He was speaking from the Arab shepherd's standpoint. Sir George looked at him and said, " What do you mean by the door ? " Said the shepherd, " When the light has gone, and all the sheep are inside, I lie in that open space, and no sheep ever goes out but across my body, and no wolf comes in unless he crosses my body ; I am the door."

Let that illuminate these words of Jesus.

John x. 22–42.

" AND it was the feast of Dedication." Here we have the record of the presence of our Lord at another of the feasts, and that in Jerusalem. The feast of Dedication might be observed anywhere, and so John names the place.

If, as we have surmised in our previous studies, the incidents from chapter seven through the twenty-first verse of chapter ten took place in close connection with the feast of Tabernacles, then between verse twenty-one, and verse twenty-two where this record begins, there had been a gap of about two months in the ministry of our Lord.

The feast of Tabernacles fell about the middle of October. The feast of Dedication was always observed on the twenty-fifth Kislev, that is December. Incidentally that is interesting. I do not know that it is important, because I do not know that it has ever been proven that December 25th was the actual birthday of our Lord. But if it were so, then this thing took place on His birthday.

The feast of Dedication was not one of those arranged for in the Divine economy as given by Moses. It was a comparatively recent one, instituted to commemorate the cleansing and dedication of the Temple under Judas Maccabæus, after it had been desecrated by Antiochus Epiphanes. It was a feast of rejoicing, characterized by illuminations, the carrying of palms, and the singing of hymns. It was commonly called the Feast of Lights.

This was the last visit of Jesus to Jerusalem before His final coming to His Cross. The story falls quite naturally into four parts. First, we have the record in verses twenty-two to twenty-four of the challenge that met Him on this occasion. In verses twenty-five to thirty we have the account of His answer to that challenge. In verses thirty-one to thirty-nine we have the record of the discussion which resulted from His answer to the challenge. In verses forty to forty-two we have the account of how He left the city, and of where He went.

The challenge given to Jesus was definite, specific, and very arresting. John first tells us where it took place, " Jesus was walking in the Temple in Solomon's porch," a sheltered portion of the Temple, and He was walking there because " it was winter." There is a graphic touch in the story. " The Jews therefore came round about Him." That means that they literally surrounded Him, hemmed Him in, in order that He might not escape. They did it because they were determined to get an answer to the question they were about to put to Him.

Here is the question; " How long dost Thou hold us in suspense ? If Thou art the Christ, tell us plainly." The question was explicit, and it certainly was put with great plainness. There was no room for doubt as to what they wanted to know. The suggestion was that He had not been explicit, that He had not been plain, that He had not made a definite claim to Messiahship.

I do not think that all the people who put this question to Him were necessarily hostile. It may have been a very sincere question. Most probably this was a mixed company, some hating Him and trying to get something by which they could cause Him to be arrested and arraigned ; and others quite honestly perplexed. Was He really the Christ ? Or rather, would He claim to be the Christ ? So they said, " Tell us plainly," let us hear from Thy lips, in plain language, the claim, I am the Messiah.

Now He certainly had claimed Messiahship, in quite definite ways ; but His claims to Messiahship had never coincided with their conception of the Messianic office. All His claims had been from their standpoint, uncertain. Our Lord was ultimately rejected because His claim to Messiahship, and His interpretation of the Messianic office, and Kingdom, did by no means square with their ideas. They ever listened to Him with their foregone conclusions, with their degenerate ideas of the Kingdom of God. Their ideas were circumscribed by that which was material and earthly and sensual. They were looking for someone who should come and break the Roman yoke, and set up the throne of David actually there in Jerusalem, liberate the people, and give them material prosperity. Even John at one time was perplexed as to whether Jesus was the Messiah, after he had identified Him as such, asking " Art Thou He that cometh, or look we for another ? "

If we remember that, we have to admit that so far as we have found in the records, He had never claimed Messiahship along such lines. Yet He had made the claim quite definitely. So they caught Him in the morning, in winter time, as He was walking in Solomon's porch, and they surrounded Him, and said, Now we want a plain answer. Tell us plainly, art Thou the Messiah ?

There are some things that cannot be stated in that way, things which are incapable of merely mathematical and logical precision. The greatest things in God's universe cannot have an answer of that sort. Nevertheless, we shall find that He was very explicit in His answer, though He did not give them the kind of answer they wanted.

How did He answer ? First He said, " I told you, and ye believe not." They said in effect, You have never been clear about this matter. Tell us plainly. He said, I have told you, but you would not believe. How had He told them ? He said, " The works that I do in My Father's name, these bear witness of Me." They asked for a plain, categorical answer to their question. He replied that the answer had been given through all His ministry. He had told them in His works.

Now it is interesting to remember that He had certainly been explicit twice, but in each case to an individual. In Samaria He had said to a woman, " I am He." She said, " We know when Messiah cometh, He will declare unto us all things." To that one lone woman, outside the realm of privilege, held in despite, He had made the explicit claim, " I that speak unto thee am He." The other case was that of the blind man, whose eyes He had opened. " Dost thou believe on the Son of God ? " " Who is He, Lord, that I may believe on Him ? " " Thou hast both seen Him, and He it is that speaketh with thee." The word Messiah does not there occur, but it was an explicit claim to Messiahship.

Moreover, to the twelve apostles, He had consented to the confession of His Messiahship. We have no record of His ever telling the twelve He was the Messiah explicitly, or as

this crowd said, " plainly." But He had challenged them
as to Who He was ; and when one of their number said,
" Thou art the Messiah, the Son of the living God," expressing
as I always believe, the conviction of the group, He said,
" Blessed art thou, Simon Bar-Jonah ; for flesh and blood
hath not revealed it unto thee, but My Father which is in
heaven." That acceptation of the confession was an explicit
claim. These are the only occasions when we find anything
approaching the explicit to the woman of Samaria, the blind
man, whose sight had been given to him, and to the group
of His own.

Nevertheless, to these enquirers He said, You have been
told, and went on to claim that His works constituted His
claim. Of course, that referred to all He had done ; but
let us keep to the outstanding works that had been wrought
in Jerusalem, where the question was asked. First there
had been the cleansing of the Temple in the first year.
Secondly in that same period, the healing of the derelict
in Bethesda's porches. And now, more recently, the opening
of the eyes of the man born blind. Three great works. These
works bore witness of Who He was.

Moreover, in connection with them He had said things of
supreme importance. When He cleansed the Temple, and
they asked Him by what authority He did it, He gave them
the strange answer, which they did not understand : " Destroy
this temple, and in three days I will raise it up." When
He healed the derelict they challenged Him, and He said,
" My Father worketh even until now, and I work." Then
they understood Him accurately to claim equality with God,
and there began their definite hostility. When He gave
sight to the man born blind, not only physically but spiritually
through a process, and as a result they had flung him out
of the synagogue, excommunicated him, Jesus found him ;
and on the basis of that finding and admission to the new
fellowship, He had uttered two things distinctly about
Himself, " I am the Door of the sheepfold," " I am the Good
Shepherd." Thus as we go back and look at the works

and listen to the words, we see how definite His claim had been.

Then He told them the reason why they did not understand. You believe not because you are not of My sheep. In saying this He reverted to the subject of His discourse two months previously concerning the Shepherd as King, the fold as the Kingdom, and the sheep as members of the Kingdom ; in which He had claimed Himself to be at once the Shepherd, and the Door, or the way of entrance into the true order. It is as though He said, Do you remember all I said, and all I claimed then ? The reason why you do not understand Me is that you do not belong to this fold. You have not entered into it. You are not My sheep.

Then He applied this from a new angle. " My sheep,"— those who enter by the Door, and come into the fold over which I am Shepherd,—" hear My voice, and I know them, and they follow Me ; and I give unto them eternal life ; and they shall never perish, and no one shall snatch them out of My hand ; My Father, which hath given them unto Me, is greater than all ; and no one is able to snatch them out of the Father's hand. I and the Father are one."

They said, " Tell us plainly," be specific, be logical. He replied, I have told you ; the works that I have done, and the works that you have seen Me do, have not been Mine. They have all been demonstrations of My union with God.

Then came these final words, " I and the Father are one." In the Greek the word " one " is neuter. " I and the Father are one." Not one person, but one substance, one essence. " I,"—Jesus, the One Who was speaking to them, the One Whom they had surrounded and hemmed in, the Man at Whom they were then looking. He did not say, the Son and the Father are one ; but *I*. Moreover, He did not say here, *My* Father. He used the word that could only be applied to God in Himself, " the Father," " I and the Father are one," in substance, in essence. Said they, Tell us plainly, if Thou art the Messiah. We have been looking for the Messiah. We have been looking long for a Messiah Who

shall come and break the power of Rome, and set us back
in the place of privilege. Tell us plainly if Thou art the
Messiah. His answer was bigger than their thinking. It
overwhelmed and submerged the thought of Messianic
office, in a claim to identity of substance with God, " I and
the Father are one."

Then mark what followed. Again they took up stones.
What is the meaning of " again " here ? The answer is found
in chapter eight, which records how once before they had
taken up stones. Why did they do it then ? Because He
had said, " Before Abraham was born, I am." Again when
He said, " I and the Father are one " they took up stones.
In each case the stones were taken up when His claim was
that of essential Deity.

Notice that they did not fling them. They were quite
powerless. Hemmed in by a little circle of men ? Never
hemmed in ! They took up stones, but they could not fling
them. His hour was not yet come. He was invincible
against all hostility until, as Peter said on the day of
Pentecost, He " was delivered by the determinate counsel
and foreknowledge of God." We cannot read the story
without seeing the things of infinite and awe-inspiring majesty.
The taking up of stones shows that they understood His
claim. He had been explicit enough for them to understand
that He claimed oneness with God, to be of one substance
with God.

Then He protested. He said, with what was certainly a
touch of playful irony, " Many good works have I showed
you from the Father ; for which of these works do ye stone
Me ? " He knew why they had taken up those stones. He
knew the reason of their definite desire to kill Him, but He
ignored it. He took them back where He had them a moment
before, to face His works. The works He claimed demonstrated
the fact of His relationship to His Father. They were going
to stone Him for that claim. He knew it, and so He drove
them back on what He had said bore witness to Him, His
works, " Many good works have I showed you from the

[183]

Father." Observe the carefulness with which He declared
the source of the works. " From the Father." He always
insisted upon it that God was working in Him and through
Him. That exactly coincides with what Peter said in another
part of his address on the day of Pentecost, " Jesus of
Nazareth, a Man approved of God unto you by powers and
wonders and signs which *God* wrought through Him." Peter
does not say, Which He wrought, but " God wrought through
Him." That was what our Lord ever claimed. I have
showed you many good works from the Father. For which
are you proposing to stone Me ?

Mark carefully the answer they gave Him. " For a good
work we stone Thee not, but for blasphemy ; *and* because
that Thou, being a man, makest Thyself God." It was not
mere blasphemy. It was something more than that. Again
we are face to face with the fact that they understood Him.
They understood what He meant. They did not believe
Him, but they knew what He meant. He was telling them
plainly in another way than the way they intended, and so
plainly that they did not miss His meaning. They said that
the reason for their hostility was that He was claiming Deity.
They were quite right. They understood ; and yet they
refused to face the works that demonstrated God, and
demonstrated His unity with God. They simply ignored
them. That is what they consistently did. They ignored
the derelict at Bethesda's pool. They never saw the man
for looking at what they thought was a desecration of the
Sabbath. They did not see that the thirty-eight years'
dereliction was ended, and that the man was delivered from
his limitation. They did not see the works. Hemmed in
by tradition, held by false conceptions, and prostituted ideas
of God, they charged Him with blasphemy, and with making
Himself God.

Our Lord then appealed to them from their Scriptures.
" Is it not written in your law, I said, Ye are gods ? " He was
quoting from the Psalms. Therein those to whom the Word
of God came were called gods. They were dignified with

the very name of God, because they were the instruments through whom the Word of God came. And He declared that this was perfectly justifiable. Whatever they were in themselves, the office of being the bearers of the Word of God warranted those who spoke of them as gods.

But between such and Himself there was a great contrast, and He suggested the contrast. If you call " them gods, unto whom the Word of God came," do you say, " of Him, Whom the Father sanctified and sent into the world. Thou blasphemest ; because I said I am 'the Son of God ? " In their scripture the word was used, and justifiably, of those to whom the Word of God came. There was however an infinite distance between those to whom the Word came, and the Son of God sanctified and sent by the Father. This line of argument depended for its value entirely upon His claim that He was sanctified and sent of the Father.

Then again He appealed to the witness of His works. " If I do not the works of My Father, believe Me not." The cleansing of the Temple ; the healing of the derelict man ; the opening of those eyes that had never seen ; if they are not the works of God then do not believe Me. If they were not the works of God, to whom could they be attributed ? But if they are the works of God, and you do not believe Me personally, believe the works. If you believe the works, and admit that they are the works of God, you will know and understand the truth about Me. " The Father is in Me, and I in the Father." That was explicit. " Tell us plainly." He had told them plainly.

What followed ? " They sought again to take Him." They understood Him. They did not believe Him, and so they sought to take Him. Once more we have the revelation of His august majesty. He departed, and went out from them. A little cordon was round Him ; they hemmed Him in. They were going to get an explicit answer. They had it, and became so angry they took stones up, but they never flung them. Then they were going to arrest Him and take Him to the Sanhedrim. They never touched Him. He departed and moved away. It appeared so easy to hem Him in, to get Him. But they could not. They never did. At the last moment when with a band of soldiers and torches they came, and felt sure of Him, the first thing that happened was that they fell backwards and fell to the ground. They never arrested Him, until His hour had come.

Then finally, the account of His leaving. " He went away again beyond Jordan." This is very full of interest. " He went away again beyond Jordan into the place where John was at the first baptizing." In chapter one, verse twenty-eight, we have the place named. In the third chapter we are told John changed his location and went to Ænon near Salim. Jesus now went back to the place where John had identified Him as Messiah. He went back to the place where He began His ministry after the identification ; and this very man John who is writing, was one of the first disciples to follow.

" And many came unto Him." There is no doubt that in all that region the effect of John's ministry was still felt ; and evidently there were those who remembered the identification. They were talking. The tense of the verb expresses the general conversation. John did no miracles, but John was right. Everything he told us about this Man has come true. The last sentence is, " Many believed on Him there." Put the emphasis on " there." If Jerusalem had rejected Him, many believed on Him *there*.

This, as we have said, was His final visit to Jerusalem prior to the Cross ; and on this occasion His claims for Himself reached their climax. What were these claims ? That He was sanctified and sent of the Father. The implicate is that of His pre-existence. The declaration is that He, the pre-existent One, had been specially sanctified, consecrated to the work that He was to do ; and being consecrated, sanctified, set apart, He was sent. Moreover He said " I am the Son of God." That was explicit. And again, " I and the Father are one," in substance. That was explicit. And once more mystically, but explicitly, " The Father is in Me, and I in the Father." These were His claims when they asked Him to be explicit.

John xi. 1–27.

IT will readily be conceded that the story found in the first fifty-three verses of this eleventh chapter of John is one of the most wonderful in all the records of our Lord's ministry. It is full of colour, of life, of movement. In it there is a remarkable merging of pathos and of power. It is at once a threnody of sorrow, and an anthem of victory. In this story are manifested essential human conditions, and the power and glory of the Lord.

In the first twenty-seven verses we have the story leading to the account of the final sign, the raising of Lazarus. From verse twenty-eight to fifty-three we have the story of the sign itself.

We are now considering the story leading to the sign. The movement alternates between Bethany and the region beyond Jordan. Verses one to three take us to Bethany. Then we cross over Jordan in verses four to sixteen. Finally we return to Bethany in verses seventeen to twenty-seven.

In Bethany there was trouble, and Jesus was not there. That tells the story of the first three verses. The trouble was that Lazarus was sick. Lazarus was the brother of Mary and Martha. John is careful to identify Mary : " It was that Mary which anointed the Lord with ointment." The account of that anointing is found later, in chapter twelve. John was writing long after the event, and in his mind was the memory of that which marked Mary out, and made her supremely remembered among the twelve.

We know something of these sisters, because Luke has given us a glimpse into that Bethany home. At the end of chapter ten we have the story. Luke, in speaking of the sisters, makes it plain that Martha was the house-keeper, when he says that she received Jesus into her house. To Mary he simply refers as the sister of Martha. John puts Mary first, and suggests by so doing that the whole village belonged to Mary. A good woman may own a house, and run it, and herself to death ; while another sort of woman will hold a complete village by her love and ministry. It is quite evident that this was a home to which Jesus loved to go, as it seems to me, the one place where, if I may use that wonderfully familiar and yet beautiful phrase, He was " at home."

And now Lazarus was sick, and Jesus was not there. I think we are warranted in thinking that Lazarus was younger than the sisters. He never appears as having any responsibility. Lazarus was sick. Jesus was not there. If He had been there, everything would have been different, so the sisters thought, and probably they were right.

In their trouble they did the natural and beautiful thing, they sent a message to Jesus, saying, " Lord, behold, he whom Thou lovest is sick." It is interesting to note that they did not make any request. They simply told Him the facts, showing that they knew Him ; showing that they felt quite confident if He knew that He would come.

The word they used to describe the love of Jesus for Lazarus, was the Greek verb *phileo*, which is the verb which describes affection and emotion in its fulness. We notice this now, to return to it presently.

Now, from verses four to sixteen we find ourselves beyond Jordan. There the messenger arrived, bearing the message. Then we have a most amazing thing, a most startling thing, the sort of thing that challenges faith, and raises every kind of suspicion and question in the heart, in what we read next. When Jesus received the message He said ; " This sickness is not unto death, but for the glory of God, that the Son of God may be glorified thereby." The statement, " This sickness is not unto death " did not mean that Lazarus would not die. As a matter of fact Lazarus was dead when the messenger arrived. The word of Jesus meant that death was not the final word. He knew Lazarus was dead. The distance between Bethany and the place where Jesus was took a day to travel. Jesus stayed there two days. Then He took the day's journey back. That makes four days. Presently Martha said, " he hath been dead four days " already. It is evident then that when the messenger arrived with the message, Lazarus was already dead. Yet the Lord said, " This sickness is not unto death." Death is not the last word in this matter.

Then what was the last word ? " This sickness is not unto death, but for the glory of God, that the Son of God may be glorified thereby."

In dealing with the story of the opening of the eyes of the man born blind, I changed the punctuation, and read thus, " Neither did this man sin, nor his parents. But that the works of God should be made manifest in him, We must work the works of Him that sent Me while it is day." I gave the reason for the change that the other punctuation necessitated the view that the man was born blind and allowed to remain blind in order that God might have an opportunity to show His power. This is absolutely unbelieveable. Now it has been suggested that this statement about Lazarus gives that same view. But the difference is infinite. In the one case the idea would be that a man was born blind, and allowed to live until he was of age, seeing nothing, waiting for an hour when God's power should be manifested in him. Here was a sickness which ended in death. Of that fact that Lazarus had died Jesus said, " This sickness is not unto death," that is not the end. The end will be the glory of God, and the glorification of the Son of God.

The cases are entirely different. Nevertheless it was a remarkable statement. Lazarus was already dead. What Jesus said was practically this ; Yes, he is gone, and the fact creates an opportunity for the display of the glory of God, in that the Son of God may be glorified thereby.

At that point in his narrative, John interpolated this statement; "Now Jesus loved Martha, and her sister, and Lazarus." Undoubtedly he did so because of what he was going to write next; "When therefore He heard that he was sick, He abode at that time two days in the place where He was." Mark the "therefore." He stayed because He loved Martha and Mary and Lazarus.

Here we return to what we said about the word the sisters used concerning the love of Jesus for Lazarus. It was the verb *phileo*, which speaks of emotional affection. That is how they thought of the love of Jesus for their brother. But when John writes this, "Now Jesus loved Martha, and her sister, and Lazarus," he employed a word having an entirely different significance, the verb *agapao*. That is love, but it is the love of intelligence and judgment and consideration. It is not easy to draw the distinction between the Greek words in our English language. I am inclined to think Dr. Goodspeed comes nearest to a true interpretation of agapao when he uses our word devotion. Devotion means much more than mere emotion. I am resolutely going to use that word here—Jesus was devoted to Martha and Mary and Lazarus. They knew the affection Jesus had for Lazarus. Hence their message, "He whom Thou lovest is sick." John now shows that His love for them was more than that. He was devoted to them; and therefore, He did not hurry. He stayed where He was. He let enough time to elapse for the death to be so certified that there could be no doubt about the power manifest.

After this, when the two days were over, He said to His disciples, "Let us go into Judæa again." Judæa was the centre of hostility to Him, the place where, as these disciples said, they had taken up stones. "Rabbi, the Jews were but now seeking to stone Thee; and goest Thou thither again?" That was a natural and beautiful protest by His lovers. They loved Him, and they did not want Him to go back into the danger zone.

Now observe the majesty, the calm dignity of His answer.

Judæa was hostile. He knew it. His disciples knew it.
He was going back. His disciples said, They want to kill You.
Now listen to Him. " Are there not twelve hours in the day ?
If a man walk in the day, he stumbleth not, because he seeth
the light of this world. But if a man walk in the night, he
stumbleth, because the light is not in him." Applied to Him,
it meant ; I certainly am going back to Judæa. You need
have no fear. There will be no stumbling. There will be no
accident. Hostility cannot touch Me until My hour has
arrived. I am walking in light, and not in darkness. I am
making no experiments. Do not be anxious about Me.

Then He told them, " Our friend Lazarus is fallen asleep ;
but I go, that I may awake him out of sleep." Sleep, said
the disciples, that is a good thing ; if he is asleep, he will
recover. Then He used their language, came down to the
level of their apprehension, " Jesus therefore said unto them
plainly, Lazarus is dead. And I am glad for your sakes that
I was not there, to the intent ye may believe."

That does seem to suggest that the sisters were right, if
He had been there, Lazarus would not have died. " I am
glad for your sakes that I was not there." But why was
He glad ? " To the intent ye may believe."

His view of what we call death was sleep. Their view is
revealed in what He said to them, which literally was not
" Lazarus is dead," but, " Lazarus died." When He talked
He talked in the present tense. He was thinking of Lazarus
in the essential fact of his personality. He said, He is asleep.
When He had come to their level and had to speak in a past
tense, and the experience through which he had passed, He
said, Lazarus died. That is what happened. That was their
language.

" I am glad for *your* sake." The tarrying was for their sake.
The disease had been permitted to run its full course, and
snap the vital cord, and the man was dead. For their
sakes, always that. He is always saying " for your sake."
He tarried because He loved Martha and Mary and Lazarus.
He went because He loved Martha and Mary and Lazarus.

For their sake, the tarrying. And now for their sake, the going.

The next scene is just outside the village of Bethany. He had arrived. Lazarus had been four days in the tomb. " Jesus saith, Take ye away the stone. Martha, the sister of him that was dead, saith unto Him, Lord, by this time he stinketh ; for he hath been dead four days." Four days dead meant that in that Eastern land corruption had already set it. No doubt Martha was right. He had raised the dead on two earlier occasions. Jairus' child, swiftly after the spirit had left the body, He called her back. The son of the widow of Nain, only a few hours after the passing of the spirit, as they were carrying him out to burial, He had called him back. But here He waited until the thing should be absolutely supreme in its evidence of power.

Martha hurried from the house to meet Him. In doing so she violated the conventionalities of the East. Mary observed them. She sat in the house, remaining in the seclusion of the home. Martha, honest, angry, as I cannot help believing, hurried to meet Him, and when she met Him, she said, " Lord, if Thou hadst been here, my brother had not died." Of course it is very difficult to interpret dogmatically, but when Mary came she said exactly the same thing. But surely there was a tremendous difference between the intention of Martha and the intention of Mary. I have no doubt whatever that Martha's intention was that of honest, sincere, protesting disappointment. As though she had said, Why did You not hurry ? " If Thou hadst been here, my brother had not died." But she still believed in Him. She still had confidence in Him, and that in a very wonderful way, as witness her words ; " And even now I know that, whatsoever Thou shalt ask of God, God will give Thee." She had tremendous confidence in Him, and yet, as a matter of fact, she did not quite mean that. She thought she did. She was perfectly honest, but she did not expect her brother back. This is proven by the fact that when presently the Lord said, " Take ye away the stone," she said, It is no good. He has

passed into the realm of corruption. Evidently she did
not expect the thing was going to happen which did happen.

Then Jesus said to her, " Thy brother shall rise again."
Possibly in saying this, our Lord was not referring to the fact
that He was going to raise him from the dead.   I think rather
it was a general reference, and a reminder to her of the fact
of resurrection, and a reminder that this life is not all.   As
though He said to her, Martha, it is not all over when death
comes.   There is resurrection.   Of course He may have
referred to what He was going to do.   I do not so understand
it.   I think it was a general reference, and so Martha evidently
understood it, for she refused the comfort of a postponed
resurrection.   That brought no immediate comfort.

Thus we reach the sixth great " I am " of Jesus, which
John has recorded ; " I am the resurrection and the life."
" I am "—the eternal present tense.   Wherever I am there
is resurrection ; and more than that, for resurrection is but
an incident.   The greater part of the statement is not "I am
the resurrection," great as it is.   The greater part is " I am. . .
the life."   I am warranted in saying that, because He went
on to interpret what He had said, and His interpretation was
not concerned with resurrection.   It was concerned with life.

" He that believeth on Me, though he die, yet shall he live."
That is a very simple sentence, but let it be most carefully
read.   Jesus did not say, He that believeth on Me though he
die, yet shall he live *again*.   That would be resurrection.
He said, " Though he die, yet shall he live."   In other words,
he that believes on Me, though he die, by all the appearances
as interpreted on the level of the earthly, he is not dead.   He
was saying, Your brother is not dead.   He that " liveth and
believeth on Me shall never die."   That is the great Christian
declaration.   We have hardly grasped its significance.   We
say, What has become of So and So?   The reply often is,
He is dead, She is dead.   We still talk that pagan way.
They are not dead.   " He that believeth on Me, though he
die," the death is a fact so far as you see, but he is alive.
When our Lord recalled Lazarus He talked to him as though

N   [193]

he could hear Him.   He muttered no incantations over him. He said, " Lazarus, come forth."   He expected to be heard, and He was heard.   Lazarus was not dead.

Then He looked at Martha, and He said, " Believest thou this ? "   Very tender and very beautiful, and I think perfectly wonderful was her answer.   She said, " Yea, Lord," and then as though she halted and was almost afraid of what she had said, " I have believed that Thou art the Christ, the Son of God, even He that cometh into the world."   She made the full confession there, but yet she seems to have hesitated. " Believest thou this ? "   What ?   That there is no death to those who believe on Me ; that though he die, yet shall he live ; and consequently he that liveth and believeth in Me never does die.   There is no death for such.   " Believest thou this ? "   " Yea, Lord " ; and yet she could not affirm belief in that definitely, but she affirmed the faith she had, the faith that was hers, gloriously, " I have believed that Thou art the Christ, the Son of God, even He that cometh into the world."

In these preliminary things two matters impress us.   First the disciples.   We do not see the critics here, though the Jews were round about.   Hostility is not manifest so far.   The twelve were there.   Thomas has spoken, and so has Martha. What do you see ?   Faced by death, they were groping in darkness, and filled with despair.   Over against them we see the Lord, the Lord of life walking in the light, and inspired in all He did by love.

John xi. 28–53.

THIS paragraph completes the story which began at the first verse of the chapter ; that of the last sign in John's selection, namely, the raising of Lazarus.

The meeting and converse with Martha had taken place

outside the village of Bethany, as the thirtieth verse in parenthesis makes clear ; " Jesus was not yet come into the village, but was still in the place where Martha met Him." During all this time Mary sat in the house. Martha, with splendid honesty, had violated the conventionalities which demanded that those thus grieving for their loved ones should remain in the seclusion of the home at least for a period of seven days.

Martha came to Mary, unquestionably sent by Jesus, for she said, " The Master is here, and calleth thee." That is enough. We know perfectly well that Martha would not have said that if it had not been true. All the conversation between Martha and our Lord is evidently not recorded. Having said to her what He said, and uttered His great claim, " I am the resurrection and the life," He told her to go and call her sister. Martha came to her, and said secretly, evidently with the intention that she should find her way to Jesus, without there being anyone else there. But, as the Eastern custom was, there were friends in the house, to mourn with her and comfort her ; and when they saw her quietly get up and leave the house, they followed her ; and so were present when she and Jesus met.

So we have, before the actual sign, that matchlessly beautiful picture of Mary and Jesus. She uttered the same words as Martha had ; " Lord, if Thou hadst been here, my brother had not died." But it is evident that there was a different tone in Mary's voice than in that of Martha. I am not criticizing Martha. I never do. She was magnificently honest. But I think that Martha meant, Why didn't You hurry when we sent for You ? I think Mary meant, I wish it had been possible for You to be here. The same words, with a different emphasis, and intention.

When Mary arrived she went to His feet. Martha did not. She stood upright. Mary went to His feet in the attitude of adoration and discipleship. I think we only get the value of that, if we go back to the incident Luke records, the only glimpse we have of these women before this occasion, when

Jesus came to the house, and was entertained in the house of
Martha, who also " had a sister called Mary." " Mary sat
at His feet." She had taken her share in the work of the
house. Then, prosperity was their portion ; then the sun
was shining. Jesus was a doubly welcomed Guest in that
home. Martha magnificently tried to express her love in
service, and broke down. If amid the pressure of service
there is no time for quietness and meditation, we always
break down. Martha became distracted herself, and then she
grumbled at her sister, and criticized her Lord. Mary took
time to sit at His feet. Now, when the clouds had blotted
out the sunshine, when sorrow had come, and her heart was
breaking, she went back to the same place, back to His feet.
Presently we shall find her there again.

At His feet she expressed her regret, but she was swept
with grief. If we glance on for a moment, to the thirty-
third verse, we read, " When Jesus therefore saw her weeping,
and the Jews also weeping which came with her." Observe
that Mary was weeping, and the Jews were weeping. In
verse thirty-five we read, " Jesus wept." The words are not
the same. The word that described the weeping of Jesus
is not the word used to describe the weeping of Mary and of
the Jews. We ought to translate the word used about
Mary and the Jews as wailing. It was a moaning, wailing
expression of grief. Not so with Jesus. The word translated
weeping about Him really means that tears were running
down His face. Mary went to His feet wailing, but it was
to His feet.

When Jesus saw her wailing, and the Jews wailing which
came with her, " He groaned in the spirit, and was troubled."
That is a most unfortunate translation, missing the whole
point. The word rendered " groaning " has one particular
signification, which is missed entirely by the translation.
Moreover the word " was troubled " is a reflexive verb. Let
me render the statement in another way. " When He saw
her wailing, and the Jews with her wailing, He was moved
with wrath, and troubled Himself." There is no sentence

in all this New Testament more full of revelation. He was moved with indignation. He was angry. And being angry, He troubled Himself.

It was then He said, " Where have ye laid him ? " This is the only occasion in all the records of Jesus asking anyone for information. One does not imagine for a moment He needed the information. It would seem to have been a question indicating that He was now going to act. Then follows the sentence, " Jesus wept." Many things have been written about that brief sentence. How are we to understand it ? The whole situation was that He stood in the presence of death. Death was the outcome of sin. All the wrath of God surged through Him in the presence of the whole of human misery, resulting from human sin, and issuing in death, and the breaking of hearts. He was moved with indignation. Then He " troubled Himself." He took into His own heart all the agony, the reason for which moved Him with indignation. He made Himself responsible, and gathered up into His own personality all the misery resulting from sin, represented in a dead man and broken-hearted people round about Him. This was voluntary indentification with the sorrow that issues from sin, and was the outcome of righteous wrath against the sin that caused the sorrow. It is a most remarkable unveiling of the heart of Jesus.

Then He wept. What were those tears ? I do not hesitate for a moment to interpret those tears. They were the tears of sympathy with Mary, and Martha, with all the sorrow caused by sin and death. It may be said that they could hardly be tears of sympathy, because He knew that within, shall I say half an hour, perhaps less, but at any rate immediately, He would remove the cause of those tears, and bring joy in place of mourning. When we are inclined so to think, and to say, we are revealing our lack of understanding of the sensitiveness of the heart of God to all human sorrow. What I mean is simply this. Supposing—forgive the absurdity of the supposition—but supposing I could come into your house where the loved one lay dead, I do not think I could

shed tears of sympathy with you if I knew that I was going to
give you back your loved one. That is because I am dull,
and callous, compared with the keen sensitiveness of the
heart of God. " Jesus wept." " The Word made flesh,"
weeping is a revelation of God's sympathy, so quick, so sensitive. In a little while He will wipe all tears away ; but while
they are there, even though He will dry them, and end the
sorrow, He enters into fellowship with the sorrow. That is
true to-day. This is microcosmic ; make a macrocosmic
application of it. Our sorrows God is sharing with us. His
ultimate purpose is to wipe the tears from all eyes, and He
knows that presently, as we look back, it will seem so short
a time, this time of sorrow, when all the agony is over, the
rapture of eternity has begun. That does not mean He is
not with us in our sorrows now. And if I may put it so, in
those tears of compassion there was relief for Him also in
the hour when He was ploughed to the depths with the sorrows
of indignation. He was angry ; He troubled Himself ; and
He wept in sympathy with those who were sorrowing.

That leads us to the account of the sign itself. It is very
interesting to follow the Jews, and listen to them. When
they saw those tears, they said, "Behold how He loved him ! "
They felt they were tears Jesus was shedding because He had
lost Lazarus. They were very blind. Look at those tears ;
they said, they prove He loved Lazarus. He did love him,
but that was not the cause of those tears we have seen. Then
some of them said, " Could not this Man, which opened the eyes
of him that was blind, have caused that this man should not
die ? " I do not think anyone can be certain as to what
they meant, or why they said that. It may have been a
cynical remark ; or it may have expressed their unbelief
in that earlier miracle. Or it may have been a very sincere
statement. We have seen Him do that, open the eyes of a
man born blind, and could not a Man doing that, prevent
this man's dying ? Whatever the motive, the question
remains, Could He not have prevented this man's dying ?
Of course He could ! And yet He could not ! If it is a

question of power, yes. His power was unlimited. But it is not a question of power ; it is one of purpose. There are things in which God is limited, limited by His own purpose. Listen again to what He had already said : " I am glad for your sakes that I was not there, to the intent ye may believe." Purpose means the resolving of all that appears to be discord into the harmony of God's perfect will and perfect action.

Following on we read, " Jesus therefore again groaning "— the same word—" again moved with indignation within Himself."   He was in the presence of everything that marked human failure. Death is the final thing ; sorrow the resultant thing, and blindness characterized the attitude of all those round about Him. He was angry, He was moved with indignation, and so He moved towards the tomb. Now watch the process. He acted in the raising of Lazarus against unbelief, or rather, in spite of unbelief. I am not now thinking of the unbelief of His enemies, but the unbelief of Martha. He had said to her, " Believest thou this ? " She had said, " Yea, Lord ; I have believed that Thou art the Christ, the Son of God." Honestly she could not make the full affirmation for which He had asked, but she made the great confession. Now we come to this moment, the crucial hour, the critical moment. Christ stood in front of the grave, and the dead body lay within it, four days dead. He said, " Take ye away the stone." Immediately Martha protested. She had not grasped the full significance of the things He had previously said to her, showing that she was still lacking in perfect understanding of Him. So Martha failed in faith. But He went straight forward. Then " Jesus lifted up His eyes, and said, Father, I thank Thee that Thou heardest Me." Evidently He had been holding communion with His Father all the way through. But what made Him say that ? All we have to do to find the answer to that question is to read on. He was still speaking to His Father, and in doing so He revealed the reason for what He had said : " I knew that Thou hearest Me always ; but because of the multitude which standeth around I said it, that they may believe that Thou didst send Me." If I may reverently say so, it was as though our Lord said to His Father : Father, I am not surprised, I thank Thee. Thou hearest Me always ; but because of the multitude which standeth around I said it that they may believe that Thou didst send Me. He was about to work a sign, but He was doing it in fellowship with God, and He took this means of making the multitude face that fact. All the way through we have seen that to be His claim. Nothing by Himself ; He and the Father together. He and the Father one. Perfect co-operation.

"And when He had thus spoken, He cried with a loud voice, Lazarus, come forth." Someone says, Why did Jesus have to cry with a loud voice. That is a child's question, and therefore it is the sort of question that admits to the Kingdom of heaven and truth. It does look as though He had to cry in a loud voice to make Lazarus hear. But we know that is not so. Profundity is in the simplicities. He raised His voice that the crowd might hear. He had prayed to His Father that the multitude may believe, and now that all may hear what He does, He raised His voice. With a loud voice He spoke. Moreover, the habit of that time, and indeed of to-day in the case of all sorts of sorcerers and wizards communicating with the dead, was and is that of muttering incantations, that nobody understands but themselves. I am not sure that this was not also the reason of the loud voice. " He cried with a loud voice, Lazarus, come forth."

But far more important than that, He spoke as to somebody who could hear Him. Martha would not have thought of calling Lazarus. Mary in her wailing might have called upon her brother, O Lazarus, Lazarus ! But she would never have dreamed that he could hear her. Jesus spoke as to one who could hear. He knew that Lazarus was not dead. That is what He told Martha, he was asleep, he was not dead. When He went into the house of Jairus, He said, " Talitha cumi," that exquisitely beautiful little phrase, so badly rendered, " Damsel arise," which should be, " Little lamb arise." He expected her to hear Him. She did ! That was His attitude now. His was the voice which needed no raising for that purpose ; but that carried over the border-line, and could be heard on the other side.

Immediately there was response. Lazarus "came forth, bound hand and foot with grave-clothes." How could he come forth, if he was bound with grave-clothes, some one may ask ? It depends on the method they took in the sepulture of Lazarus. If they had taken the Egyptian method of swathing the limbs separately, and not bound all together, he could move, but he could not loose himself. He struggled up by himself, a living man, and he "came forth," but found it difficult to go further. Jesus at once said, " Loose him, and let him go."

That was the great sign. What did Jesus do ? Was that a resurrection ? No, not in the sense in which our Lord's was resurrection. That was the calling of the spirit back to the body ; but that was not resurrection in the full sense ; that was resuscitation. When Jesus was raised, He needed no loosing from grave-clothes. When John and Peter went to the tomb, they saw the grave-clothes all in their wrapping as they had been round His body, and the napkin about His head, but He was not there. That was resurrection. We talk about the raising of Lazarus. That is correct, but it was not a raising in the sense in which our Lord was raised from the dead. It was the bringing back of the spirit to the same body ; and in the coming, the healing of the body, with all that had happened to it, to which Martha had referred. " These things are written that ye may believe that Jesus is the Messiah, the Son of God." That was a sign of God acting through Him.

As we do not come in this study of the Gospel to another incident like this, I pause to say that it is a significant thing that whereas He went about doing good, healing the sick, casting out demons, and bringing all kinds of blessing to men in the physical, He is recorded as having only raised three from the dead. There seems to have been a reticence in the operation of His power in that direction. It would seem that our Lord was very reluctant to bring back those who had escaped from the earthly life. He knew He was bringing them back to limitation, bringing them back probably to sorrow.

This last sign was wrought when death was certified at its worst. He raised that man from the dead, resuscitated the body by calling the spirit out of the spirit world to take up its residence again in the temple that had been left.

Finally John recorded the effects of the sign. There was division. "Many. . .believed on Him," as the result of what they saw. Some reported to the authorities. That report ensured His arrest finally on the human level. The result of the report to the authorities was the calling together of the council. It was a very special gathering of those in authority. We read, "The chief priests therefore and the Pharisees." Who were the chief priests? They were Sadducees, every man of them, diametrically opposed in philosophy and religion to the Pharisees. They made no terms with each other as a rule, but that which had manifested itself earlier, now came to a final activity; a coalition between Pharisees and Sadducees. It is a very brief report of what went on, but it is complete. First of all the council, then the consultation, and finally the counsel.

The council held a consultation, which resulted in the counsel. The subject under discussion was, What were they going to do about this Man Jesus? What could they do to stop the whole business? We have no detailed report of the speeches made. I have no doubt they were characterized by confusion. At last Caiaphas spoke. In all literature, there is on record no more clever and damnable speech than that! It was the voice of the politician at his worst who was not prepared to say with blunt brevity what he means, but would clothe a dastardly intention in elegant phrases. Caiaphas began very cleverly. I never read it without thinking it is a wonderful way to begin a speech, if you are taking part in a debate, or are on a committee. He begins by saying, "Ye know nothing at all." That is the way to dismiss the previous

speakers. Well, what do you know, Caiaphas? Now mark
the elegance of the phrasing. " It is expedient for you that
one man should die for the people, and that the whole nation
perish not." That is all. A very brief speech. It simply
meant ; There is only one thing to do, kill Him, get Him out
of the way at any cost. It would not do to put it like that,
so he put it on the ground of political expediency and national
well-being. It was the most dastardly speech, but it won on
the human level. Pilate at last consented to that policy.
When Pilate saw that a tumult was arising, he gave Jesus
over. It is expedient! What devilry can be done in the
name of expediency!

What was the counsel they took? They determined to
kill Him. That is how it ended. " From that day forth
they took counsel that they might put Him to death."

Now observe that marvellous comment which John inserted.
It is as radiant with light and beauty, as that speech from
Caiaphas' standpoint was dark with sin and iniquity. He
declares that Caiaphas had said more than he understood;
more than he intended. " This he said not of himself."
That is, he did not mean what John now said. " But being
high priest that year," God over-ruled and compelled him,
when he was uttering a thing of diabolical obscenity, at the
same time, in the same words to utter a prophecy full of light
and beauty. " This he said not of himself; being high
priest that year, he prophesied that Jesus should die for the
nation ; and not for the nation only, but that He might also
gather together into one the children of God that are scattered
abroad." Caiaphas was a politician, and he said something
characterized by political sagacity, indicating the right thing
to do. John in reporting it, said in effect ; Yes, and what he
was saying was more than he knew. He was uttering a great
word. It was expedient that He should die, and not for the
nation only, but for all the world, that He might also gather
together into one the children scattered abroad. Thus we have
the most tragic and dastardly and diabolical speech on record ;
and side by side with it, a statement that the devilry is

gripped and mastered by God, until the very thing said is transfigured, and becomes the statement of the Gospel of hope for a dead world.

John xi. 54—xii. 19.

The raising of Lazarus had intensified the hostility of the rulers to Jesus. That in itself is an amazing fact and a terribly revealing one. Two notable instances of it have been seen before. One occurred in the first year of His ministry. When, passing through Bethesda's porches, He healed the derelict who for thirty-eight years had been in his infirmity, the rulers were angry because, according to the technicalities of their traditions, He had caused this man to break the Sabbath day by carrying his mattress. They seem to have been entirely indifferent to the wonder wrought for the man. Again, in the case of the man born blind, exactly the same thing was manifested. The creation of sight for a man who had never seen was of small moment to them. They excommunicated the man, and their whole objection was to the fact that Jesus had wrought the wonder on the Sabbath day. A derelict for thirty-eight years given back to life and health and strength, and moral cleansing. A man born blind, gaining his sight. A dead man brought back to life. To these they were indifferent. What a picture we have of what traditional religion can do. It had killed their capacity for compassion. They were concerned because their traditions were violated. Moreover, they saw that these signs wrought by Jesus, and very especially this last and supreme one in many senses, were drawing men after Him. The multitudes were coming to Him, and they felt they were losing their hold upon them. It was because of these things that the council had been gathered together, and the counsel had been decided upon to kill Him.

Therefore Jesus withdrew, until His hour came in the economy of God. In this passage we have the story of that withdrawal; then the story of His coming back, and the supper at Bethany; and finally that of His coming to Jerusalem for His hour, for the final things.

The reading breaks up quite naturally into three sections, and we may mark the sections by geographical names. In chapter eleven, verses fifty-four to fifty-seven, we are in Ephraim with Him; in chapter twelve, verses one to eleven, we are in Bethany with Him; and from verses eleven to nineteen in the same chapter we are in Jerusalem with Him.

Ephraim. " Jesus therefore walked no more openly among the Jews, but departed thence into the country near to the wilderness, into a city called Ephraim; and there He tarried with the disciples." We have no means of knowing how long that tarrying was. Possibly for forty days. During that period He was with His disciples, in quietness in the country. A period of quietness with His own before the storm broke upon Him, and the billows swept over Him.

Then John carries us to Jerusalem, and tells us what was happening there, towards the end of the time that Jesus was in Ephraim. " Now the passover of the Jews was at hand; and many went up to Jerusalem out of the country before the passover, to purify themselves." Arriving from all that countryside, from over Jordan, and from Galilee—as they did at the Passover season, when Jerusalem became crowded with pilgrims,—they sought for Jesus. Jerusalem is seen without Jesus. This seeking of the people shows the place He occupied by this time in the public thought. They were familiar with His name, and largely with Himself. Now they sought Him here at Jerusalem, centre of the national and religious life. The interest was general. They were seeking Him—the verb should have that rendering—and they were speaking one to another as they stood in the Temple. All these people, gathered to celebrate the Passover, seeking ceremonial purification for the observance of the feast, were

discussing the situation. " What think ye ? " they said one
to another. What they were inclined to think is revealed
in the fact that they put the next question in the negative
form. They did not say, Will He come to the feast ? They
said, " That He will not come to the feast ? " John reveals
immediately why the people talking about Him, put the
question in that form. " The chief priests and the Pharisees
had given commandment, that, if any man knew where He
was, he should show it, that they might take Him." Quite
evidently this was an authoritative proclamation issued by
the Sanhedrim that if any one found the location of Jesus,
he should signify to them, and they would arrest Him. The
people knew it, and were wondering, and talking about what
He would do. Would that proclamation keep Him away ?

In the wilderness Jesus was quietly spending the period
with His disciples, while the city was beginning to fill with
the crowds coming up to the feast, and He was the subject
of discussion.

So we turn to chapter twelve, and now He was coming.
John selects three incidents from the events of these final
hours of Jesus' public ministry. First that of the supper at
Bethany ; secondly that of His entry to the city, coming to
it for His hour ; and finally that of the coming of the Greeks.
In this paragraph we have the first two.

" Six days before the Passover " Jesus came to Bethany.
This was a purely social gathering. That was the intention.
" They made Him a supper." Matthew and Mark tell us
that the supper was given, not in the house of Martha, but
in the house of one Simon. It was a happy occasion. It is
arresting and remarkable how often during the ministry
of Jesus, they invited Him out ; and it is more amazing that
·He went. He knew the motives in the invitations. Apart
from the day when He went to the house of Martha and Mary
this would appear to be the only occasion when the invitation
was that of pure hospitality.

Look at the gathering. What was Martha doing ? Serving ! Martha would serve to the end. That is what she was

doing before, in the incident recorded by Luke. That is all
we are told about her now. It was not her house, but she
was acting as hostess in Simon's house. Is that all there is
to say? No. When we met her in Luke, so far as we have
any means of knowing, she was preparing a meal for Jesus,
and Mary, and Lazarus, and herself; four people. How
many had she here? Jesus, and twelve disciples, that is
thirteen, and Mary, fourteen; and Lazarus, fifteen; and possibly Simon, the host, sixteen, and Martha herself, seventeen.
Four only on the previous occasion; seventeen now, and there
is not a word here about being distracted. Martha had
learned something on that sad, dark day, when Jesus talked
to her, when she came to Him in hot and angry protest,
created by her very love. He had talked to her, and said
strange and mighty things. She passes off the scene now,
and we see her still serving, but there is not a word about
being distracted. Her service had not ceased, but some
secret had been learned, which kept her from distraction.

At this social gathering two things happened, two most
revealing things, two things which stand in almost startling
contrast to each other. The act of Mary, and the attitude
of Judas are recorded side by side.

What did Mary do? And why did Mary do what she did?
First observe that Mary is seen at His feet. She has returned
to the old trysting place. In the day of sunshine, when
Martha became cumbered with serving, Mary had learned
the lesson that there must be time for quietness and discipleship and adoration. She sat *at His feet*, when the sun was
shining. Then when the darkness was round about her, and
Lazarus was dead, and her heart was breaking, she came
when He sent for her, and went straight to *His feet*.
Now it was His day of approaching sorrow, and again
she went straight *to His feet*. Do we understand
what she did? Should we ever have understood if it
had not been for our blessed Lord? After the protest
of Judas, He said, " Suffer it now." I like the old rendering
here, " Let her alone." She hath done it " against the day

[207]

of My burying." That is surely a revelation of what was in the heart of Mary. When that day she looked into His eyes, she saw the sorrow there. In a very little while after we shall hear Him say, " Now is My soul troubled." Mary saw that. She remembered the day of her own sorrow, how she had seen those eyes first flash with indignation in the presence of the dead ; and then melt into tears of tenderest pity and sympathy ; and on this day she saw, as did none other, the sorrow unto death ; and she said to herself, I wonder what I can do to show Him that I see. Love then became prodigal, and according to the meanness of Judas, she became wasteful. " Why this waste ? "

The question arises, Had she done what she wanted to do ? Had she made Him feel that somebody at least in this hour of approaching sorrow, sensed His sorrow, knew the darkness of the hour in measure, to which He was going, and was in fellowship with Him ? Yes, he knew. That is what He meant. " Let her alone ; against the day of My burying hath she kept this." And if, with great daring, I may change the wording without interfering with the thought, it is as if He said, She sees and understands. Once a woman's touch drew from Him virtue. Here a woman's act gave Him comfort. I would rather be in succession to Mary of Bethany than to the whole crowd of the apostles.

Then, in contrast, Judas. She, perceiving, sympathizing, sacramentally expressing it ; Jesus, accepting the offering, knowing the intention, and seeing a gleam of brightness in the wasteful and glorious act ; Judas—" Why was not this ointment sold for three hundred pence, and given to the poor ? " Then John becomes sarcastic. " This he said, not because he cared for the poor ; but because he was a thief." Judas, having no understanding of the situation, was blinded by selfishness, and spoke in criticism. Mary, seeing to the heart of things, expressed her sympathy in a prodigality of activity. A social hour ; Jesus the honoured Guest. Round about Him the disciples. The radiant loveliness of Mary's action shines like a rainbow of God over the dark clouds that were gathering about Him. In the words of Judas hell flashed itself out in deep and dire animosity.

And now, the hostile priests see they have more to do than to put Jesus to death. It is very significant. Caiaphas in that council had said, " It is expedient that one man should die." They are finding out now that one won't do ; " Lazarus also." That is a great phrase, " Lazarus also." We shall have two to kill, instead of one. And that was but a beginning. Hostility to God as manifested in Christ, has been the characteristic of the world ever since, and it has ever been trying to get rid of Him. How many have they put to death in the endeavour ? Pilate probably thought he had done the business presently when he put Jesus on the Cross. When he handed Him over it was with a sort of sense of relief, that it was done with. Done with ! Within a couple of generations the power he represented had to repeat the martyrdom of Jesus ten thousand times in Rome itself. " Lazarus also." We do not know if they did put Lazarus to death. Probably not. He was, however, in peril. This may be the reason of their passing out of the picture. We do not read of either of them at the Cross, or after the resurrection.

This hostility, how futile it is. It is expedient Jesus should die, it will suffice. No, " Lazarus also." And following Lazarus, the long succession of the martyrs of Jesus ; and " the blood of the martyrs is the seed of the Church."

Then, what next ? John says, " On the morrow," and there follows the story of our Lord's coming to Jerusalem. He is now seen coming deliberately to Jerusalem for His " hour." His foes had tried to take Him and trap Him, had issued a proclamation that if anyone should know where He was to report, that they might take Him. Now He was coming of His own volition for His hour. We speak of His entry as triumphal, and such it was from the side of the heavenly, the determinate counsel and foreknowledge of God.

There were three entries ; the first day, He rode into the city, came to the Temple, and looked round upon all things, and left without saying a word. On the next day He went

o

to the Temple and cleansed it.   On the third day the rulers
gathered round Him.   John only records the first of these
three entries, and that in a very condensed form.   His purpose,
undoubtedly, was rather to show the effects of that coming,
than to describe its details.   He tells of the greetings of the
crowds to Jesus as He came.   They took down palm branches,
waved them, and flung them on the highway.   As He
approached, they sang sentences from the great Hallel.
" Hosanna ; Blessed is He that cometh in the name of the
Lord, even the King of Israel."

" Hosanna," being simply translated, means, " Save now."
And then, " Blessed is He that cometh in the name of the
Lord, even the King of Israel."   It was a most remarkable
thing for the crowds to sing, when Jesus was coming.   The
rulers were hostile, the crowds themselves were fickle ; and
yet there came this sudden outburst of enthusiasm.   Another
evangelist tells us that the rulers objected, and said, Command
these Thy disciples that they be silent. To which Jesus replied,
If these should hold their peace the stones would become
vocal, would cry out.   In that popular outburst of quotation
from one of the greatest of the Hebrew songs, He was pro-
claimed as the " King of Israel."   It has sometimes been
said that the very voices which that day cried " Hosanna "
very soon after cried " Crucify."   I am not sure that they were
the same voices.   I am rather inclined to think the crowd
that gathered around Him, and marched in with Him, and
cried " Hosanna," was a Galilean crowd ; and that the crowd
that hissed " Crucify," was largely Judaean.   There is no
proof of that, but it is more than probable.   However, even
though it was a Galilean crowd, they also all forsook the
King of Israel they confessed, presently.   And yet mark
this, He accepted it, and rode in regally.   He chose to
ride in, in Kingly fashion.   The ass was the beast of kings.

John declares that all this was in fulfilment of prophecy,
and he gives the prophecy in Zechariah. Then he immediately
adds, that at the time the disciples did not understand this,
but when Jesus was crucified, when presently He was risen

and ascended, when He was glorified, then they saw the relationship between the sign and the song, and understood what He did. John saw at last that however poor and paltry on the human level that entry was; nevertheless in the economy of heaven, it was the entry of the King. So He arrived. The hour was at hand.

John xii. 20–36.

THIS paragraph contains the story of the last incident in the public ministry of Jesus which John records. Moreover, it is the last incident on record. It took place later than that great day of question and answer in the Temple, which Matthew records so fully. It would seem that after this, He retired, possibly to Bethany. One can imagine those last hours spent in the quietness of Bethany.

In this paragraph there are two very distinct movements; first the story of the coming of the Greeks which occupies verses twenty to thirty-three; and then John's account of the questions of the crowd in verses thirty-four to thirty-six.

In the story of the coming of the Greeks, there are two things to notice; the request which they preferred; and the response of Jesus to that request.

These men were not Hebrews. They were Greeks. There are two different words in Greek, which are unfortunately translated the same way in the New Testament; the Greek words *Hellenes* and the *Hellenistae*. The first is always used of those who were Gentiles. *Hellenistae* were Greek-speaking Jews. The word here is *Hellenes*, which marks them at once, not as Jews, but as Gentiles. But they were evidently Gentile proselytes, for they had come up to worship at the Hebrew feast. These men came to the place where Jesus was teaching, surrounded by the group of His apostles; and they preferred their request. They said,

speaking to Philip, " Sir, we would see Jesus." The fact
that they addressed Philip with the title of great respect,
" Sir," would at least suggest that there was something
about this Jesus, Whom they had not seen, but of Whom
they had heard, which commanded respect.

There we tarry a moment, wondering why they wanted
to see Jesus. It may have been mere curiosity. It is possible
that it was so. At that time Jesus was the supreme Centre
of interest in all the countryside, and especially in Jerusalem.
They were gathered from everywhere for the Passover feast,
and as they gathered, they were talking about Him, " What
do you think ? " " That He will not come ? " He was the
subject of discussion throughout the length and breadth
of the city ; wherever they were crowding, they were talking
about this Jesus, Who had been conducting His ministry
for three and a half years, and to Whom their rulers had
become bitterly hostile. These Greeks said, We want to
see Him, possibly out of mere curiosity.

On the other hand it may have been, if we could but know
the history of these men, that disillusioned and disappointed
in the religion of paganism in which they had been brought
up, they had turned in their quest for God to the Hebrew
religion. And it may be that their connection with the
Hebrew religion had left them still disillusioned and disappointed ; for the Hebrew religion at that time was utterly
dead and degenerate within itself. They may have heard
of some of the things Jesus had been saying and doing,
and their very coming was a further quest for something
they had never yet found.

It is interesting that they went to Philip. Philip is a
Greek name. Andrew is a Greek name, and they were
both dwellers in the same town of Bethsaida. Probably
these men had known them before. Then we have the
interesting hesitation of Philip and Andrew. Philip did not
go straight and tell Jesus that there were certain Greeks
wanting to see Him. He consulted with Andrew, and after
consultation, they came. Why the hesitation ? I do not

know that there is a dogmatic answer to that question ; but the possible reason was that they knew these men were Gentiles, and they were not quite sure, now absolutely convinced of the Messiahship of Jesus, as to whether He would be prepared to receive Gentiles.

The response of Jesus to the request was amazing. Glance at the end of the paragraph for a moment. It begins by Gentiles asking to see Jesus. How does it end. What is the last thing ? The last thing is that He hid Himself. It opens with a request to see Him. It ends with a declaration that He hid Himself. I am not suggesting that these men did not see Him with the eyes of their flesh. I think they probably were near enough to see Him, and to hear all He had to say. And yet the last thing recorded is that He hid Himself.

His response to the request is not exhausted in verse twenty-three. We have no right to stay there. What follows ? " Verily, verily, I say unto you." Our Lord used the arresting formula " Verily, verily," which ever meant that something was now going to be said of supreme importance.

" The hour is come that the Son of man should be glorified. Verily, verily, I say unto you, Except a grain of wheat fall into the earth and die, it abideth by itself alone."

First note His reference to an hour. The first occasion He made such reference was to His Mother, " Mine hour is not yet come." Then to His brethren, " My time is not yet come." Again, " No man laid hands on Him, because His hour was not yet come." And yet once more, " No man took Him ; because His hour was not yet come." Now He said, " The hour is come that the Son of man should be glorified."

All that follows interprets that statement. First the illustration of the grain of wheat with applications. Then the great cry of His soul in its travail, " Now is My soul troubled." This followed by heaven's voice ; and certain human opinions. Finally the cry of triumph, " Now is the judgment of this world ; now shall the prince of this world be cast out. And I, if I be lifted up from the earth, will draw all men unto Myself." Then John says, "This He said, signifying by what manner of death He should die."

"The hour is come that the Son of man should be glorified." What hour? "Now is My soul troubled . . . now is the judgment of this world . . if I be lifted up out of the earth, I will draw all men unto Myself." The hour had come to which He had been moving through all the public ministry, the hour which evidently, in His own mind, from the beginning, was the consummation and the culmination of everything. In that first year of His ministry they had challenged Him when He first cleansed the Temple, as to what right He had to do it; and He had given that mystical answer, "Destroy this temple, and in three days I will raise it up." He was then looking to the consummation and the culmination. Now He said that hour had come.

Mark carefully how He referred to it. It would have seemed natural had He said; The Greeks want to see Me; the hour has come in which I am going to die. But He did not say that; He said, "The hour is come that the Son of man should be *glorified*." Our Lord's vision of that hour to which He was going was that it was the hour in which He would be "glorified"!

The writer of the letter to the Hebrews says that He was "crowned with glory and honour, that by the grace of God He should taste death for every man." It does not say He was crowned with glory and honour because He tasted death, but rather that God conferred upon Him the glory and honour of the right to die for men. He had already said, "No man taketh My life away from Me, but I lay it down of Myself. I have power to lay it down, and I have power to take it again. This commandment received I from My Father." "The hour is come that the Son of man should be glorified."

Then continuing, He interpreted. He began with that matchless illustration from Nature: "Verily, verily, I say unto you, Except a grain of wheat fall into the earth and die, it abideth by itself alone ; but if it die, it beareth much fruit." In the realm of Nature that is perfectly true. Its application to Him is arresting. Jesus said in effect, These Greeks cannot see Me. There is only one way by which they may see Me, know Me, apprehend Me ; and that is through the " hour " that has now come, and that is through the way of the Cross. That is the only way.

" Except a grain of wheat fall into the earth and die, it abideth by itself alone." Have you ever seen a grain of wheat ? Imaginatively put a grain of wheat in your hand. Are you looking at it ? Can you see it ? Of course you can see it. But really you cannot see it. How can you see it ? Drop it into the earth, let it die, and wait and watch, and presently the grain becomes the blade, then the ear, and then the full corn in the ear. That was all in the grain, but you could not see it. You have not seen it yet. Husk that grain, and get out all the grains, and put them back again, and watch, and if you keep the process up, one day you may see what lay hidden in the grain of wheat that lay hidden in the hand. My mind goes back to the Old Testament song,

" There shall be abundance of corn in the earth upon the
     top of the mountains ;
The fruit thereof shall shake like Lebanon."

Christ was saying, These men cannot see Me. There will be a day when men will see Me. It will be the result of My going down into death, and of My emerging out of it ; and of the process being carried on through the running centuries ; through death into life, through death into life, through death into life. The harvest is not yet in its completeness.

It is very remarkable that He took a natural illustration, Man in the Divine economy is not natural ; he is supernatural. Man fell on to the level of the grain of wheat, of things that die to live. Man never would have died if it had not been for sin. He fell. Jesus never fell. He did not have to die.

He was transfigured. But now He was going down into the realm into which man had fallen, which can be illustrated in Nature, because man has become merely natural, and no longer supernatural.

Then He applied the principle. " He that loveth his life loseth it ; and he that hateth his life in this world shall keep it unto life eternal." There is marked difference here in the words rendered " life." " He that loveth his life " (*psuche*) " shall lose it ; and he that hateth his life in this world "—that is, life conditioned here—(*psuche*), " shall keep it unto life eternal " (*zoe*). *Psuche* refers to the mental. Whenever Paul talks about the " natural man," we might accurately read " the psychic man," the man living on the lower plane of the merely mental. If you love that life, said Christ, you shall lose it. If you hate that, mental activity conditioned in the cosmos, then you gain life (*zoe*) in all its fulness. Men who have fallen on to the level of the natural, must abandon all the calls and claim of the merely natural, if they would enter into the fulness of life.

Again, " If any man "—not the Greeks only—" If any man serve Me, let him follow Me." My hour is come. If men want to see Me, they must come My way, " and where I am," on this pathway to death, " there shall also My servant be." In all that teaching, our Lord was insisting upon the necessity for that to which He was going ; the necessity for the Cross, as the Cross leads to resurrection, and all the life that lies beyond. " We would see Jesus," they said. Here was His answer. There is only one way to see Me. Men must come My way. It is the way of the Cross, through death, into life.

He then revealed the nature of the hour. " Now is My soul troubled," not *zoe*, but *psuche*, that very realm of life, that man must be content to lose in order to find fulness of life. " Now is My soul troubled." I hear Him say that, and am conscious of sorrows that I cannot fathom, of a travail that baffles me when I try to comprehend it. " My

soul is troubled." The trouble was such that He went on:
" What shall I say ? " Shall I say ?—I am inserting these
words to give the sense—" Shall I say Father, save Me from
this hour ? " But there was no hesitation. He declared:
" But for this cause came I unto this hour." What then did
He say ? Not, Save Me from this hour, but " Father, glorify
Thy name." It is true that John does not tell us about the
Garden of Gethsemane, but he does here reveal Gethsemane's
experiences. Gethsemane was more than an experience of
an hour or two in the darkness of the night. Gethsemane
was the experience of His soul all the way to Calvary. Shall
I say that ? Father, save Me from this hour ? No, I have only
one passion ; to glorify My Father's name, " Father, glorify
Thy name."

Very daringly let me say, and yet I say it resolutely, it
seems as if God could not have kept silence then. Heaven
answered, and the voice was articulate with words for
those who were able to follow it. " I have both glorified
it, and will glorify it again." " I have both glorified it."
All the past was in that, all the past of human history, specifically and specially in the ministry of His Son, in His revelation of the meaning of human nature, in His unveiling of
the Divine heart in speech and word and deed. " I have
both glorified it," and what I have done, I will do. So
heaven broke the silence for the third time in the course of
His life.

But why did heaven break silence ? Notice first the
different opinions about what had happened. Some said that
it thundered. Others said an angel had spoken to Him.
It is an arresting illustration of the fact that people often
hear the same thing quite differently according to what they
are in themselves. Some heard the thunder. Some, perhaps
with a little more spiritual perception, knew it was articulate,
and said it was an angel. He knew. He heard. He understood. Then He told them that it had not come for His
sake, but for theirs. The voice that broke through, which
they heard as thunder or as angelic, even if they did not

hear what was said, and understand it, was a supernatural manifestation, intended to arrest them anew.

The moment that voice had spoken, He continued, and the final thought of glorification was revealed. " Now is the judgment of this world." Judgment ? Yes, now the world stands judged ; the verdict is found. Necessarily and un-hesitatingly the sentence is pronounced on this world. There He stood. Presently they would take Him, and put Him on a Roman gibbet. In view of that, He said, this is the crisis in human history.

What next ? " Now "—not has the prince of this world been cast out ;—but, " Now shall the prince of this world be cast out." It is a process. It began when presently He bruised the head of the serpent. It is not over yet. The process is running on.

The way of the casting out is then revealed ; " I, if I be lifted up from the earth." That should be " out of the earth." That includes more than the Cross. It includes the resurrection. It includes the ascension. It includes His exaltation to the right hand of His Father. " If, if I be lifted up out of the earth, will draw all men unto Myself." That does not say that all will yield, but it does say He will be the gathering point for men, that men will be drawn towards Him.

Then it was that the multitude asked Him two questions. That is to say that somebody in the crowd expressed the attitude and thinking of the multitudes. The first was a theological question, and the second a personal one.

The first one was, " We have heard out of the law that the Christ abideth for ever ; and how sayest Thou, the Son of man must be lifted up ? " They knew the teaching of the law, that when Messiah came, that would be final. They also understood that Christ had claimed to be Messiah ; and further, they understood that He said He was going to die. There seemed to be a discrepancy between the law, and the claims of Christ, and what He was saying about Himself. The law said Messiah abideth for ever ; but

He said He was going to die, and yet He claimed to be Messiah.

Therefore their second question. " Who is this The Son of man ? " I put the definite article in, because it is in the Greek, and I think we have lost something by omitting it. Evidently they were quoting Him, for that was His name for Himself, and nobody is ever recorded as using it except Himself. They meant, What do You make Yourself ? " Who is this, The Son of man." It was a cynical question.

It is nevertheless an arresting thing that this crowd asked the very question He had made the test question of His ministry. John does not record it, but at Caesarea Philippi, He had asked His disciples Who the people said, He, the Son of man was. The crowd are now asking the same question.

Well, what did He say to them ? He ignored their theological problem, and said, " Yet a little while is the Light among you." In the Temple He had said, " I am the Light of the world ; he that followeth Me shall not walk in the darkness, but shall have the light of life." Now He said, " Yet a little while is the Light among you." They were going to put out the Light. They were going to put Him to death. So He said, " Walk while ye have the light, that darkness overtake you not ; and he that walketh in the darkness knoweth not whither he goeth. While ye have the Light, believe on the Light, that ye may become sons of light."

When going to the grave of Lazarus, He had talked about walking in the light. He was not walking in the darkness, He was walking in the light. He walked in the light all the way, even into the darkness. There did seem to come a moment presently when, for Him, the light passed ; but that was when He was where I ought to have been, when the pains of hell got hold on Him.

In His answer, five times the word " light " occurs ; four times with the definite article, " the light," once without it, " light." If you want to know Me, said Christ in effect, Follow the light, the light you have. To fail to do that is to go into darkness. Mystic, majestic, infinite in beauty. "Who is this, The Son of man?" they said. And He did not argue with them. He said, Follow the Light!

John xii. 37–50.

IN this paragraph we have the very last things in connection with the public ministry of Jesus. No incident is recorded here. John had already completed his account of that public ministry, and now before going on to tell of the last teaching which He gave to His own, he surveyed the field, and gave us two summaries. From verse thirty-seven to verse forty-three he gives a summary of the results of the public ministry of our Lord, as he saw them. Having done so, from verse forty-four to the end, he gives a summary of the teaching and claims of our Lord, in words of our Lord Himself.

John summarizes very briefly the results by saying, "Though He had done so many signs before them, yet they believed not on Him." John had selected from the many signs, eight in the realm of works. We have seen them as we have followed through; the turning of water into wine, the cleansing of the Temple, the healing of the nobleman's son at a distance, the healing of the derelict in Bethesda's porches, the feeding of five thousand, the stilling of the storm, the opening of the eyes of a man born blind, and the raising of Lazarus from the dead. In that little closing paragraph at the end of chapter twenty, with which we began our meditations, he says that they did not exhaust the story; "Many other signs did Jesus . . . which are not written in this book." The ministry of our Lord had been a ministry of signs. Now John surveyed the field. He had been with Him through the whole period of that public ministry. He had seen Him and listened to Him. Looking back to

the period when it ended, when our Lord had said the last
thing, and wrought the final sign of His earthly ministry in
public, John said, "Though He had done so many signs
before them, yet they believed not on Him." The statement
has almost a touch of hopelessness in it ; and yet we all
know that it was by no means a hopeless statement, but it
was the facing of a fact in the public ministry of Jesus. That
was the general result. Of course, there were those who had
believed on Him. There was the group around Him of His
own disciples, His apostles. There was a larger company
we are familiar with; on the day of Pentecost, one hundred
and twenty were gathered together ; and as Paul tells us,
five hundred brethren met Him after His resurrection. The
ministry had not been without definite and positive results
that could be tabulated. And yet if we add them all together,
the result would still seem meagre. Twelve, and one of them
a devil. So I think we had better say eleven. One hundred
and twenty. Five hundred. Statistically nobody would say
it was a great success. But who is going to call the ministry
of our Lord a failure ?

There were also His signs in the realm of words, with all
the discussions and the discourses gathered round about them.
Six of them had passed His lips, " I am the Bread of life,"
" I am the Light of the world," " Before Abraham was, I am,"
" I am the Door," " I am the Good Shepherd," " I am the
Resurrection and the Life." All of them great claims, uttered
in the presence of the crowds, in the midst of discourses and
discussions. There had been marvellous evidences that
God was working through Him in the works ; and evidences
supremely that He was God, in the words that had thus
fallen from His lips. Many signs, many signs, " *Yet* they
believed not on Him." No sign had been wrought, or could
be wrought, that could bring complete revelation and complete
conviction. The sign equal to that had yet to be wrought.
They had asked Him for a sign in the first year of public
ministry, and He had replied, " Destroy this temple, and in
three days I will raise it up." The only sign that could bring

complete revelation and create ultimate belief would be the sign of His Cross and resurrection. By another evangelist the same thing is recorded in other words. On another occasion Jesus said, " An evil and adulterous generation seeketh after a sign ; and there shall no sign be given to it but the sign of Jonah the prophet ; for as Jonah was three days and three nights in the belly of the fish ; so shall the Son of man be three days and three nights in the heart of the earth."

Then John explained the unbelief : " That the word of Isaiah the prophet might be fulfilled, which he spake,

Lord, who hath believed our report ?

And to whom hath the arm of the Lord been revealed ? " It is as though John had said, Of course we need not be surprised ; this is the fulfilment of prophecy. The prophetic utterance of old anticipated it. This is a most interesting sidelight on prophecy. When Isaiah wrote those words, or uttered them, there is no question that they had local applica- tion, but they implicated abiding principles. " Who hath believed our report ? " that is our message, the word we have had to say. " And to whom hath the arm of the Lord been revealed ? " The arm which is always the symbol of strength. Said Isaiah in those olden days, " Who hath believed our message ? " Who has been convinced by the things of power seen ? Jesus had wrought many signs ; signs in the nature of a report from heaven, words spoken ; signs in the nature of the manifestation of the activity of God ; the arm of the Lord in strength. They did not believe. John has now quoted that word from Isaiah, and says in effect : The principles that were manifested in the prophetic age, have now come to their ultimate fulfilment and expression in the ministry of the Messiah.

But he went further. " For this cause they could not believe, for that Isaiah said again,

He hath blinded their eyes, and He hardened their heart ;

Lest they should see with their eyes, and perceive with their heart,

[222]

And should turn,
And I should heal them."
That is a definite statement that these people could not
believe because God had hardened their heart and blinded
their eyes. But it must be remembered that God never
hardens a man until the man has hardened his own heart.
John has quoted freely from Isaiah. Let us go back and read
it, in Isaiah, verse ten in chapter six: "Make the heart
of this people fat, and make their ears heavy, and shut their
eyes; lest they see with their eyes, and hear with their ears,
and understand with their heart, and turn again, and be
healed." That was the command to the prophet. Now
look at the previous verse, verse nine; "He said, Go, and
tell this people, Hear ye indeed, but understand not; and
see ye indeed, but perceive not." It was because of this
that He confirmed their own decision. It is exactly the same
in the story of Pharaoh. The Lord at last hardened Pharaoh's
heart, but not till Pharaoh had hardened his own heart.
The word used for Pharaoh's action and the word used for
God's is not the same. In all the earlier movements God
made strong the heart of Pharaoh, that is, held him in the
strength of his manhood to make his own choice. Pharaoh
did not make strong his heart; he calloused it, he hardened
his heart. Then there did come a moment when God sealed
his own choice, and the other word is used of the action of God.
    We are certainly not to understand by this summary of
John that unbelief was the result of a Divine action, preventing
belief. God does not do that. He does ratify human decision.
If in spite of all the signs, men refuse the evidence of the
signs, there comes the hour when that choice is ratified by
God, and they pass into the realm of blindness. That
summarizes the whole of that mission of our Lord. "Many
signs," and the signs were intended to bring men to a recognition of truth, and to submission to it. "Many signs . . . yet
they believed not." The reason for the unbelief was foretold
by Isaiah. God ratified a decision and an attitude, to which
men had come of their own choice.

Then he ends, shall I say, in some senses surprisingly, after what he had said about not believing ; " Nevertheless even of the rulers many believed on Him ; but because of the Pharisees they did not confess, lest they should be put out of the synagogue ; for they loved the glory of men more than the glory of God." That is by no means a contradiction. I think the most illuminative sentence concerning that came from the pen of Bishop Westcott, when writing of it, he said, " This complete intellectual faith is really the climax of unbelief." That is what John has shown. It is the severest indictment of them. He said they knew, they believed the truth, they had been convinced of the truth, but they would not confess it ; and they would not confess it because of that most unworthy attitude of loving the glory of men rather than the glory of God. So the outlook covers all the ground. During three and a half years of public ministry He had given them many signs, signs that would remain, signs that would be recorded, signs ultimately that would have their influence. Yet He was refused, He was rejected. This record of the man who had been with Him all the time, is characterized by simple honesty. When he wrote it he was looking back, and knew the ultimate. He knew the final sign of the Cross and the resurrection, the sign producing complete revelation ; but looking back he says in effect : when our Lord came to the end of His public ministry, when He had uttered the last word in public, when He had wrought the last wonder supernaturally, they believed not on Him. All the teaching, and all the supernatural working of Jesus failed to bring about the final results. To-day when I am told that all we need is the teaching of Jesus, and a determination that we will obey His teaching, it is not according to truth. Or when I am told, on the other hand, all we have to do is to believe in the supernatural element in the doing and teaching of Jesus, that also is not enough. There is only one final sign that brings complete revelation concerning our Lord, and that is the sign of the Cross and the resurrection.

Then we have the summary of Christ's teaching. The question arises as to whether John is here recording an actual address of our Lord, or summarizing. In any case he introduces the paragraph by the words, " And Jesus cried." The word " cried " we have noticed twice before. It is a word that reveals a manner and a method ; it suggests a strong emotional appeal. I personally believe that John here was summarizing on the claims of Jesus. First, emphasizing the fact that these claims had been made so definitely and positively, that there can be no doubt about them ; he said, " Jesus cried," and then summarizing the claims so made.

Unquestionably these were the claims of our Lord. " He that believeth on Me, believeth not on Me, but on Him that sent Me. And he that beholdeth Me beholdeth Him that sent Me." That is the first movement. There we have our Lord's definite claim to relationship with God. We have seen how He had insisted upon it. He was sent, and everything He had said had been on the authority of the One Who sent Him. So now.

He that believes on Me, believes on God ; and he that seeth Me, seeth God. Later He said the same thing to Philip, " He that hath seen Me, hath seen the Father." Christ consistently declared that He stood before men in the place of God, and that if men believed on Him they were believing on God ; and that if they had seen Him, they had seen God. That is the first movement in the claim ; relationship to God insisted upon.

Then followed the definite personal note. " I am come a light into the world, that whosoever believeth on Me may not abide in the darkness. And if any man hear My sayings, and keep them not, I judge him not ; for I came not to judge the world, but to save the world. He that rejecteth Me, and receiveth not My sayings, hath One that judgeth him ; the word that I spake, the same shall judge him in the last day." We must not disassociate this from what He had already said. Nevertheless this is personal : I am come a

P

light into the world. I have brought into the world that which it had lost, the light of life that comes when God is there, and is recognized. That is the light. I am come a light into the world ; and if any man hear My sayings, *rhemata*, not the word, but the sayings, the individual sayings ; and keep them not, I do not judge ; I did not come to judge. I came to save. But that man is judged. And how is he judged ? By the very words that having heard, he refuses to obey. They are the words that judge him in the last day.

The last movement was a return to the first. He goes back to emphasize His relationship with God. " I spake not from Myself ; but the Father which sent Me, He hath given Me a commandment, what I should say, and what I should speak. And I know that His commandment is life eternal ; the things therefore which I speak, even as the Father hath said unto Me, so I speak."

What self-emptying all through. And yet what daring. He had been speaking. Men had heard His sayings. They were not His. They are the sayings of God. They are the words of God. Who else ever made that claim. For nineteen hundred years the sacramental host has grown and multiplied of those who have found it to be true, that in the words of Jesus they have heard the voice of God.

Thus the account of the public ministry of Jesus ends. Fourteen signs have been grouped, eight in the realm of works, six in the realm of words ; and as John distinctly says, " many other signs." We have no complete list either of His words or His works ; but we have illustrations of them in this grouping of John. So many signs, yet they believed not. If we take this Gospel of John, and also Matthew, and Mark, and Luke, and end there, with their account of the saying and doing of Jesus in beneficence and in revelation, then we are face to face with failure. Yet we know the story is not that of failure. The Christian Church, using the word in its fine, catholic, universal sense, all down the ages proves that it has not been failure. And why not ? Because He did not end there. His teaching, wondrous teaching ; His beneficent doing in the realm of miraculous exercise of power, wondrous and amazing ; left the mass unbelieving. They were all unbelieving in a measure. You get little glimpses of it after the resurrection. In Matthew, in the last chapter when they went up to meet Him in Galilee, it is said that some disbelieved. Ultimate saving faith only broke in waves of possibility and power after the death and the resurrection and the ascension, when the Holy Spirit was poured out upon men.

So the story ends. The final sign was not yet. When the Greeks came Jesus had said, " Except a grain of wheat fall into the earth and die, it abideth by itself alone ; but if it die, it beareth much fruit." To the story of that final sign we shall come presently.

John xiii. 1-20.

WE now begin the third and last division of the Gospel. And particularly, we begin a section occupying five chapters, thirteen, fourteen, fifteen, sixteen and seventeen. For the devout student of the oracles of God, the wonder of this section never ceases. Like the alternating lights and shadows on the Urim and Thummim upon the breastplate of the high priest of old, the story proceeds, radiant with glory, and yet almost terrible with deep darkness.

A group of thirteen men is seen, presently and quickly becoming twelve, as one of the number is excluded. All the way the central figure is that of Jesus. The other six names are those of Peter, John, Judas, Thomas, Philip, and Jude. These presently become five, leaving six of the twelve unnamed. These are all seen grouped around our Lord. Our attention throughout is held by Jesus Himself. The others are seen in their relationship with Him.

[227]

He was now about thirty-three and a half years of age. The pathway of His earthly life was ending. The pathway of ministry had been brief indeed, only three and a half years. In these five chapters we have glimpses into the mind of Jesus that are very revealing. I cannot help thinking that as He talked, He was remembering His own childhood, thinking of His mother. I think His own mother was in His mind in the course of His discourses when He said, " A woman when she is in travail hath sorrow, because her hour is come ; but when she is delivered of the child, she remembereth no more the anguish, for the joy that a man is born into the world." When He looked at that little group, He called them *teknia*, " Little children." It is the only time recorded that He used that name for them. It was the diminutive plural of the word Mary had used for Him when she found Him in the Temple at twelve years of age, " Child." Now He called the group " little ones," or " little children," perhaps catching the accents of His mother's tender voice. In the seventeenth chapter we discover the quietness of His soul in the sense of life well lived, and perfect service rendered ; as He talked to His Father.

The key phrase to this section is " His own." The thirteenth chapter begins, " Having loved His own which were in the world, He loved them to the end." His public ministry completed, our Lord devoted Himself for a brief period of a few hours to the inner circle of His apostles, those here designated " His own," those whom God had given Him, as He said presently in talking to His Father, out of the world. " Thine they were, and Thou hast given them to Me."

This period is divided very clearly into two parts as to location. During the first period, chapters thirteen and fourteen, they were together in the upper room. The occasion was that of the Passover feast observed, and then relegated to the past. At the end of chapter fourteen it is recorded that He said, " Arise, let us go hence." Unquestionably they then left the upper room. Then follow chapters fifteen, sixteen, and seventeen, when the location was elsewhere.

The paragraph now under consideration deals with an incident at the Passover feast. John gives us no account of the Passover feast itself ; nor does he give any account of the institution of the new Feast. It was the hour of the merging of the old and the new, and John has recorded incidents in connection with the two Feasts, the old and the new, the Passover and the Eucharist. The first incident is an unveiling of His grace. The second is an unveiling of His government. In the first we see Him girded with the towel, the badge of slavery ; in the second we see Him excluding the traitor. Here, as everywhere, is that infinite and marvellous merging of meekness and of majesty, but He is with His own. The world is shut out. All the clamour of the voices of His foes is silenced, all the hubbub of the curious and questioning crowd is hushed.

The first thing that impresses us is the consciousness of Jesus which led to the symbolic act of grace. The symbolic act was that of the washing of the feet of the disciples ; but the consciousness of Christ is the arresting thing in the story as John tells it. Let us read those opening sentences once more, putting an emphasis on certain words.

" Now before the feast of the Passover, Jesus *knowing* that His hour was come that He should depart out of this world unto the Father, having *loved* His own which were in the world, He *loved* them unto the end. And during supper, the devil having already put into the heart of Judas Iscariot, Simon's son, to betray Him, Jesus, *knowing* that the Father had given all things into His hands, and that He came forth from God, and goeth unto God, riseth."

In that emphasis the consciousness of Jesus is revealed. The causative consciousness of Jesus, that is, the consciousness that led Him to the action recorded here is revealed in the word " knowing." The resultant consciousness is revealed in the word " loved."

What then were the things that John said our Lord knew ? First that the hour was come. His first recorded reference to that hour was when He said to His mother, " Mine hour is not yet come." Now He knew " that His hour was come." He knew too that it was the hour when " He should depart out of this world unto the Father." Not a word is said here and now about the way of His going, but only the fact that His going would bring Him to the Father. When the Greeks came, He said, " The hour is come that the Son of man should be glorified." So here the reference was not to the method of His going, but to the fact, and to the issue of it. " Knowing that His hour was come that He should depart out of this world unto the Father." It is of supreme importance that we should understand the Scripture's teaching about the mind of Jesus as He approached His Cross. Too often the death of Jesus is spoken of as a martyrdom, the heroic surrender to the inevitable in circumstances. There is no scintilla of truth in that view of the Cross. The New Testament accounts all reveal Him as moving with the mien and attitude of One carrying out a Divine programme ; His soul troubled, but always seeing through the gloom to the glory. " Knowing that His hour was come that He should depart out of this world unto the Father."

But again, " Jesus knowing that the Father had given all things into His hands." That statement is significantly placed : " The devil having already put into the heart of Judas Iscariot, Simon's son, to betray Him, Jesus knowing that the Father had given all things into His hands." Judas had willed, and the devil had willed ; but Jesus knew that He was already by the Father's appointment in supreme authority. Presently He will say to this self-same group, " All authority hath been given unto Me in heaven and on earth." He knew it now.

Thus, when the strident voices of His foes were hushed, and the hubbub of the curious crowd was still ; and He was alone with His own, He knew that the hour was come ; He knew the issue of the hour, He was going to His Father ; He knew His Father's confidence in Him, He had given all things into His hands. Moreover, He knew the certainty of

His victory. " Knowing . . . that He came forth from God, and goeth unto God."

And " knowing," He " loved." " Having loved His own which were in the world, He loved them unto the end." The words, " unto the end," *eis telos*, mean to completion. It has been rendered beautifully, " to the uttermost." I am going to dare to render it in another way, which I maintain reveals the very spirit of it. " Having loved His own which were in the world He saw it through." The hour was come. The issue was that He was going to His Father. His Father trusted Him, confided in Him, had put all things into His hands. He was proceeding with the consciousness of certain victory. He had come from God. He was going back to God. Yes, but He had said, " Now is My soul troubled, and what shall I say ? Father, save Me from this hour ? " And a little later, though John does not tell us the story, beneath the sombre shade of the olive trees in Gethsemane, He said, " Father, if it be possible, let this cup pass." Now John, writing after the event, says, " Having loved them " He saw it through, " He loved them to the uttermost, He loved them to the end," *eis telos*, to perfection, to completion, to realization. So I dare to use the phrase which is not translation, but which is interpretation, " Having loved His own, He saw it through."

" Love perfecteth what it begins."

Thus the mind of Jesus is revealed !

Of this He gave them a revelation, a symbolic unveiling. Three words mark the activity, *riseth, girdeth, washeth.*

" He . . . riseth from supper." He broke in upon the ritual of the Passover feast. The washing of the feet was not the ordinary washing of the feet of guests. This was something new, something startling, something intended to arrest their attention. He took a towel and girt Himself with it. The towel girt about the loins in the East was the sign and badge of slavery. They saw Him rise, and gird Himself with a towel. They saw Him assuming the badge

[231]

of slavery. And then He bent down, and poured the water, and began the washing of their feet.

Now Peter protested. Nobody knows the order in which He washed their feet. There is a legend that He went to Judas first. There is no proof of it. I think it was to Peter that He first went. I think if some of the others had submitted, he would not have been so vehement. Peter said, " Lord, dost *Thou* wash *my* feet ? " The emphasis should be placed on the two pronouns to understand Peter. " *Thou* . . . *my*." The amazement of it, his " Teacher," his " Lord," the One Who had instructed him, the One to Whom he had yielded himself ! " Dost *Thou* wash *my* feet ? "

The pronouns were used again when Jesus replied, " What *I* do *thou* knowest not now ; but thou shalt understand hereafter." The same contrast is recognized. But He said more : " But thou shalt understand hereafter." Full of self, Peter did not understand Him then. But he would understand.

Peter was still vehement. " *Thou* shalt never wash *my* feet." Jesus was equally emphatic. " If *I* wash *thee* not, *thou* hast no part with *Me*." " If *I* . . . *thee* . . . *thou* . . . *Me*." Peter at once yielded : " Lord, not my feet only, but also my hands and my head." It was a great word, showing that to Peter the thought that he should have no part with Him was intolerable.

Then again the words of Jesus tenderly corrected and explained. His own were already clean, because they were His. The act was symbolic of that which ever will be necessary, the cleansing of defilement contracted by the way. The whole picture is that of the Roman baths. When men walked from the bathing place to the dressing place, they might contract some dust by the way, and so always the last thing, after the robing, was the washing of the feet in order to remove the dust that had been contracted on the march from the central pool to the dressing room.

Then our Lord applied what He had done. First He asked a challenging question. Do you know what I have done ?

He had told Peter that he did not know. " What I do thou knowest not now ; but thou shalt understand hereafter." So He was going to help Peter, and began with a question. Do you know what this means ? I rose, girt Myself with a slave's apron. I have taken the place of a slave, the lowest place of service possible. Do you know what I have done ? Then, resuming the relationship of dignity and authority, He said, " If I then, the Lord and the Teacher, have washed your feet, ye also ought to wash one another's feet."

Now there are certain sections of the Christian Church even to-day who take that very literally, and observe this ritual as carefully as the Lord's Supper and baptism. While we may not share their practice, we must at least not lose the significance of it. Said Jesus, As I have done, so ought ye to do. What had He done ? Stripped Himself of dignity, taken the lowliest place of a slave to serve them, in their highest interests. So ought we to do for each other ; strip ourselves of all our dignities, and take the lowliest places of service.

He ended with a beatitude, " If ye know these things, blessed are ye if ye do them, happy are ye if ye do them." In effect Jesus said, the theory of service is no use, it is its practice which is of value.

In conclusion. I turn to the first letter of Peter in chapter five and verse four. " And when the chief Shepherd shall be manifested, ye shall receive the crown of glory that fadeth not away. Likewise ye younger, be subject unto the elder. Yea, all of you gird yourselves with humility." The King James' Version reads, " clothe yourselves with humility." Peter, where did you learn that ? I think if I had asked him, he would have said, On that Passover night, in the upper room I saw Him do that. I saw Him gird Himself with humility. It is a remarkable word that Peter used here, rendered in the Old Version " Be clothed with," and in the Revised, " Gird yourselves." The Greek noun from which the verb is derived has as its root a word signifying " Knotted." Being clothed or girded, is being dressed in a knotted garment.

The Greek noun for that garment is used in two applications. It was the garment of a slave, but it was also the garment of princes. Whether the garment was a slave's or a prince's depended upon the material of which it was made.

It seems to me that possibly Peter saw the knotted garment of slavery on Jesus, and before He was through, he saw that it was the knotted garment of royalty. He was writing now to young people, and to old people ; and he gathers us all up, and says, " All of you, put on humility as a slave's garment," and so learn to wear the garment of true royalty. I think he learned this in the upper room, when Jesus rose, and girded Himself, and washed the feet of His disciples, both as Servant, and Sovereign.

John xiii. 21-35.

JOHN gives no account of either the Passover or of the institution of the new feast. Some account of these may be found by a study of the other evangelists. John does record incidents that took place on that memorable night when He—according to the desire of His heart, as He said, " With desire I have desired to eat this Passover with you,"— was with them at the Passover feast, and then instituted the new feast of the Christian Church.

At this point a question arises, which I am not proposing to discuss, but to which I am bound to make passing reference. Was Judas present at the observance of the new feast ? There has been a great deal of discussion around that question ; and the findings are by no means unanimous. However, I think I am warranted in saying that the general consensus of careful and scholarly opinion is that he did not partake of the new feast, that he was excluded before it was observed. Personally that is my conviction.

In this paragraph we have the account of our Lord's

action in excluding Judas from the company of the twelve. In it there are two movements. Verses twenty-one to thirty, give the account of the exclusion. Verses thirty-one to thirty-five give the account of the comments of Jesus, as the result of that exclusion. Everyone realizes the tragic solemnity of this story. It is not possible to come to it without that consciousness.

Many have felt the story of Judas to be a difficult one; and there have been attempts to exonerate him from blame. I suppose the principal one was that of Thomas de Quincey. Based upon de Quincey's article, a novel was written by Marie Corelli, in which she strenuously sought to prove that Judas meant well, but failed. With that view Dr. Parker in one of his volumes agreed. I refer to these to show that there have been honest differences of opinion.

Let us note three plain statements of the New Testament about Judas; two of them from the lips of Jesus, one found in the book of the Acts. The first is found in this Gospel of John, in its sixth chapter. When our Lord was referring to His disciples as chosen, He said, "One of you is a devil." The other equally plain saying was a reference to Judas, recorded in the seventeenth chapter, where He called him "the son of perdition." In the Acts, in chapter one, the inspired writer tells us that he went "to his own place." The references are: John vi. 20, xvii. 12, Acts i. 25. I believe each one of those statements to be literally true. I do not believe Judas was a man as other men. I believe he was a devil incarnate; I believe he was the son of perdition; and I believe that after his death, by his own hand, he went "to his own place." My own conviction has long been that Judus was raised up to do the darkest deed in human history, and that he was actually a devil incarnate.

Now if that were so, his story is not without significance for us, because Judas is nevertheless presented to us as a human being, acting on human levels, using human intelligence, mastered by human emotion, deciding with human volition. As Jesus was God incarnate, and the reality of the humanity of Jesus no one will question, who nevertheless believe that He was the Word made flesh ; so the reality of the humanity of Judas equally cannot be questioned, even though he were a devil incarnate.

So we proceed to look at the story. It is graphic and tragic. In the earlier part of this chapter, in the eighteenth verse, there is a reference to which we turn. Jesus said to them, " I speak not of you all ; I know whom I have chosen ; but that the Scripture may be fulfilled, He that eateth My bread lifted up his heel against Me." I have only referred to it to show that our Lord knew all the truth about Judas.

But now mark how this story opens. " He was troubled in the spirit, and testified, and said, Verily, verily, I say unto you, that one of you shall betray Me." He knew ; and He was troubled in the spirit. We have had that same word about Him twice already in the course of our readings. At the grave of Lazarus He was troubled. When the Greeks came, and He spoke of His approaching hour, He was troubled. There is a difference, however, in the form of the statements. At the grave of Lazarus the reading should be " He troubled Himself." There He was first moved with indignation in the presence of death, and all that of sin which made death inevitable. He was angry ; and then He troubled Himself. He took upon Himself all the sorrow. When He broke out into that great cry in the twelfth chapter, " Now is My soul troubled," it was " My soul," the area of the mental. Here our Lord is seen in the presence of evil at its worst, of treachery beyond all treacherousness, and He was troubled in spirit. Here trouble had reached its deepest depths. That is the spirit in which our Lord approached this action.

But the hour had come when it was absolutely necessary to take action, and therefore He " testified " to the group sitting there around Him, as I believe, the Passover feast ended, and the new feast not yet instituted. He said, " One of you shall betray Me." Troubled in spirit, He testified. The hour had come for action.

Then John tells us about the twelve with great naturalness. They looked at one another. They were speechless. They were filled with consternation. They were conscious of their own failure oftentimes, but that one of them should betray Him seemed incredible. John reclining on Jesus' breast, partly turned toward Jesus in response to Peter's suggestion that he should tell them who it was. Then John leaning further back, asked, and the Lord gave him a sign. " He it is, for whom I shall dip the sop, and give it him."

The act of the giving of a sop must be interpreted by the customs of the East, and of that particular time. In our country, people, at a banquet or a dinner, have the habit, if wine is being drunk, of lifting the glass, and saying, I drink to you. That is exactly what the giving of the sop was at an Eastern meal. It was a sign of friendship. We do not understand this incident if we miss that. That is what Jesus did. He was troubled in spirit. He knew what the issue would be. But foreknowledge is not causation. He knew from the beginning who it was who should betray Him ; and yet up to the last, He gave Judas the chance to halt, to turn from his wickedness. If he was a devil, he was a devil incarnate, and in his human life he was representing responsibility and opportunity. Up to the last our Lord was keeping the door open for him.

Judas took the sop. He responded to the friendly gesture. Then Satan entered in. How did he get in ? Judas let him in. Judas sat there, the nefarious purpose in his heart. He had already made up his mind. When Jesus handed him the sop, He said by the action, The door is still open to come back. Satan was on hand. There does not seem to have been hesitation ; but for a moment at least, Judas stood between the friendly gesture of Jesus, and the appeal of Satan to carry out the nefarious business. He yielded. Satan entered. In that moment his doom was sealed. The sop was his last opportunity.

Then followed the command of Jesus, " That thou doest, do quickly." That was authority ratifying a choice. It was as though our Lord had said : I offered thee the symbol of friendship ; thou hast made thy choice ; now do not hesitate. " That thou doest, do quickly." Judas immediately went out ; and the arresting sentence follows : " It was night." He went out into the night. He that had eaten bread with Jesus had lifted up his heel against Him. Our Lord had clung to him all through, had taken him about with Him, had given him every opportunity. Evil incarnate had now manifested itself in its ultimate, and at its worst.

Then what followed ? " When therefore he was gone out." " He was gone out." The very form of the statement shows that his going was voluntary. It was self-excommunication. I have spoken of our Lord's excluding him. That is true, but the method here was that which is always the method of the Divine. God never excludes a man from His heaven. It is the man who excludes himself ; and God ratifies his choice in the necessities of the order of the universe. " God willeth not the death of a sinner, but rather that all should return to Him and live." We talk about God sending men to hell. There is a sense in which that is so ; but God never sent any man to hell that did not send himself there. He ratifies human decisions.

It was necessary now, however, that evil should be put out ; and so we have the group without Judas, which means that treachery was absent. Evil expelled, was compelled to co-operate in the purposes of God. That is the meaning of what our Lord said to him, " That thou doest, do quickly." The word rendered betray in our New Testament is a remarkable word. The Greek word means to deliver up. It is used of the action of Judas. But in a little while, six weeks or a little more, Peter, talking about the Cross to which Judas betrayed Him, or delivered Him, says He was " delivered by the determinate counsel and foreknowledge of God." Evil will deliver up Christ, but the infinite love and compassion of God will over-rule that betrayal, so that it becomes the very means by which redemption is provided for a race. Thus Judas, and the devil behind Judas, are seen under the control of God. He was over-ruling all. Expelled was evil, and so compelled to carry forward the Divine programme.

Then Jesus said : " Now is the Son of man glorified." It was night, and Judas had gone into the night to carry out the purposes of darkness. A little later on Jesus said to a company of men, with Judas leading them, " This is your hour, and the power of darkness." He went out into the night, and when he was gone, He said, " Now is the Son of man glorified." The hour has arrived, the great " *Now*." The process was working itself out, even in the going of Judas, and in the nefarious business he had on hand.

That is the last occasion which John records on which Jesus used the title " the Son of man " for Himself. The first is found in chapter one. When Nathanael came He said to him, " Ye shall see . . . the angels of God ascending and descending upon the Son of man." There the great title emerged in this Gospel. Ten times John used it on the way through. That is the first. This is the last.

Now He was at the end. He had said to the guileless Nathanael, " Thou shalt see . . . the angels of God ascending and descending upon the Son of man." Now, tragedy on the human level, darkness all about Him, treachery hounding Him to death, He says, " Now is the Son of man glorified." The rainbow arch was shining around the dark thunder-clouds. All the wickedness of humanity in treachery, had gone out into the night. To that little group of His followers, He said, Do not look on the darkness merely. Know that through that very process, and in the very way, in all that results from the thing so dark, the Son of man is glorified.

And more, " God is glorified " in the same way, and by the same process. And yet again, " God shall glorify Him in Himself, and straightway shall He glorify Him." Who ? The Son of man. Here then, as presently in His great prayer in chapter seventeen, He saw beyond the darkness to which He was going, His return to the glory of which He had divested Himself. God would take Him back to that glory, but this darkness was the process through which the glory would be gained, and God would be glorified.

Thus He saw through, He saw Himself taken back to the glory that He had with the Father ere He came, but taken back to it as the Son of man. So that, for evermore identified with God, at the heart of the universe, is humanity, as represented in Him.

Then He dropped into infinite tenderness in speech as He said " Little children." He had never talked that way before, so far as the records reveal, teknia, " Little children." It is a word of infinite tenderness. It is the diminutive plural of the word His mother used to Him when she found Him in the Temple, having lost Him. She called Him " Child," always a word of tenderness, and always a word that recognized peril, and the necessity for care over the little one. The very method of address is suggestive of all that was in His heart at the time. Troubled in the presence of treachery, confident as He moved along the line of a Divine programme of victory to glory ; and then He looked round to those that were left, and He said, Little ones ; I am with you for a little while. " Ye shall seek Me ; and as I said unto the Jews, Whither I go, ye cannot come ; so now I say unto you." He said something to the Jews He did not say to these. To them He said, " Ye shall die in your sins." He did not say that to these men. He was simply stating the fact that the way He was now going, they could not come. He was going alone ; they could not travel with Him then.

But " A new commandment I give unto you, that ye love one another ; even as I have loved you, that ye also love one another." Judas the traitor was gone, but that little group of eleven were still with Him, and He gave this command as the sum total of everything. " By this shall all men know that ye are My disciples, if ye have love one to another."

When He said, " A new commandment," what did He mean ? There is a sense in which it was not a new commandment. In the Mosaic economy the word is found, " Thou shalt love the Lord thy God with all thine heart, and with all thy soul, and with all thy might ; " and " Thou shalt love thy neighbour as thyself." What did He mean when He called it new ? This word for new means something that is fresh, as opposed to that which is effete. When He said that they were to love as He loved, the word indicates result, having the value of the phrase " seeing that." If we love, seeing He has loved, it is true that our love will be on the pattern of His. That is the sequence. But the point is this : I am giving you, said Jesus, a commandment that is new in its inspiration. Seeing I have loved you, let My love for you be your inspiration for loving each other ; and then consequently, of course, it will mean love of the same nature. Stripped of His dignities, girded with a towel, the badge of slavery, He had washed their feet ; and He had said, What I have done to you, you ought to do to one another. This then was His one, final, and inclusive commandment, that they love one another.

Then followed the arresting statement, " By this shall all men know that ye are My disciples." Not by the creed you recite. Not by the livery you wear. Not by the hymns you sing. Not by the ritual you observe. But by the fact that you love one another. Tertullian tells how in those early days, the exclamation that was made about the Christians was, " See how these Christians love one another." The measure in which Christian people fail in love to each other is the measure in which the world does not believe in them, or their Christianity. It is the final test of discipleship, according to Jesus.

John xiii. 36–xiv.

THE Passover had been observed and superseded. The new feast had been instituted and observed. Then immediately converse followed between our Lord and the group gathered round about Him, Judas being excluded. These men were in trouble, and what wonder. Four of them spoke. The rest listened, and shared unquestionably in the troubled feelings, expressed by the four, and answered by Jesus. When we reach the end of the chapter, we find them quiet, hushed into peace.

In this paragraph we have the account of their questions, and of our Lord's replies. There are four questions and answers recorded between verse thirty-six of chapter thirteen, and verse twenty-four of chapter fourteen. Right in the heart of this we have the seventh sign of our Lord in the realm of words. In what remains, verse twenty-five to verse thirty-one, we have the summing up of Jesus at the close of those intimate conversations.

It is very arresting that all the questions were concerned with super-earthly matters. Their supreme consciousness at the moment, a poignant one, a painful one, filling them with sorrow, was that our Lord was going. He had been telling them about this for six months, insisting upon it since Cæsarea Philippi; and the way of His going He had clearly indicated; that it was to be the way of suffering and death, leading to resurrection. Those men had never understood the reference to resurrection. It was quite self-evident to them that He was going. Of course, they could not have listened to Him without knowing that His attitude was never that of despair, but rather that of a consciousness of majesty, as He was moving along a Divinely marked course. But for them the terror of it was He was going; that soon, as they thought, He would be dead, and with them no longer. All their questions therefore moved into the realm of super-earthly matters; Peter, " Whither goest Thou ? "; Thomas, " Lord, we know not whither Thou goest ; How know we the way ? "; Philip, " Show us the Father, and it sufficeth us "; Jude, " What is come to pass that Thou wilt manifest Thyself to us, and not to the world ? " Every one of them moved in a high realm, the realm of super-earthly consciousness.

The story of Peter begins at the thirty-sixth verse, and runs through chapter fourteen and verse four. The cause of unrest in the soul of Peter was that of the absence of Jesus from the earth. " Lord, whither goest Thou ? " The Lord was going away. Where ? It is patent that he knew by this time, as they all did, that Christ was going to death. So Peter said, Where are You going ? We shall not have you here. Where will You be ?

Then came the remarkable answer of Jesus, all of which must be considered. The first thing He said to him was not a definite answer as to where He was going. He said, " Whither I go, thou canst not follow Me now ; but thou shalt follow afterwards." Peter never said a finer thing than he said in response to that. " Why cannot I follow Thee even now ? I will lay down my life for Thee." He was perfectly sincere. The difficulty was that he did not know himself, nor understand the weakness of his nature.

This the Lord proceeded to declare to him as He said, " Wilt thou lay down thy life for Me ? Verily, verily, I say unto thee, the cock shall not crow, till thou hast denied Me thrice. Let not your heart be troubled ; ye believe in God, believe also in Me."

I recognise that objection may be taken to reading these sentences thus in close connection on the ground that in the first verse of chapter fourteen the pronouns are plural, while the pronouns are singular at the end of chapter thirteen. That is quite true ; but when He said, " Let not your heart be troubled," while He took them all in, He did not exclude Peter. Luke tells how on this same occasion He said to Peter, " Simon, Simon, behold, Satan asked to have *you* "— plural—" that he might sift *you* "—plural—" as wheat ; but I made supplication for thee, that *thy* faith fail not "— singular. But He did not exclude the others from His interest and prayer by saying that. So here. He began with the individual, and including the rest, He did not exclude Simon.

Simon had said, I will lay down my life for Thee. To which

our Lord replied in effect :—Is that so ? Is that how you feel ? Is that your will ? Simon, I know you better than you know yourself. I know the worst that is in you. I know before the flush of morning is on the Eastern sky, you will have betrayed Me ; but do not let your heart be troubled.

Then He told them the condition upon which their heart might be free from trouble as He said, " Ye believe in God, believe also in Me." Our translators, most of them, have rendered that sentence with one indicative, and one impera- tive. " Ye believe in God," indicative ; " Believe also in Me," imperative. I think they should both be rendered as imperatives. " Believe in God, believe in Me." He thus asked for equal confidence in God and Himself.

Then He gave the larger answer to Peter's first question. He said, " In My Father's house "—that is in the whole universe, " are many abiding places. If it were not so, I would have told you." If this earth were the only abiding-place, I would not have deceived you. You are all troubled as to where I am going. I am only going from one abiding-place in My Father's house, to another. I am going " to prepare a place for you. And if I go and prepare a place for you, I come again, and will receive you unto Myself ; that where I am, there ye may be also." He was telling him now where He was going. He was going, still in the Father's house, to some other abiding-place ; and He was going to prepare it for Peter and the rest. I am going from this abiding-place, to another ; so that when you come, you will be at home there, for you will find Me there. I am going to prepare it for you. I will be there when you come. And if I go, I come,—not I come again, but I come,—and will receive you unto Myself.

Now again quite simply and bluntly, to review the whole movement. I am ready to die for You, said Peter. Peter, said Jesus, is that your will ? You will not be equal to it. Before the morning dawns, you will deny Me thrice. But let not your heart be troubled ; believe God, believe Me. I am going to prepare a place for you, and if I prepare a place, I will come and get you. In other words, I know the worst that is in you, Peter, but if you trust Me, in spite of the worst that is in you, I will realize all your highest aspirations, and fulfil your life for you.

In all this we have a great revelation of His attitude towards life. These men were earth-bound in their thinking, engaged in a quest, asking strange questions in an honest, blundering way ; and He flung round them the vastness of the universe ; and the fact that it was unified as being the Father's house ; and therefore the fact He was out of sight, did not mean He was lost to them. I come to you. Now how are we to interpret that " come " ? There have been various ways. I think they are all included. He came to them in resurrection. He came to them in a full and new sense when the Paraclete came. He came to receive the majority of them as they passed to Him through violent death. He met them as they passed over. The ultimate reference was undoubtedly to His second Advent.

Peter had said, Where are You going ? What is the mystery of this life that lies beyond ? Can't You tell us something about it ? If there were nothing beyond, said Jesus, I would have told you. There are many abiding-places in this house of My Father. I am going out of sight, but I am coming for you, and I will prepare the home for you ; and in the meantime I come to you, and at last I will receive you to myself. And He ended by saying : "Whither I go ye know the way."

Then Thomas the magnificent, the honest—the man who would not pretend to have a faith he had not, or a knowledge he lacked—bluntly contradicted Jesus, broke in upon what He was saying, and said, We do not know where. You have not answered Simon. You have not told us where. How can anyone know the way who does not know the destination ?

Then in answer to that honest expression of disagreement with Jesus, came that great claim ; " I am the way, and the truth, and the life." The implicate of that is that He had said to them incidentally, that He was going to the Father. I am the way unto the Father ; therefore I am the way to all the abiding-places in the Father's house. I am the truth about the Father, and therefore ultimately about all creation, all the universe, all being. And I am the life, the very life of the Father ; and therefore the One in Whom, as Paul put it presently, " all things consist," or hold together. That word of Jesus illuminated all the darkness that was resting upon the minds of these men. Whether they entered into it then or not, who shall say ? Peter's Where are You going ? ; Thomas' How can we know the way ? ; Philip's Show us the Father ; Jude's What means the method of hiding the manifestation of Thyself from the world ? ; the whole realm of difficulty was illuminated by this claim. I am the way to the Father, and to all the universe. All the highways that baffle our thinking, and leave us dreaming dreams and seeing visions, are unified in Me, I am the way. I am, moreover, the truth, the ultimate interpretation of everything. And finally of all that universe, I am the life.

When we commenced these studies, I insisted upon, and I want to emphasize again, the fact that the works we call miracles, do not demonstrate His Deity. They do demonstrate the fact that God was working through Him. It is His words that demonstrate His Deity. Put these words into the lips of any other than Jesus. It is unthinkable and impossible. In the midst of that little group, hell outside through priests and enemies, and Judas' treachery, waiting to murder Him and to those enquiring souls who were trying to know something about the life beyond, He said, " I am the way, and the truth, and the life." Follow Me, and you have direction anywhere in God's universe. Follow Me, and you have, ultimately, the interpretation of all secrets, the ultimate in truth. Follow Me, and you will know the fellowship of the ages, " I am the way, and the truth, and the life ; no one cometh unto the Father, but by Me." He was going to the Father. He was the way there. He was the truth about the Father. He was the very life of the Father.

Then Philip spoke, and I never read this word of Philip

without feeling that whatever he may have meant, it was the great cry of humanity voicing itself through this quiet, simple, unobtrusive man, because that is what Philip was. In a myriad tones still, many of them discordant, many of them wails of agony and sobs of distress, that is what the world is saying, Show us God and it sufficeth us.

Now listen to Jesus. " Have I been so long time with you, and dost thou not know Me, Philip? he that hath seen Me hath seen the Father." Thus He claimed to be the Revealer of God. When we introduce some man or woman, youth or maiden, to Jesus Christ, we are bringing such face to face with God. That is what Christianity means.

He did not finish there. He went on to show that if in Himself was the revelation, by the coming of the Holy Spirit, there should be an interpretation of the Revelation. " I will send another Comforter," an Advocate, and His business shall be that of interpreting Me. As the Spirit interprets the Christ, men find God. " He that hath seen Me, hath seen the Father." The Spirit shall be the Interpreter of the Revelation. That is the only way in which humanity's need will be met. Men will never find God by groping after Him in Nature. A man tells me he has given up going to Church, and worships in the country. He is deluded. He never gets near to God in that way, so as to meet humanity's dire need. A man may have an æsthetic titillation of his senses in the country, but for God's sake don't let him call that religion. Don't let him imagine that so he is dealing with God. " No man cometh unto the Father, but by Me." I will send the Spirit, and He shall interpret Me, and so men will find God. There is no other way.

And then He spoke of manifestation, and Jude fastened upon the word " manifest," How is it come to pass that You are abandoning the world? " What is come to pass that Thou wilt manifest Thyself unto us, and not unto the world? "

The answer was not in some senses a direct answer, but it was a complete answer. His answer to Jude's enquiry was to talk about love, and the keeping of commandments. He went on to tell Jude and the rest of them that when they, or any, loved Him, and proved it by keeping His commandments, something would happen. What? "We"—My Father and I—"will make Our mansion with him." The word here rendered "abode" is exactly the same word Jesus used, when He said, "In My Father's house are many abiding-places." He had said that, referring to the whole universe. Now He said in effect: You ask Me, Jude, why I have abandoned the world? I have not abandoned the world. My Father and I are coming to dwell in you, and in all who shall, like you, love Me.

The implicate of that statement is the answer to Jude's question. Given a man or a woman in whom God and Christ are living, the world receives illumination. One of His great claims in one of the earlier days of ministry was, "I am the light of the world." It is not in John's record, but in His ethical Manifesto He had said to those disciples, "Ye are the light of the world." Thus He answered Jude by showing He was not abandoning the world, but finding those in whom God and He could live, and shine upon the world in manifestation.

Then in final words He summarized on the whole fact of that which was coming. He told them of the coming of the Comforter for interpretation. Very tenderly He said to that little group of troubled men, I will not leave you desolate, I will not leave you orphans, unloved and straitened and uncared for. He had called them *teknia*, little children. He said, I am not going to leave you like little children, with no one to care for you. I am sending an Advocate, a Paraclete, One called to be by your side, and Who will interpret these things, to bring all things to your remembrance that I have said; to interpret to you the revelation you have, but have not yet understood.

And then finally, "My peace I give unto you." "I go unto the Father." When He said that He was looking through the conflict to the issue. "The prince of the world cometh; and he hath nothing in Me," nothing on which he can fasten that can give him the victory. Then He was considering the victory in the conflict. I go " that the world may know." Then He was referring to the final purpose, and showing that it was still the world.

In view of all that He said, " My peace I give unto you." Literally, I will give unto you the peace that is Mine. Had He not said something like that before ? Yes, a little earlier He had referred to " the commandments that are Mine." In the next chapter He spoke of " the love that is Mine " ; and a little later, " the joy that is Mine."

He is going. The commandments, the peace, the love, the joy that were His, He committed to them ; commandments to be obeyed, peace to be entered into, love to be yielded to, joy to be experienced.

Then He said, " Arise, let us go hence." The conversations were over. There were no more interruptions. The key note to the whole is, " Let not your heart be troubled." Do not let these questions cause you unrest. " I am the way, I am the truth, I am the life." There is direction for you in Me. There is the solution of all problems ultimately for you in Me. There is life sufficient for the fulfilment of your being and service in Me. " Let not your heart be troubled ; believe God, believe Me."

John xv.

THE closing words in chapter fourteen of John are these, " Arise, let us go hence." At that point they left the upper room, where the Passover had been observed, and the new feast had been instituted. When they left the upper room where did they go ? Did they immediately leave the city ? Chapter eighteen begins, " When Jesus had spoken these words, He went forth with His disciples over the brook Kidron, where was a garden." Does that mean that He went forth from the city then ? It may do, but not necessarily so.

There are those who believe that when they left the upper room, they took their way to the Temple, for it was the Passover season, and at that time it was the custom at Passover season to leave the great outer gates of the Temple open all night so that those desiring to enter in might do so for preparation for Passover observance. If Jesus took His disciples there, as they passed in through those gates, their eyes would very probably rest upon the golden vine which adorned the gates, and which was the symbol of the national life. That may have been so. I cannot tell.

Personally I am inclined to believe that they left the upper room, and left the city, and went somewhere on the slopes leading down to the place where the winter torrent, or the Kidron, was running on its way ; and that halting there, He uttered this great allegory of the vine. If that were so, in all probability at that time in the night, with the Passover moon shining upon them, they could see almost everywhere the vines growing, those stunted, gnarled, little vines of Palestine ; and here and there, perhaps, they would see the flicker of a flame from the fires in which branches were being burned. Be the location what it may have been, wherever they went, He uttered this great final discourse.

The questions and answers recorded in chapters thirteen and fourteen were concerned with super-earthly matters, as we saw. The troubled hearts of His disciples were peering out into the mystery of all that lay beyond the here and now ; asking Him where He was going, and telling Him they did not know the way, asking for a glimpse of God, and wondering why now, He was manifesting Himself to them, and not to the world. He had answered their questions, and hushed them into quietness and peace.

Now, in this great discourse He brought them back to the earth life in a very definite way ; and that with regard to their relationship with Him in service on behalf of the world. They naturally, wistfully were staring out beyond, to where He was going, and asking their questions. He answered them, and then in effect, He said, Come back now with Me, and see what I plan for you on the earth level. The allegory itself in its entirety is briefly given, and is followed by exposition and enlargement, in interpretation of this, His final sign, in the realm of words. As we have been travelling across this Gospel, we have listened to Him on varied occasions, using the personal pronoun " I " in conjunction with the simplest form of declaration concerning being, " I am," and linking it with human symbols. This is the last, the final sign in the realm of words, uttered to that little gathered-out company that were round about Him. The whole chapter is needed for an understanding of the allegory of the vine and the final sign ; and indeed, the greater part of chapter sixteen is also needed. We begin with the sign itself, and then rapidly survey His interpretation thereof.

Said He, as we have read it all our lives, and very beautifully, " I am the true vine." To me, however, there is suggestiveness in the Greek form in which those words are recorded. It may be said that it is merely a matter of idiom, and we have changed it from the Greek into the English idiom. The words are identical, but their arrangement is slightly different. This is how it reads : " I am the vine, the true," There is a difference of suggestion, the Greek form gives us at once a sense of intended contrast. " I am the true vine " is perfectly accurate, but when we hear it thus, " I am the vine, the true," we immediately see that He was intending to put Himself, under that figure of the vine, in contrast with all that had gone before. " I am the vine, the true."

The figure of speech in itself was perfectly familiar to those who heard it. We can only appreciate its value as we remember that our Lord was not making use of a new figure of speech, but one which in their religious literature had had its place for long years ; and in their national life had become definitely and positively symbolic.

This figure of the vine emerges in the Biblical literature in Psalm eighty. There, in the midst of national declension, a singer, singing a song with national intention, said,

" Thou broughtest a vine out of Egypt."

[251]

That was a symbolic reference to the beginning of their national life.

Then we find the prophets made use of the figure. Hosea, Isaiah, Jeremiah and Ezekiel, all employ the figure of the vine. Hosea in his tenth chapter says, " Israel is a luxuriant vine, which putteth forth his fruit." That means that Israel was failing. It was not bringing forth the fruit it was intended to bring forth. It was bringing forth its own fruit. The following statement shows this : " He hath multiplied his altars." Later, Hosea speaking of God's restoration of His ideal through a spiritual Israel, says that in that day, " Ephraim shall say . . . from me is Thy fruit found," that is, fruit according to the purpose of God.

In Isaiah we find two great passages. In the fifth chapter, " Let me sing for my wellbeloved a song of my beloved touching his vineyard. My beloved had a vineyard in a very fruitful hill." God was looking for fruit from the vine, and wild fruit was brought forth. That was failure. Then in the twenty-seventh chapter, Isaiah is looking on to a time when there shall be realization, and he says then the vine shall be fruitful. He " will water it every moment." So Isaiah uses the figure, first of failure, and presently of fruition.

Jeremiah in his second chapter speaks of that nation as being " a degenerate vine."

Ezekiel uses it on different occasions. The first is in the fifteenth chapter, when he employs it with caustic satire, as he declares that the wood of the vine has no use, especially when it is burnt at both ends. Then in chapter nineteen he uses the figure as he speaks of one that caught up the vine, and carried it away, and planted it somewhere else ; thus referring to the captivity of the people of God. Again in satire he speaks of the branches in the vine becoming rulers over the vine, so referring to the fall of Israel to monarchy, when they clamoured for a king, when God alone was appointed to be King.

During the Maccabean period they had made the vine, on

the basis of these references by psalmists and prophets, the symbol of their national life.

Now Jesus stood among them and said, " I am the vine, the true." Not many hours before, He had made use of the same figure. Matthew in the twenty-first chapter records the parable of the vineyard. Servants sent, who were beaten and stoned and killed ; the son sent, who was cast forth and killed. In that connection, when He had used the figure of the vine as illustrating the national life, He had excommunicated the nation, " The Kingdom of God shall be taken away from you, and shall be given to a nation bringing forth the fruits thereof." His disciples had heard Him say that solemn and awe-inspiring thing. Now He was giving them His last consecutive teaching, and He took hold of that figure, so familiar, the vine, the emblem of national life, which the prophets had used to show national failure, and to predict ultimate realization. He stood there amid the ruins of the vine so far as the nation was concerned, and having excommunicated it from the position of responsibility and privilege which it had held, He said in effect, God has not failed, if the nation has failed. The purposes of God are not abandoned. He Who created the vine to bring forth fruit for the world is not defeated. " I am the vine, the true." Thus in that great word He transferred the privileges and responsibilities from the Hebrew people to Himself, and those associated with Him, for in the fifth verse He repeats the figure, not using the word now, " the true," but indicating the relationship of all such to Him, " I am the vine, ye are the branches."

It is impossible to conceive of anything more startling, august, splendid, final than that. Hell was all round about Him. Through the treachery of a man, and the animosity of a degenerate priesthood it was getting Him now, and was about to put Him on His bitter Cross. Then it was He said, " I am the vine, the true " ; " I am the vine, and ye "—that little group of men—" are the branches."

Then followed His interpretation. In the first ten verses He interpreted the fact of union between Himself and His own. "I am the vine, the true, and My Father is the Husbandman." "The Husbandman," the One Who cares for the vine, Who sees to it that it bears fruit. Nowhere in the Gospel narratives does that word husbandman occur, except in His parable of the vineyard, which He had uttered a few hours before, in excommunicating the nation. There He had spoken of "wicked husbandmen," to whom the care of the vine had been committed, the whole order of priests and rulers who had all broken down, killing the prophets, killing the Son. After that parable this word becomes the more arresting. He said, Now no longer will the care of the vine be entrusted to husbandmen on the earthly level ; "My Father is the Husbandman." All intermediation in care of the vine is abandoned, superseded.

Then He told of the process ; pruning, cutting out fruitless branches, and committing them to the burning ; and the purging, or cleansing of the branches that remain, in order to more fruitfulness. Thus He said, Now the care of this vine is in My Father's hands. He and He alone will do the pruning ; He will do the cleansing necessary to produce fruitfulness.

Then He revealed the vital condition of fruitfulness. "Abide in Me, and I in you. As the branch cannot bear fruit of itself, except it abide in the vine ; so neither can ye, except ye abide in Me." Then, "I am the vine, ye are the branches ; He that abideth in Me, and I in him, the same beareth much fruit ; for apart from Me, severed from Me, cut off from Me, ye can do nothing." The condition is that of abiding.

What then is the value of this new union ? He stated it in words which I am going to render a little differently. "If you abide in Me, and My words abide in you, you shall demand as your due whatever you are inclined to, and it shall be generated unto you." That rendering is certainly warranted, and is an amazing statement. But do not let us forget the flaming sword which guards the way, *If ye abide in Me!* If we do that, what then ? You shall demand as your due.

The Greek word certainly warrants that rendering. It is one of the strongest words used with regard to prayer. If you abide in Me, and My words abide in you, utter your demands, whatever you are inclined to. It shall be done, and the word means generated, caused to be; creative power shall operate. If we are abiding in Him, and His words are abiding in us, we shall not be inclined to anything out of harmony with His will. That is the condition. But if we are there; then we may demand as our due, and God generates, if necessary, that which is so demanded, as the result of living union with Christ.

The intended issue is fruit. " Herein is My Father glorified, that ye bear much fruit." The value of the union is that we are admitted into a relationship that makes us free of the franchise of heaven; and access to God enables us to make demands upon God through which, when we make them, God can do things that He does not do except upon those conditions. Such demand always issues in fruit-bearing. Any prayer which does not react upon my life, and make it a more fruit-bearing life, is not prayer at all. The value of the union is the franchise of asking, and the reaction of fruitfulness.

Then He revealed the nature of this union in those wonderful words, " If ye keep My commandments, ye shall abide in My love; even as I have kept My Father's commandments, and abide in His love." The nature of the union is that of the love-mastered life that demonstrates our loyalty to our Lord, and allows Him to express Himself through us in fruit.

Having thus interpreted the new union, He went on to show what it means with regard to His disciples and Himself. " These things have I spoken unto you, that the joy that is Mine may be in you, and that your joy may be fulfilled." What then is the purpose of the union so far as the disciples are concerned? That they may have His joy. This is the first time in the ministry of Jesus that we have it recorded that He referred to His joy. He referred to it when He was approaching His unfathomable sorrows. " My joy "! I think

[255]

the writer of the letter to the Hebrews had that somewhat
in mind when he said, " For the joy that was set before Him
endured the Cross, despising shame." Union with Him means
that we have His joy. Those who do so know what joy really
is, their joy is fulfilled. The measure in which we know
anything of His joy, is the measure in which all other joys
are like the crackling of thorns under a pot, the attempt to
satisfy life with apples of Sodom.

Then is revealed the law of this union; " This is My
commandment that ye love one another, even as I have
loved you." Always, in these last discourses He was keeping
these men face to face with love as the supreme matter.

Then, very tenderly and beautifully He told them of the
new name He was now giving to them. " No longer do I
call you bond-slaves, but friends; for the bond-slave knoweth
not what his lord doeth; but I have called you friends."
I am interpreting to you the things from My Father; and
because you are coming into an understanding, you will be
My friends. I call you friends.

Then followed that wonderful statement, " Ye did not
choose Me, but I chose you . . . I appointed you." He
was talking to the eleven, of course; but through them He
was talking to all whom they represented. His Church was
in His mind, as we shall see by and by, when we get to His
prayer in the seventeenth chapter. I chose you, and appointed
you, what for ? " That ye should go and bear fruit, and that
your fruit should abide ; that whatsoever ye shall ask of the
Father in My name, He may give it you." I chose you and
I appointed you to two things, to fruit-bearing, and to asking.
The same two things already referred to, only now He put
the ultimate first, and the secret behind it. I chose you in
order to bear fruit, and in order that you may do so I chose
you to ask, and so to get into touch with God, that fruit
may abound.

Once more He repeated His command : " These things
I command you, that ye may love one another." If we really
love Him, we have fellowship with Him in suffering. " If

the world hateth you, ye know that it hath hated Me before
it hated you." The world loves its own, and hates that
which is not of itself and its own nature. Therefore it hates
Christ. So long as the world is of the world, living by the
philosophy of the world, conditioning life wholly within the
earthly, the materialistic order, it loves its own, its own people,
its own ways, and its own self-satisfaction. The world, so
mastered, is bound to hate Jesus Christ Who comes crashing
across everything in His first requirement, " If any man
would come after Me, let him deny himself, and take up his
cross daily, and follow Me." Therefore the world hates
Christ's people, that is, if they can see Christ in them. The
measure in which the world agrees with us and says we are
really a fine type of Christian, we are so entirely broad,
is the measure in which we are unlike Jesus Christ. Union
with Christ means fellowship with Him in suffering in this
world.

But He had something else to say. " But "—I am glad
that " But " is there, against that solemn passage. " But
when the Comforter is come, Whom I will send unto you
from the Father, even the Spirit of truth, which proceedeth
from the Father, He shall bear witness of Me ; and ye also
bear witness, because ye have been with Me from the
beginning." Thus the last thing He said was not merely
that we are to suffer in fellowship with Him, but we are to
witness in fellowship with the Holy Spirit. The chapter is
over. He had more to say to which we come in our next
meditation.

" I am the vine, the true." God's purposes are not failing.
They never have. They never will. His instruments have
failed almost continuously and disastrously ; but through
the ages, the " one unending purpose runs." Or in those
wonderful lines of Russell Lowell,

> " Standeth God within the shadow,
> Keeping watch above His own,"

not merely His own people, but His own purpose, His own

R [257]

passion, His own redeeming intention. "I am the vine,
ye are the branches," so fulfilling God's purpose in the world
of bearing fruit that will meet the world's hunger, and satisfy
its deepest necessity.

John xvi.

BETWEEN chapters fifteen and sixteen there should be no
break. It would seem that at the point which we reach in
verse sixteen in chapter sixteen, the Lord paused, and the
disciples are seen talking together, " They said one to another."
They were talking of their perplexity, perplexity concerning
that which Jesus had just said. After that conversation,
He, being aware of their difficulty, and what they were
enquiring, resumed, and replied to that enquiry. Again
the disciples spoke, this time not of perplexity, but affirming
their confidence in Him, " Now speakest Thou plainly . . .
now . . . we believe . . . Now we know." To this the
Lord replied in a very remarkable way. Not questioning
their confidence, He indicated to them that however confident
they were, they would break down ; ending everything with
that tremendous word, " I have overcome the world." At
that point His teaching ceased.

Let us begin with the sentences at the end of chapter
fifteen :

" When the Comforter is come, Whom I will send unto
you from the Father, even the Spirit of truth, which
proceedeth from the Father, He shall bear witness of Me ;
and ye also bear witness, because ye have been with Me
from the beginning."

These words followed immediately upon what He had told
them about the world's hostility. They were going out into
a hostile world, hostile because it was ignorant of God and
of Himself. Therefore He had told them of the coming

double witness in the world, which nevertheless would be
one witness, and the only witness capable of bringing conviction
to the world ; the witness of the Spirit, and the witness of
the Church. " He shall bear witness of Me ; and ye also
bear witness, because ye have been with Me from the
beginning." Now, in close connection He ran on, in these
sixteen verses.

First, having spoken of the fact that in the hostile world
this double witness would be borne by the Spirit and by the
Church, He showed the relation between the world and the
Spirit ; verses one to eleven. The world was in His mind,
the hostile world. God so loved the world that He had
given this Son of His love. If the world was hostile to Him,
He was not hostile to the world. He was about to die for it ;
and looking on to those days when these men would go out
into the hostile world, He had told them that the Spirit would
bear witness to the world, and they also.

He first shows that the world's hostility will be very
definite and very bitter. He said, The hour will come when
they will think they are doing God service when they kill
you. That was actually true in the case of these men, and of
the early Church ; the world thought it was serving God if
the witnesses going forth were slain.

Then He showed that the reason for the hostility was still
the world's darkness, " Because they have not known the
Father," and because they know not Me. That is still the
trouble with the world. The world is hostile to Christ. Why ?
Because it does not know God.

Then He showed them what their equipment would be for
going out into that hostile world. It was here that He made
that remarkable statement ; " It is expedient for you that
I go away." Look at that little group of men. In a little
while, they would all forsake Him, yet they were all loving
Him, all loyal to Him. The one terror filling their heart
was that of the apprehension of the future without Him.
And now He said, " It is expedient for you that I go away."

It is an arresting word, that word " expedient." It is an

interesting fact that it is the word Caiaphas had used about
His going. That superbly brilliant and damnable politician
had said to the Sanhedrim, " It is expedient . . . that one
man should die for the people, and that the whole nation
perish not." Caiaphas said more than he knew, when he said,
It is expedient that He die. Jesus was now close to the
Cross, with Caiaphas in the background ; and He now said
to this group, " It is expedient for you that I go." The
high line of politics, said Caiaphas, is that we get rid of Him.
The higher line of God's policy, said Jesus, is that I go. Thus
all the folly and wickedness of man is at last resolved into
the harmony of the Divine government and the Divine
authority. It is expedient, said the politician ; it is expedient,
said the King Redeemer.

Thus Jesus told these men that it was better, not only
better, it was best, the only right thing, that He should go.
But why ? " If I go not . . . the Comforter will not come."
It is better that I am not here. My going is a gain. My
going out of this relationship that I have borne to you is in
order to progress. This physical intimacy is a poor thing
compared to that which begins when the Comforter comes.

Then straightway He told them what that coming of the
Spirit would mean for the world. " He when He is come,
will convict the world," not *of* in spite of the translations,
but " in respect of," that is about, or concerning. The
witness of the Spirit in the world has to do with three things ;
sin, righteousness, judgment.

These are inter-related. Sin, the fact of failure all men
know, whatever name they give it. Righteousness as an
ideal is admitted if the fact of sin is recognized. If there is
no such thing as righteousness, there is no such thing as sin.
Judgment is the principle at work everywhere in human
thinking, which differentiates between right and wrong.

Said Jesus, When the Spirit is come, these are the things
He is going to deal with in the world, the things which
constitute the cardinal consciousness of every human being,
when that human being gives attention to its spiritual nature.

Then He told them what the Spirit would have to say concerning those things. "Of sin, because they believe not on Me." Jesus said in effect, My being in the world has created a new centre of sin, and given a new meaning to sin ; and the Spirit is coming to show the world that sin now, is rejection of Me. Sins are symptoms. Sin is a malady. Because of the coming of Jesus into the world, the sin which blights and blasts and may damn, is rejection of Him. All sins can be dealt with if men believe on Him.

The Spirit would also witness concerning righteousness. "Of righteousness, because I go unto the Father." Righteousness would now have a new interpretation, and a new potentiality, because He was going back to the Father. There was the Cross. That is the way He was going. It was in His mind all through these intimate conversations and discourses. He was going that way, and because of that, because He was going through to the Father, victorious, righteousness would be made possible.

And of judgment. The Spirit was coming to show to the world that this principle of discrimination had its central manifestation in the fact that the prince of this world was judged and condemned. In Me, said Jesus, there is the power that deals with sin. If men reject that, that is sin. In Me, said Jesus, is the power that enables for righteousness. I am going to the Father, and through Me righteousness has been set forth before the world. In Me, said Jesus, the fact of the condemnation of evil and the glorification of righteousness is seen.

At this point our Lord made this revealing statement,

"I have yet many things to say unto you, but ye cannot bear them now."

It was something said, as it were, in passing. He looked at them ; He had told them these things. He knew how frail they were, how faulty they were, how they were failing to apprehend His teaching. He understood it all, and yet with great tenderness He said, "I have yet many things to

say unto you, but ye cannot bear them now." A little earlier
He had said, " They shall put you out of the synagogues ;
yea, the hour cometh, that whosoever killeth you, shall
think that he offereth service unto God. These things will
they do, because they have not known the Father nor Me.
But these things I said not unto you at the beginning, because
I was with you." There were things Jesus did not tell them
at first. He did not tell them of the hostility that would
come. He never told them about His own Cross until He
had been with them three years. And now He was going,
and He said, " I have yet many things to say unto you,
but ye cannot bear them now." A wonderful principle is
revealed there, namely that He tells us things, reveals things
to us, as we are able to bear the revelation. I look back
over my life. Thank God that He did not tell me all about
it at the beginning. He teaches us, as we are able to bear.

Yes, but that is not all. " Howbeit." There are many
things that I have to say to you which at the moment you
are quite unable to bear. "Howbeit when He, the Spirit
of truth is come, He shall guide you into all the truth ; for
He shall not speak from Himself ; but what things soever
He shall hear, these shall He speak ; and He shall declare
unto you the things that are to come."

Do not exhaust that phrase, " the things that are to come,"
by making it a prophetic reference only. It is that, but it
is far more. Look at that group of men. When He left them,
they had very little idea how to proceed, except that they
must do so in the power of the Holy Spirit. All subsequent
unveilings to the Church of God as to methods of work and
service, have come by the growing interpretation of the Spirit.
" He shall show you things to come." In that word of Jesus
we find warrant for many things the Church of God, in the
line of true authority, and under the guidance of the Spirit,
has had to do in the running centuries, for which we have
no instructions in the words of Jesus.

He will guide you. A guide always means a pilgrimage,
and a guide always means a process. The whole Church of

God to-day has a fuller apprehension of truth than had those twelve men. The Spirit has been guiding us into the truth.

Finally in this regard, the whole mission of the Spirit is to glorify Me, said Jesus, by interpretation of the things of the Father which are all Mine. The world is hostile, but God so loved it that He gave His Son. The world is hostile because of its ignorance of God, and of His Son. Out into the world He sent His own, in partnership with the Spirit of God ; and the ministry of the Spirit in the world is to deal with the cardinal elements of spiritual consciousness ; sin, righteousness, and judgment, and relate them to Him. And about the disciples ? The Spirit needs them. It is through them the work must be done, and in order that they may do it, Jesus went as to bodily presence. The Spirit came to guide them into truth, to show them, all the way, things that are to come ; and that, in order that the Christ may be glorified ; and in the glorification of the Christ, the things which are the things of God, be revealed to the world. So the great allegory of the vine ended.

Then He said to them something that puzzled them, and what wonder. He said, " A little while, and ye behold Me no more ; and again a little while, and ye shall see Me." " Behold " and " see " are two different words in the Greek New Testament, as in ours. Ours do not quite convey the force of the difference. " A little while," and you will not be looking at Me as you are looking at Me now. That is what you are frightened at. In a little while I will be gone out of sight. That is your trouble. " Yet a little while . . . and ye shall see Me." If you are going to lose sight of Me in the way you have been accustomed to look at Me, you will see Me in a new way. It is expedient for you that I go, and in a very little while it will be so, I will not be here with you, to meet you on the shores of Galilee. You will not behold Me ; but in a little while you will see Me, see Me as you have never seen Me before.

Then the perplexed disciples talked to each other. They were very serious. What is this He is talking about : A little while, you will not behold Me, and a little while and you shall see Me. "We know not what He saith."

Then He told them explicitly what He meant. "A little while" was the little while of darkness into which they then were passing. "Verily, verily, I say unto you, that ye shall weep and lament." He was looking at the Cross, their weeping and lamenting, while the world would be rejoicing. The world will think when they have put Me on the Cross they have gotten rid of Me, and so will it seem to you. You will be weeping and sorrowful ; and the world will be glad.

Then the high, wondrous, beauteous declaration : "Ye shall be sorrowful, but your sorrow shall be turned into joy." Not after your sorrow you will obtain joy. No, the very sorrow, the very thing causing your sorrow will be transmuted into joy. The joy will come out of the sorrow. "Your sorrow shall be turned into joy."

In that connection He employed that fine, tender, exquisite illustration of a woman in travail, to interpret the sorrow in the hour to which they were going, and in the hour to which He was going. In effect He said ; Your sorrows will be birth-pangs, leading to life. A little while that you will not see Me, the little while of your darkness, and pain, and tears ; but that is going to be turned into your joy. He was telling them beforehand. I do not think they understood Him at the time, but I am sure they came to understand Him by and by.

Running on, in verses twenty-three to twenty-seven, we find these wonderful words, "In that day ye shall ask Me nothing." In this paragraph we have two Greek words both rendered "ask." This one means, In that day you shall ask Me no question. Why not ? Because the Paraclete will be there, guiding you into truth. I think there was an application here to the things that had been happening. They had been asking questions. Peter, "Whither goest Thou ?" Thomas, "We don't know where You are going, how can we know the way ?" Philip, "Show us the Father, and it sufficeth us." Jude, "What is come to pass that You are revealing Yourself to us, and not to the world ? " And now, what does He mean by a little while ? We do not know. He now said, When that day comes, the day that dawns with the coming of the Spirit, you will not ask Me questions. Why not ? You will have the Interpreter, the Spirit guiding you, leading you, teaching you. You will ask Me no question, because of the interpreting Paraclete.

In that day, moreover, you will find you have a new relationship with the Father. He said, I am not saying that I will ask the Father to do things for you, for you will ask Him yourselves. Notice two things here. You will ask in My name ; and the Father will give in My name.

Then in verse twenty-eight, completing everything, we have His summary of His whole mission, the mission of which they were to bear witness, the mission of which the Spirit will bear witness, the mission concerning which the world will gain the truth in the united witness of the Spirit and the Church.

Listen to the majesty of it. " I came out from the Father," Nativity and Incarnation ; " and am come into the world," all His mission, His teaching, His ministry ; " again, I leave the world," by the way of the passion, the Cross ; " and go unto the Father," the ascension and the return to the glory. " I came out from the Father," the Virgin Birth and Incarnation. I " am come into the world," His identification with humanity in its limitation, by His teaching, and mighty works, " He went about doing good." " I leave the world," I am going by the way of the Cross. I am going " to the Father," assurance of victory, and the ascension foreshadowed.

Then they said to Him, " Lo, now speakest Thou plainly, and speakest no proverb. Now know we that Thou knowest all things, and needest not that any man should ask Thee, by this we believe that Thou camest forth from God." It was a great word. Two things they said, Now we know, and now we believe ; and they were perfectly sincere ; and our Lord did not question their sincerity. He said, " Do ye now believe ? " The " now " there is different from their " now."

The Greek word indicates a crisis. He was not denying what they affirmed, but He was saying to the whole of them what He had said to Peter in the conversations in the upper room. He said to them in effect, Have you arrived so far? You will break down in spite of it. The knowledge that you have, and the belief that you have so far, will not be enough to hold you. " Do ye now believe ? " He knew their coming failure. " The hour cometh, yea, is come, that ye shall be scattered every man to his own," his own house, his own home, his own pursuits, his own affairs, anything you like ; " and shall leave Me alone." " Do ye now believe ? " Is that so ? That is not enough to hold you ; the hour is coming and it is right here, when you will all be scattered ; you will go to your own, you will leave Me alone ; and if I had none to depend on save you, I would be desolate. Yet I am not alone, the Father is with Me.

Then the final words. " These things have I spoken unto you, that in Me ye may have peace." I have spoken these things to you, things of comfort, and things of terror ; and the last thing is that you will all forsake Me. These things I have told you, " that . . . ye may have peace." Peace ? Yes, peace. There is no peace so fine to the human soul as the sense of realizing that He knows me, even the worst that is in me.

And then the great final word, " Be of good courage, I have overcome the world."

John xvii.

I WOULD ever be careful lest I should appear to differentiate between the value of one part of Holy Scripture and another, but no one will deny that when we come to this chapter we are at the centre of all the sanctities. The mission of our Lord on the earth was ended, completed. I emphasize that phrase " on the earth." In the fourth verse we hear Him saying, " I glorified Thee on the earth, having accomplished the work which Thou hast given Me to do." That is " on the earth." The greatest work yet remained. That was to be done by His lifting up out of the earth. His work on the earth level was already accomplished, completed ; and His converse with His own was consummated in the allegory of the vine. Now we are permitted to come into His presence as, under the very shadow of the Cross, He held communion with His Father ; and did so audibly, in the presence of our representatives, the first disciples. Who can doubt that the uttering of this great prayer at the close, while it was strictly communion with His Father, was uttered audibly for the sake of that group of men that were round about Him. They, through this prayer, and we through this self-same prayer, are permitted to come into the sanctity of the thinking of Jesus in the presence of His Father, immediately before His Cross.

The prayer moved on a very definite plane as is revealed in the words He employed with reference to it. Thrice over in verses nine, fifteen, and twenty, we find the words, " I pray." Once in verse twenty-four we find the word, " I will." These words reveal the plane upon which He prayed.

The word, thrice rendered " I pray," in our Version, has a marginal note, which says, " or make request of." Personally I do not like that marginal note, because the Greek verb He used there means literally, to interrogate. But etymology may often be insufficient for interpretation. The word in use describes a desire uttered in perfect fellowship with the one to whom it is expressed. This word for prayer often occurs in the New Testament, but it is never used of prayer except by John ; and he never uses it of any prayers other than the prayers of Jesus.

So that I would render it, " I desire." That may not be strictly correct etymologically, but I believe that it is strictly spiritual interpretation. He was talking to His Father.

He was not asking favours; but in communion, expressing the things upon which His heart was set. In the twenty-fourth verse the American revisers have rendered another word, " I desire," I think quite missing the mark. I much prefer there, the translation, " I will." The word there means, I determine. That is all technical, but it does introduce us to the atmosphere of the prayer. Our Lord was talking to His Father. He had said the last thing to the world. He had said the last thing to the group of men God had given Him out of the world. Now with these men in mind, and with the world in His heart, He was talking to His Father, expressing His desires, and His determination. So we are admitted into the heart of Jesus, and the mind of Jesus, and the will of Jesus, in those over-shadowed moments just before His Cross.

The movement of the communion is threefold. His expressed desires at first, concerned Himself. These are found in the first five verses. Then from verse six to nineteen He prayed for the men who were then about Him. At verse twenty we come to the final movement. He said, " Neither for these only do I pray, but for them also that believe on Me through their word." From there to the end, He was praying for His whole Church, for all who are Christians, all members of the Church of God. All who are members of the one Church of God are so because they have believed on Jesus through apostolic teaching, that is, through these men then gathered about Him, through their witness in speech and by writings.

So our blessed Lord is heard talking to His Father about Himself, about that group round about Him, and through them, looking on down the years that have multiplied into decades and centuries, and now nearly two millenniums, all the hosts who have believed on Him, thinking of them. Into the circle of His thinking, and of His passion, and of His desire, all His Church to the consummation passed as He prayed; Himself, His first messengers, apostles; and all the sacramental host. The plane of prayer was that of

expressing in communion, His desires and determination.
The subjects of prayer ; Himself, His first messengers, and
all who should believe on Him through their word. In the
first five verses which concerned Himself there were two
expressed desires. In verses six to nineteen, concerning the
men around Him, there were three expressed desires. In
verses twenty to twenty-six there were two desires, and one
determination expressed.

In the first five verses, two desires were expressed. What
were they ? Mark the arresting words with which He began :
" Father, the hour is come." All through John we have
found references to that hour. It began away back, when
talking to His Mother at Cana He said, " Mine hour is not
yet come." Now He said, " Father, the hour is come." To
this hour He had been looking forward from the beginning ;
for it, He had been preparing in all His teaching, and all
His doing ; it was this hour which had constituted the
underlying passion, urge of His life. " Father, the hour
is come." In the presence of that consciousness, He expressed
two desires for Himself. The first is contained in the early
verses, " Glorify Thy Son, that the Son may glorify Thee ;
even as Thou gavest Him authority over all flesh, that whatsoever Thou hast given Him, to them He should give eternal
life. And this is life eternal, that they should know Thee
the only true God, and Him Whom Thou didst send, even
Jesus Christ. I glorified Thee on the earth, having
accomplished the work which Thou hast given Me to do."

What is the desire ? " Glorify Thy Son, that the Son may
glorify Thee." He did not say, Glorify Me that I may glorify
Thee. Of course that is what is meant, but the very method
of statement is significant. It was not personal, but relative.
He was thinking of Himself in His intimate relationship with
His Father, " Thy Son . . . the Son." Whereas the prayer
is personal, as we have said, the first expressed desire
maintains His sense of relationship, and all which that meant
at that hour. " The hour is come ; glorify Thy Son, that
the Son may glorify Thee." He was expressing His desire

[269]

that the Son might be glorified. What for ? That the Son may glorify the Father. The deepest passion of His heart was the glory of God. The deepest passion of the heart of Jesus was not the saving of men, but the glory of God ; and then the saving of men, because that is for the glory of God.

How that applied to Himself is discovered as we read on. " Even as." That phrase introduces us to interpretation. " Even as Thou gavest Him authority over all flesh, that whatsoever Thou hast given Him, to them He should give eternal life." Glorify Thy Son, that He may glorify Thee, even as Thou hast given Him authority to give eternal life.

How had God given Him that authority ? What does He mean by that " as " ? In the tenth chapter we hear Him say, " Therefore doth the Father love Me, because I lay down My life, that I may take it again. No one taketh it away from Me, but I lay it down of Myself. I have authority to lay it down, and I have authority to take it again. This commandment received I from My Father." The authority to lay down His life that He might take it again, was in order to place it at the disposal of men. Now He said, " Father, the hour is come ; glorify Thy Son, that the Son may glorify Thee, even as Thou gavest Him authority . . . to give eternal life." He was praying for the Cross, the glory of the Cross. Here we miss the whole thinking and heart of Jesus if we imagine that at that moment He was first of all desiring the glory of which He had divested Himself when He came into time and human condition. He was desiring the Cross, because by the way of the Cross, and by the way of the Cross alone, He would put life at the disposal of humanity, according to the purpose of His Father. It was the desire of a great consent. In the twelfth chapter we heard Him say, " The hour is come that the Son of man should be glorified " ; and then, " Now is My soul troubled ; and what shall I say ? Father, save Me from this hour ? " He did not say that ; He said, " Father, glorify Thy name." Now, right on the margin of the hour, He was still assenting, consenting to the Cross, and saying to His Father that the first, surging, urging, passionate desire of His soul was the Cross. God crowned Him with glory and honour that He might taste death for every man, said an apostolic writer. He had done all that led up to the hour, finished, accomplished everything on the earth level. Now, said He, " Father, glorify Thy Son, that Thy Son may glorify Thee."

Then we reach His second desire in verse five. " And now, O Father, glorify Thou Me with Thine own Self, with the glory which I had with Thee before the world was." He does not now say, the Son, that relative description. It is now personal, " Glorify Thou *Me* . . . with the glory *I* had with Thee before the world was." Now He was expressing His desire for return to that of which He emptied Himself when He became a Servant, and was made in the likeness of men ; and being found in fashion as a man, became obedient unto death, even the death of the Cross. But the desire of Jesus for return to the glory of which He had divested Himself, was only a desire that He might reach it by the way of the Cross. When next we sing,

" In the Cross of Christ I glory "

let us remember that was the mind of Jesus Himself, as He went to it. The glory of the Cross ! The shadows were gathering. Presently He crossed the winter-torrent of the Cedars into Gethsemane. Then all the darkness of the Cross enveloped Him ; but even there He said, " Nevertheless not as I will, but as Thou wilt." There was never a moment's deflection from the doing of the Father's will, even though in the presence of the gathering storm there was a shrinking. Here as He talked to His Father, His desires for Himself were, first the Cross, and then the glory which comes out of the Cross. As though He had said,—let me say it softly ; there are some things it is so hard to say because they refer to matters which defy speech,—My Father, I emptied Myself to come to this level. I never want to come back except by the way that accomplishes the purpose for which I came. Glorify Thy Son by the Cross. Then give Me again the glory I had, but by that way, and by none other.

Then at verse six He began to pray for the men about Him. He first referred to the work He had already done with them. He said, " I have manifested Thy name " to them. What name ? God has only one name according to the Biblical revelation. God, is not a name. It is a designation. The Lord is not a name ; it is a title. He has only one name, and His name is Yahweh—Jehovah as we now render it. Jesus had borne that name, linked with the thought of salvation ; Jesus the Greek for Jehoshua, Jehovah-salvation, merged into one. " I have manifested Thy name." That first group of men, as Hebrews, knew that God had one name. God had said, This is My name, My memorial name to all generations. Now said Jesus, " I have manifested Thy name " to them. I have interpreted the meaning of the prophetic name that Thou didst take for Thyself in the long ago. " I have manifested Thy name unto the men Thou gavest Me." These men had by no means understood all He had said to them, or revealed to them ; but they did know, as He said, what He said was the Word of God, and that He was from God.

For these men He expressed three desires ; " Keep them in Thy name . . . that they may be one, even as We are " ; " Keep them from the evil " ; " Sanctify them in the truth." Of these the first is inclusive, while the second two interpret. The one desire for them was : " Keep them in Thy name . . . that they may be one, even as We." The two show how that will be done : " Keep them from the evil," " Sanctify them in the truth."

In this connection occurred those arresting words, " I pray not for the world, but for those which Thou hast given Me." When we read that, at first it appears that Jude was warranted in what he had said in the upper room to the Lord, " What is come to pass that Thou art manifesting Thyself to us and not unto the world ? " It looked to Jude for the moment when

[272]

he asked the question as though our Lord was abandoning
the world. Now Jude heard Him pray, and the rest heard
Him pray, and they heard Him say this thing, " I pray not
for the world." I read that for years, and did not like it.
It did not seem as though Jesus would give the world up.
Yet He said " I pray not for the world." Presently, however,
we hear Him say, " That the world may believe . . . that
the world may know." He had not forgotten the world.
The world was on His heart, for He was in union with the
God Who so loved the world that He gave His Son. What
then did He mean ? Simply this : In order that I may reach
the world, I am not for the moment praying for the world,
but for those through whom I am going to reach the world.
He was praying for the instrument He was creating, through
which He would reach the world.   If this instrument, that is,
this company of men, multiplied as they will be down the
running ages, if this instrument is to bring belief and knowledge
to the world concerning God, then " Keep them in Thy name,
that they may be one, as We are one."

" As We are one." First of all, that is vital and essential
oneness. He was one with the Father vitally and essentially.
Now He prayed that these, kept in His name, may be one
in that way ; having a vital relationship. Not the oneness
of sentiment or intellectual opinion, but the oneness that is
living. One in life, therefore one in light, and therefore one
in love. He and the Father were one in essential life. He
and the Father were one intellectually in all light and understanding. He and the Father were one in love. Keep them
there ; keep them in the name I have revealed, and manifested
to them. Keep them there, that they may be one as We ;
one in life, one in light, one in love.

Said He, continuing, " I pray not that Thou shouldest
take them out of the world." Their business is in the world.
" I pray . . . that Thou shouldest keep them from the evil."
But how ? " Sanctify them," separate them through Thy
truth " ; and then that there might be no mistaking in the
lengthening years, He said, " Thy Word is truth."

S   [273]

This desire for that first group of men applies equally to us all. To the world we are sent, the world as we have seen, hostile, gathering its forces to put Him on His bitter Cross; the world hating Him. But there is He, loving the world. He was not praying for it, at the moment, but He was praying on its behalf, for the men who were to go out into it with His messages, and His witnesses; praying for all such that they might be one, that they might be kept from the evil, and sanctified in the truth.

So we pass. "Neither for these only do I pray, but for them also that believe on Me through their word." Here for His whole Church He expressed two desires, and one determination. The first desire was "That they all may be one," not only that first group, but the continuity of believing souls through their ministry, that they all may be one, in the same way. What for? "That the world may believe." We have often quoted that, and I think perhaps permissibly, in order to show that if Christianity is divided up into all sorts of sections, we cannot expect the world to believe. I am quite sure that the division of Christendom into sects and parties has hindered, when the divisions have created bitterness and separation in spirit. The main thought again, however, is that of being one in vital relationship with each other, because having vital relationship with the Father and the Son. One, that is, in life and light and love. It is the unity, and manifestation of life and light and love according to the Divine, that brings conviction and belief in the world.

Then there is a slight change in the next expression. "That they may be perfected into one." There is the recognition of a process, the recognition of the fact that the ultimate unity may be postponed in realization; but the desire is that at last it shall come to consummation. What for? "That the world may know." That is something beyond belief. Here I think He was looking through to that hour, which has not yet arrived, to the great consummation, in which the unity of the Spirit, the unity of all believers with God and with Christ, is completely manifested. In that hour the world will not believe merely ; it will know, when Christ shall come to be glorified in His saints to perfection.

Then we have the final " I will," I determine. This is My will, this is My determination, this is My decision. That " where I am, they also may be with Me ; that they may behold My glory." Where was that ? Go back to what He was saying about Himself. He was going to the Cross, and through the Cross to the glory. My determination, My will concerning My own is that they shall have fellowship with Me, in the glory of the Cross, and so in the glory that results from the Cross. In time, with Me by the way of the Cross and in the Cross, in the ages to come, with Me for ever in the glory that is yet to be revealed.

So, our blessed Lord approaching the hour, talked to His Father. Were these prayers of Jesus answered ? As to Himself ? Yes, He went to the Cross ; He returned to the glory. As to His own ? Yes, except, as He said, in the case of the son of perdition. The requests were progressive, but they were kept in the name, kept from the evil, sanctified in the truth. As to His Church in the widest outlook ? Yes ; in the Divine economy the Church is one. The measure of our failure has been the measure of our failure to recognize the fact of unity. The belief of the world has been the result of the answering of these desires of Jesus, and that determination. The knowledge of the world will be the final issue.

There is another way of approach to this chapter. It is to ponder it alone ; and to say, How far am I a member of that one Church for which He prayed, as He prayed I might be ?

John xviii. 1-27.

THIS is the first of our last seven studies in the Gospel according to John. The seven of them will deal with the final section of John's writing from the standpoint of his own scheme. Now everything is climacteric. Chapters eighteen, nineteen, twenty, and twenty-one give us the story of the ultimate Sign. As we have followed the narrative along the line of our Lord's public ministry, we have seen sixteen signs, eight of them in the realm of works, eight of them in the realm of words.

Now we reach what I have already described as the ultimate Sign. For the interpretation of that designation we go back to chapter two, where we have the account of our Lord going up to Jerusalem, and cleansing the Temple. In connection with that He was challenged, " What sign showest Thou unto us, seeing that Thou doest these things ? " They asked Him for a sign that would demonstrate His authority for the things He was doing. To that He replied in what to them must have been mysterious language. John tells us immediately after recording His answer, that the disciples did not understand Him then, but they came to understand Him afterwards. He said, " Destroy this temple, and in three days I will raise it up." On another occasion, not recorded by John, Jesus said, " An evil and adulterous generation seeketh after a sign ; and there shall no sign be given to it but the sign of Jonah the prophet ; for as Jonah was three days and three nights in the belly of the fish ; so shall the Son of man be three days and three nights in the heart of the earth." On both these occasions our Lord declared that the only sign which would completely and finally reveal Him and the secret of His authority, would be that to which He referred at first as their destroying of the temple which He would raise ; and on the other occasion, taking the similitude of Jonah's story, declaring that He would be three days and three nights in the heart of the earth. In other words, our Lord declared at the beginning, and again on one definite occasion at least, that the ultimate sign of His authority would be His death and His resurrection. He named the two things which, in their merging, would constitute the sign, the ultimate sign, the dissolution of the temple of His body at the hands of His enemies ; and His raising of it again. Death and resurrection.

These last four chapters then, eighteen to twenty-one, have to do with these two things. It may be well to survey the whole scheme. In the first eleven verses of chapter eighteen we have the prelude, the story of the garden and the betrayal. Beginning at the twelfth verse of chapter eighteen, and running over to the sixteenth verse of chapter nineteen, we have the account of two trials, the religious and the political; before the priests and before Pilate. In chapter nineteen, in a few verses, seventeen to thirty-seven, we have the story of the crucifixion. In what remains of the chapter, beginning at the thirty-eighth verse, and running through the forty-second, a very brief paragraph, we have the story of the burial of the dead body of Jesus. Then in chapters twenty and twenty-one we see the risen Jesus.

In these first twenty-seven verses of chapter eighteen we have two movements; first the betrayal in the garden; and then, the trial before the priests.

How then do we see our Lord in this story of the garden? There are two things that are supremely evident; first His majesty, and then His meekness.

Let us look first at the things that mark His majesty. John is careful to tell us where this took place, and that in an arresting and beautiful way. "When Jesus had spoken these words, He went forth with His disciples over the winter torrent of the Cedars, where was a garden, into which He entered." Mark that word "entered." It was undoubtedly a private garden, into which Jesus had the right of entry. It was not a public place.

"Now Judas also, which betrayed Him, knew the place." It is possible to be familiar with the Most Holy Places, and do the most damnable deeds. He knew the place. "For Jesus ofttimes resorted thither with His disciples." That is to say that Jesus often gathered there with His disciples. Thus it was familiar ground to which He went.

It is evident then that when our Lord had ended His prayer, He did not hide. He went to a place where He knew Judas could find Him. With majesty He was moving forward.

He had ordered Judas, a little while before, to be quick about the business, when He said to him in the upper room, " That thou doest, do quickly." Then Jesus, when He had done with the group round about Him, went to the garden, knowing that Judas knew where He was going.

" Judas then, having received the band of soldiers," that is a cohort, a whole company of Roman soldiers. His enemies were determined to settle the business for ever. Their obtaining of a cohort undoubtedly suggested that they anticipated trouble in the arrest of Jesus. They took with them also " officers from the chief priests," that is, the Temple police. John names " the chief priests and the Pharisees." The chief priests were not Pharisees; they were Sadducees. Thus two bitterly opposed parties, theologically and politically, were united in their determination to put an end to Jesus. They came " with lanterns and torches and weapons " notwithstanding the fact that the paschal moon was riding high in the heavens. They thought He might be lurking and hiding somewhere, and might offer resistance.

Now mark the majesty of these next four verses. " Jesus therefore, knowing all the things that were coming upon Him, went forth." That statement is full of significance, bearing out and emphasizing the fact that the pathway of Jesus to His Cross was not the pathway of a Victim. All the way He knew all that was coming to Him. Perfectly familiar with it all, He " went forth," went forth in majesty, never more majestic than when His eyes were set upon His Cross.

This statement that " He went forth " means that He left the garden. He went forth from it. He went outside.

There and then happened a remarkable thing, which was a supreme evidence of His majesty. He faced them. He said, " Whom seek ye ? " They said, " Jesus the Nazarene." He then said, " I am." Our versions render it " I am He." Quite literally He simply said, " I am." When He did so, a cohort of Roman soldiers, the Temple police, the rulers themselves, Judas guiding them, went backwards and fell to the ground. Some burst of majesty halted them. There may have been the emerging of something we cannot interpret, a flaming of glory. I think rather that something in the mien of Jesus as He stood confronting His enemies caused their shrinking and fall. They could not lay a hand on Him. Right to the very margin He revealed the fact referred to again and again, as we have seen in the process of the Gospel, that no man could lay hands upon Him until His hour was come. His hour had now come, but even now, all the cohort and the police of the Temple and the elders were powerless of themselves to lay any hand on Him. "I am," He said, and they went backwards, and fell. Thus the majesty of Jesus was revealed.

Then He said to them a second time, "Whom seek ye?" And they repeated themselves, "Jesus the Nazarene." Said He, "I told you that I am; if therefore ye seek Me, let these go their way." A beautiful merging of His mercy and of His majesty. He knew perfectly well that if they were arrested, they would all break down even more swiftly and terribly. So He said, Let them go; take Me alone.

Then Simon drew his sword and struck a blow for Jesus. I like Simon. He had got something in him. I know it was wrong. It was honest zeal, but it was zeal without knowledge. The other evangelists record that the last act of supernatural and Divine surgery wrought by Jesus was rendered necessary by the blundering zeal of a disciple. I sometimes think that our Lord is still often healing wounds that zeal-without-knowledge people make on other souls. What said our Lord? "Put up the sword into the sheath; the cup which the Father hath given Me, shall I not drink it?" That was zeal with knowledge. Simon did not understand, and struck a blow. It was a poor blow. When a man unsheathes his sword, and aims at a man's head, and only gets his ear, it is a poor business. It was zeal, but he was nervous when he struck that blow.

That is not the way, said Jesus. "The cup which the Father hath given Me, shall I not drink it?" And so

Gethsemane is seen in John, although he does not tell the story. From other evangelists we know He had been talking to His Father about the cup. " If it be possible, let this cup pass away from Me ; nevertheless, not as I will, but as Thou wilt." There was shrinking, and yet complete fellowship with His Father's will. Now, John shows the result of that. " The cup that the Father hath given Me, shall I not drink it ? " Simon's was zeal without knowledge. That of Jesus was zeal with knowledge,—" the zeal of Thine house hath eaten Me up " said the prophetic writing long before, knowing all that was coming upon Him. This cup that I am pressing to My lips, so potent and so bitter, that no human soul will ever understand it, shall I not drink it ? This was the word of an ultimate majesty, and the revelation of complete meekness.

Then they bound Him. I never read it without laughing. Yes they bound Him, and see how many it took to do it ; the band, and the council, and the chief captain, he is specially named, and all the police. They rushed at Him, and they bound Him. *They* bound *Him ?* They thought they bound Him. What did bind Him ? Love for me ! Love for you ! That was what bound Him ; not the hempen cords of those foolish men, but the eternal cords of the Divine Love.

Still they bound Him, and they took Him to Annas. John only gives an account of the arraignment of Jesus before Annas, which was quite a preliminary matter. He tells us in the twenty-fourth verse that Annas bound Him again, and sent Him to Caiaphas. John omits entirely the account of our Lord's examination before Caiaphas and the Sanhedrim, recorded by Matthew and Mark. At verse twenty-eight we read, " They led Jesus therefore from Caiaphas into the palace." Thus omitting the appearing before Caiaphas, and the Sanhedrim, John gives the story of the preliminary arraignment of Jesus.

In many ways Annas was one of the most remarkable personalities flung up in Judaism at that time. Five of his sons occupied the high-priestly office. In the line of succession,

Annas should have been high priest, but on some political ground, Rome objected to him, but consented that Caiaphas his son-in-law should be appointed. Annas probably was not eager to occupy the position of high priest. He was making money too fast. He had become one of the wealthiest men of the time by extortion. He had retained, some believe, his position as president of the Sanhedrim. At any rate he was so much in power, that when they arrested Jesus, they took Him first to the house of Annas.

Two of the disciples of Jesus went as far as that house. One of them went into the court, that is, the open space in front of Annas' house. That one unquestionably was John the writer of the story. The other was Peter. The rest of the disciples seem by now to have gone. John went right in. Peter halted at the gate, and stood outside. It is at least suggestive that the man who went right in was not molested. The molestation of Peter began as he halted outside. John seems to have felt that his co-apostle was in danger, for when he got in, he remembered Peter was outside, and went to the door, and spoke to the girl in charge of the door, and she let Peter in.

I wonder why John told us it was cold that night. At that season of the year, the nights were hardly ever cold. But John says it was cold that night. I wonder if it was not the chill of fear, dread, apprehension : of the things that were happening. Peter was cold, and he stopped to warm himself at a fire built by the enemies of Jesus. A very dangerous thing to do. If any try to get warmth from fires built by His enemies, they are in danger.

The formal interrogatory before Annas was brief. Annas asked Him concerning His disciples and His teaching. It is self-evident that he was hoping to get our Lord to declare Himself, His ideals and His purposes and His teaching, and to name His disciples, and show how far they were infected or affected by His teaching. He was looking for something upon which he could fasten, in order to prefer a charge against Jesus, which would bring Him within the power of the authorities who could deal with Him, and put Him to death. This was not an enquirer, wanting to know. This was an enemy, hoping there in the flush of the morning to bring Jesus within the grip of the government. The question was probably most courteously asked. In effect, Annas said, Tell us what is it all about? What is Your teaching? And what are You and Your disciples attempting to do?

Our Lord answered in majesty and in anger. There is no question about the anger in this. That is proven by the action of the officer who struck Him. It was the tone in which He spoke which provoked the act. In what He said, the emphasis was on the personal pronoun. The " I " is emphatic. " *I* have spoken openly to the world; *I* ever taught in the synagogues, and in the Temple, where all the Jews come together; and in secret spake *I* nothing." The declaration was a contrast between His method, and that of His enemies. A secret plotting against Him had been going forward, of which He was aware. He said, Why do you ask? You know. Or, if you do want to know, ask these who are all round about Me. I have spoken in public, I have spoken openly; I have not been having secret meetings; I have not been plotting against any earthly government. All I have done is in the open. Because of the anger manifest in this reply an officer said, " Answerest Thou the high priest so? " Mark the " so." He was rebuking Annas, and the officer smote Him. He did not answer the officer concerning the method of His speech, but, again referring to all His teaching, all that which He said had been spoken openly, He said, " If I have spoken evil, bear witness of the evil; but if well, why smitest thou Me? "

It was over. Annas had no more to say. The next thing was to bind Him again, and to send Him to Caiaphas.

Simon Peter was still standing there, warming himself, and they came to him again. The first denial had taken place when a saucy servant maid had taunted him. Now they came again, asking him, " Art thou also one of His disciples? " He denied. But " one of the servants of the high priest, being a kinsman of him whose ear Peter cut off, saith, Did not I see thee in the garden with Him ? " Peter denied again. John did not tell us about the cursing and swearing. That was recorded by others, especially in the story of Mark, for which Peter himself was responsible. John tells us of the tragedy, he " denied again ; and straightway the cock crew." Neither does he tell about the look of Jesus. He leaves it there. It is a tragic story. Zeal without knowledge struck a blow, and then weakened, wavered, and three times over, before the flush of morning was upon the sky, said, he did not know Him, did not belong to Him. I read it with fear. " Let him that thinketh he standeth, take heed, lest he fall."

John xviii. 28-xix. 16.

As we saw in our last meditation, John gives us the account of our Lord's arraignment before Annas, and tells that Annas sent Him bound to Caiaphas. He omits altogether the story of the examination before Caiaphas and the Sanhedrim, and resumes at the point where they sent Him to Pilate, after the Sanhedrim had sentenced Him to death. " They led Jesus therefore from Caiaphas into the palace."

This is a most graphic story. The scene is the Praetorium, which undoubtedly was the residence of Pilate, and there he held court. As we read, we find the scene alternating between the outside and the inside of the Praetorium. There are seven movements. The first things recorded took place outside, and are recorded in verses twenty-eight to thirty-two of chapter eighteen. In verses thirty-two to the first sentence in verse thirty-eight we are inside. From the rest of verse thirty-eight to forty we are outside. In the nineteenth chapter in the first three verses we are inside. In verses four to seven we are outside. In verses eight to eleven we are inside. In

verses **twelve** to sixteen we are outside. The whole story is
that of Jesus and Pilate, with a background of priests and
rulers and a rabble. Here we have the Gentile world as
represented in the person of Pilate, confronting Jesus. Pilate
was the embodiment of the Roman Empire ; all its might
and all its majesty were vested in him as an executive. All
the way through the question about Jesus is a question of
Kingship. Everything revolves around that. Three times
over Pilate went inside the Praetorium, taking Jesus with
him, leaving the crowd outside. These two are seen confronting each other. The priestly trials were over, the
arraignment before Annas, and the examination before
Caiaphas and the Sanhedrim. Religion had decided to kill
Jesus, and now the civil trial goes forward. We see Jesus
no longer in the presence of religion, but of government.

The first movement, outside the Praetorium, is revealed
in verses twenty-eight to thirty-two. In that first movement
Pilate put an official question to the men who brought Jesus
to him. They had made up their minds that Jesus must
die. That is why they brought Him to Pilate. They were
anxious that they should not be ritually defiled, so as to
prevent them eating the Passover. Therefore they did not
enter the Praetorium. Jesus had spoken of straining at a
gnat, and swallowing a camel. That is what they were
doing. Pilate's question was in legal form. These Jewish
rulers had brought a prisoner before him. His was the
official court of appeal in all these matters. He represented
the Roman Empire, and he asked them, " What accusation
bring ye against this Man ? " Sometimes it is possible to
discover the tone in which a question is asked by the answer
that is given to it. So here. They replied, " If this Man were
not an evil-doer we should not have delivered Him up unto
thee." What made them say that ? Pilate had a perfect
right to ask. Their reply shows that the question was one
of contempt and scorn for them. As though he had said,
What now ? What accusation do you bring against this
Man ? What is the meaning of this coming to me ? He had

not yet come face to face with Jesus. That was the spirit
of Pilate as he met them. This cold, dispassionate Roman
procurator, a remarkable personality, a freed slave, rising
to a position of power through the influence of the emperor's
mother and wife, was impatient with these priests and rulers,
and this troublesome mob of Jews. Angrily they replied,
" If this Man were not an evil-doer, if He were not a malefactor,
we should not have delivered Him up unto thee. "

Pilate therefore said, " Take Him yourselves, and judge
Him according to your law." In other words, he refused to
consider the accusation ; he refused to take the case.

Then the Jews said, " It is not lawful for us to put any
man to death." Pilate saw at once that the thing was more
serious than he had understood. He discovered that what
they sought was not an investigation, but a sentence, that
they had brought Jesus there, determined upon His death.
They would not have brought Him there had they not themselves at the time been deprived of the power to inflict the
death penalty. They had gone as far as they could. They
had had their interrogatory in the house of Annas, and
before Caiaphas and the Sanhedrim. They considered Him
to be worthy of death ; and now they came to Pilate because,
while they could pronounce a sentence, they could not carry
it into effect. Pilate thus discovered that these people had
not come to him to investigate an accusation, but to promul-
gate a sentence.

The second movement in verses thirty-three to thirty-
eight took place inside. The priests and the crowd were left
out. " Pilate therefore entered again into the Praetorium,
and called Jesus, and said unto Him, Art Thou the King of
the Jews ? " While it was an interrogation, the form of the
sentence in the Greek is arresting. " Thou art the King of
the Jews ? " The emphatic word is " Thou," and is placed
first, as Pilate said it. He said, " *Thou* art the King of the
Jews ? " Quite evidently he knew the accusation they were
bringing against Him, although he had asked them for an
official statement of it. Matthew, Mark, Luke, and John all

tell us that these were the first words of Pilate to Jesus. Face to face with Him inside the Praetorium, the whole emphasis of his question is on the "Thou." There was a touch of scorn in the question. "Jesus answered, Sayest thou this of thyself, or did others tell it thee concerning Me?" Have you already had that judgment from others, or is your question the result of your own wondering? A tremendously searching question. Is that the result of your own thinking, or are you repeating what someone else has said? Pilate found himself face to face with Someone he had probably never met before, and certainly a personality such as he had never known before. He answered Him angrily: "Am I a Jew? Thine own nation and the chief priests delivered Thee unto me." Then he said this amazing thing, "What hast Thou done?" Having manifested scorn in his first question, Jesus had asked him the question that had searched him, and he was angry. Yet this Roman judge did that most unusual thing, he asked the prisoner to give him the reason for His being there. "What hast Thou done?"

"Jesus answered, My Kingdom is not of this world; if My Kingdom were of this world, then would My servants fight, that I should not be delivered to the Jews; but now is My Kingdom not from hence." What an amazing reply. The judge was asking what He was there for, what had He done, and He answered Pilate, representing the Roman Empire, and what He said concerned His Kingdom. He spoke of "My Kingdom," and the emphatic word in the Greek throughout is the pronoun "My." "*My* Kingdom is not of this world; if *My* Kingdom were of this world, then would *My* servants fight." The word He used of His disciples was arresting and suggestive. It is the only place in the New Testament where that word is applied to the followers of Jesus Christ. It is a word suggesting dignity, those holding office within a Kingdom. This was the voice of the King. The Prisoner, confronting Pilate, the embodiment of the Roman Empire, and representative of the Gentile world, when asked why He was there as a Prisoner, did not answer, but talked about His Kingdom, and told this man who represented the kingdom wholly of this world, depending for its authority upon the mailed fist, upon soldiers, cohorts, and armies, that His Kingdom was not of this world. If it were, said He, My officers, My statesmen would fight. My Kingdom is not from hence. It is not built up by the world, nor by worldly methods.

There are senses in which this reply of Jesus does not seem relevant to what Pilate was doing ; but it had a relevancy to the Divine over-ruling, of all Pilate was doing. " My Kingdom is not of this world." " Pilate therefore said unto Him, Art Thou a King then ? " Are you admitting that You are a King ? I asked You if You were King of the Jews, and You gave me no direct answer. " Art Thou a King then ? "

" Jesus answered, Thou sayest that I am a King." Thou sayest that which I am, a King. He definitely thus claimed Kingship. Then He told Pilate the nature of His Kingdom. " To this end have I been born, and to this end am I come into the world, that I should bear witness unto the truth. Everyone that is of the truth heareth My voice." His Kingdom is the Kingdom of truth. He came into the world to bear witness to the truth. If once the truth triumphed in human life and history there would be no problems left for us to solve at Geneva or London, or anywhere else ! Rudyard Kipling speaks of God somewhere, and says of Him that He is " the God of things as they are." So He is ; that is to say, He is the God of truth. Paul in writing to Timothy said that He " witnessed a good confession " before Pilate. That confession was marked by this strange, mystic dignity, claiming Kingship, not of the world ; but in the realm of truth.

Then Pilate looked at Him and said, " What is truth ? " He was arrested now. He had heard things he had never heard before. He knew much about empire on a worldly basis, an empire governed by force. But here was One, a Prisoner, claiming to be a King, and that in the realm of truth. And so he said, " What is truth ? " I do not agree with Bacon in his great essay on Truth, when he begins by saying, " ' What is truth ? ' said the jesting Pilate, and did not wait for a reply." Pilate was not jesting. Pilate never felt less like jesting than he did that day. Here suddenly brought face to face with something startling, he said, " What is truth ? " I think that probably there was cynicism in the enquiry, concerning the world in which he lived. It was as though he had said, Truth ! What is it ? He was not denying that there is such a thing as truth ; but he was saying in effect, If that is the nature of Your Kingdom, You have not much chance of realization in a world like this. " What is truth ? "

Then he again went out. The account is in verses thirty-eight, the second part, to verse forty. John again has condensed into very brief words this story. We have it far more particularly in the other evangelists, but he gives enough for his purpose. When Pilate went out, he pronounced the official sentence of acquittal. What he said was the official sentence of a Roman judge, acquitting the prisoner—Not guilty ! would be our formula. He went out and said, " I find no crime in Him," then suggested that he should release Him.

But evidently they were ready. They cried out, " Not this man, but Barabbas." From the other evangelists we learn that He was wont to release a prisoner to them at that season of the year. They were allowed freedom of choice, a prisoner, whom *they* would. But now he had limited their choice. He had offered them a choice between Barabbas and Jesus. As though he had said : It is a custom for you to ask from me the freedom of any prisoner. On this occasion you much choose between this Man and Barabbas. They cried for Barabbas.

The next section is in the first three verses of chapter nineteen. Again the happening was inside. Here we are in the presence of something that is appallingly wicked. The judge had pronounced Him not guilty, had suggested that He go free, but when they chose Barabbas, he did a dastardly thing. He took Him back into the Praetorium, and he handed

Him over to scourging. The law provided that he stand by
when the scourging was done. What was he doing ? I have
no hesitation in saying that he was making a concession to
the clamour outside, in the hope that that would satisfy them.
He was trying not to put Jesus to death, in spite of the
clamour. So he did the most illegal thing, the most dastardly
thing, gave a Prisoner to scourging Whom he had acquitted.

In verses four to seven, the scene is again outside. " Pilate
went out again, and saith unto them." He went out by
himself, and said : " Behold, I bring Him out to you, that
ye may know that I find no crime in Him." Then Jesus
" came forth, wearing the crown of thorns, and the purple
garment. And Pilate saith unto them, Behold, the Man ! "
What was Pilate doing ? He had violated all justice in having
Him scourged, and yet down in the heart and mind of him
was the hope that the scourged and lacerated and thorn-
crowned and bruised and bleeding Man would appeal to their
pity. He said, " Behold, I bring Him out to you," I bring
Him forth to you, knowing that I have acquitted Him ; but
behold the Man. As they looked at Him, the chief priests
and the officers cried out, " Crucify, crucify."

Pilate said, " Take Him yourselves, and crucify Him ; for
I find no crime in Him." Again he refused to put Him to
death. He said, Take Him yourselves, and crucify Him,
knowing perfectly well they could not do it. He was mocking
them. And again I think he thought he had found a way out.
Then immediately they said something else. " We have a
law, and by that law He ought to die, because He made
Himself the Son of God." At last they have told the truth.
He had claimed to be the Son of God, and that had been their
quarrel with Him all through, but they had never raised it in
connection with His trial before Pilate until then. Now,
driven to desperation, they told this pagan Roman—for whom
they had no respect, but whom they would get on their side
for the death sentence,—the underlying reason of their
hostility. He had claimed to be the Son of God. It was a
clever stroke on their part, and it had its effect.

The next section from verse eight to verse eleven takes us inside once more. "When Pilate therefore heard this saying, he was the more afraid, and he entered into the palace again." He went in and took Jesus with him. "He saith unto Jesus, Whence art Thou?" As though he had said, What do these men mean by saying Thou art the Son of God? If ever a man was sore perplexed and tempest-tossed, Pilate was. "Jesus gave him no answer," a most remarkable statement. The question was of fear, resulting from this declaration of the Jews, and Jesus gave no answer.

Then, "Pilate therefore saith unto Him, Speakest Thou not unto me? knowest Thou not that I have authority to release Thee, and have authority to crucify Thee?" He was telling the truth on the human level. The priests had not. He had. The right of life and death was vested in him. The answer of Jesus was, "Thou wouldest have no authority against Me, except it were given thee from above; therefore he that delivered Me unto thee hath greater sin." He was revealing His sense of the authority that rises higher than the throne of the Caesars, or any other; that all authority in the last analysis is in God. He was reminding this procurator that he had no authority except that which was derived. Moreover He apportioned guilt. Caiaphas who had sinned against the spiritual, "hath greater sin" than Pilate, even though he was violating justice.

And so we come to the last section, verses twelve to sixteen, and we are outside once more. "Upon this Pilate sought to release Him. The Jews cried out, saying, If thou release this Man, thou art not Caesar's friend; every one that maketh himself a king speaketh against Caesar." In that sentence the Jewish nation expressed, through its rulers, their final subjugation by Gentile power, and their rejection of their birthright inheritance. They bowed the neck to Caesar in order to murder Jesus. "When Pilate therefore heard these words, he brought Jesus out, and sat down on the judgment-seat at a place called The Pavement, but in Hebrew Gabbatha. Now it was the Preparation of the Passover; it was about

the sixth hour." He made one more effort to release Jesus
as he said, "Behold, your King! They therefore cried out,
Away with Him, away with Him, Crucify Him." And again
he said, now perhaps in defeat and disappointed mockery,
"Shall I crucify your King?" Then the final word of the
priests, "We have no king but Caesar." "Then therefore he
delivered Him unto them to be crucified."

John xix. 17-30.

In this paragraph we have John's account of the crucifixion
of the incarnate Word of God. Here as everywhere, his
principle of selection is manifested. There are matters
concerning the crucifixion to which he makes no reference.
Unquestionably selecting, as he has done throughout, he has
given exactly the presentation necessary for the completion
of his presentation of our adorable Redeemer.

In this paragraph we have the first movement in the
ultimate Sign. At the commencement of our Lord's ministry
He was challenged when He cleansed the Temple for a sign
demonstrating His authority ; and He then made that mystic
reply, not apprehended as to its meaning at the time, " Destroy
this temple, and in three days I will raise it up." By that
statement He meant to say that the world was asking for a
sign of His authority, and that the one, ultimate, final,
complete sign would be that of His death and resurrection.
That death, on the human level, would be brought about by
the enmity of man in sin ; such would destroy the temple of
His body. Resurrection, the triumph of love and redeeming
power over sin, would follow, the third day " I will raise it
up." These last chapters in John record that final sign, the
two sides of it, the human and the Divine. We are now
dealing with the human, the dissolution of the temple ; the
death of Jesus on the human level. Nevertheless in that

consideration we shall see that the chief glory of the death of Jesus was not brought about by human agency.

The story opens with the statement that " They received Jesus " from Pilate. We read, " They took Jesus therefore." The Greek word there means, " They received Him." Pilate delivered Him ; they received Him. Pilate, at last baffled, beaten, played the coward, compromised, stifled his conscience, and " delivered Him " to them, and " they received Jesus," *they* received Jesus ! John does not say they took Him out. They received Him, but—" He went out, bearing the Cross for Himself." We are watching Him in His majesty. Pilate has delivered Him ; they have received Him, having gained their objective ; but " He went out, bearing the Cross for Himself," no Victim, but a Victor. By all human seeming, and I am inclined to think by hell's thinking, He was beaten. He was not. " He went out, bearing the Cross for Himself unto the place called The place of a skull, which is called in Hebrew, Golgotha." They got their way, but He was treading a Divinely marked pathway. " In the beginning was the Word, and the Word was with God, and the Word was God. . . . And the Word became flesh, and pitched His tent among us . . . full of grace and truth." " *He* went forth," bearing His own Cross. All the details of circumstances are trivial and stupid things in the last analysis, when one gets the vision of Divine procedure. He went out, bearing His Cross, His own Cross. And He went to Golgotha.

They crucified Him. Only three words. I am not going to add to the reverent reticence of John, and of Matthew, and of Mark, and of Luke, any detailed description of that. The New Testament writers give us no description of the crucifying. The fact is stated. It may be a challengeable opinion, but I think the Church of God has suffered more than it knows by pictures of the crucifying of Jesus ; and sometimes by very honest and well-intentioned sermons, trying to describe the matter on the physical side. I am not denying the tragedy and the pain of it physically, but the physical suffering of Jesus was nothing compared to the deeper fact

of that Cross.   So, with reverent reticence, John tells the
story and leaves it.   " They crucified Him."

They!   Who ?   When Peter came to the day of Pentecost,
he talked to the crowd in Jerusalem, and he said to them,
" Ye men of Israel . . . ye by the hands of men without the
law did crucify and slay " Jesus of Nazareth.   " *They* " the
Gentile hands did the work, but behind them were His own
people, God's people, but renegade, blinded, depraved.   They,
they crucified Him.   Sin is there revealed in its most degraded
and degrading form, that of devitalized religion.   The most
damning thing in life is religion when it has been degraded.
All history proves it.   " *They* crucified *Him* " the Sinless.
But more.   There comes back to us the voice of His great
forerunner, when identifying Him for His Messianic mission
he said, " Behold, the Lamb of God, which taketh away the
sin of the world."   There they crucified Him, the Sinless ;
and in the Divine economy the Sin-Bearer.   They heaped
insult on Him even then.   They crucified Him with two
others, John does not name them, but he does point out
the fact that they put " Jesus in the midst."   What does
that mean ?   It was the sign of pre-eminence in guilt ; and
that is what they meant when they put Him there.   By an
act of malice they crowned Him King among sinners.   Jesus
in the midst.   " They crucified Him, and with Him two
others, on either side one, and Jesus in the midst."   And as
Redeemer He was rightly placed, for He had taken upon Him
the sin of the world.

In the meantime Pilate was somewhere there in the background.   I see him with a stylus in his hand, for John is very
particular to tell us that Pilate wrote the superscription.
What did it say ?   " JESUS OF NAZARETH, THE KING OF THE
JEWS."   He had it written in Hebrew, the national language ;
in Latin, the language of the government ; in Greek, the
language spoken of the common people.   The priests objected.
Of course they did.   We will leave them alone with their
objection.   Looking back on that scene, from the standpoint
of the Divine government, we see how all men were in the

hands of God, and guided by God, even when they are not seeking His guidance. Every human being ultimately is under the government of God. When a Roman procurator, who has sold his conscience, takes the stylus and writes, guiding his hand, is God. Pilate meant to annoy the priests. The priests hated the thing, and made their protest, and with sharp incisiveness, gathering courage in an attempt to save his face, Pilate said, "What I have written I have written." Pilate, yes! Moreover, what you have written, you have written by the authority to which Jesus referred when He stood before you, and told you you could have no authority at all except it were given you from above. Now you have written God's estimate of Him among the Jews. Moreover, in that writing, from the Divine standpoint is an evidence that He had fulfilled God's intention in the creation of the Hebrew people. The Hebrew people had failed in casting Him out ; but God, out of that Hebrew nation, has lifted up the King. As King of the Jews, He will realize God's programme for them, that of providing a Witness for all the world, and a way home for humanity. What Pilate meant, and what God meant !

The rest of the story very briefly brings us into the presence of the Crucified. From verse twenty-three He is seen on His Cross. There are two groups about the Cross, the soldiers, and the friends of Jesus.

Soldiers gambled for His garments, the four pieces under the over-wrapping robe. They gave one piece to each soldier ; and then the soldiers saw that the robe was a peculiar one. Not a costly one, but woven from the top throughout. It was the garment of the simple folk, home-made. That garment of Jesus was woven by the deft fingers of some woman. Who shall doubt it was His Mother's work ? Those Roman soldiers were not accustomed to that kind of robe, so rather than rend it, they cast lots.

Here John inserted the statement, " That the Scripture might be fulfilled, which saith,

They parted my garments among them,
And upon my vesture did they cast lots."

Thus once more John drew attention to the fact that the trivialities of men are resolved in the knowledge and purpose of heaven. Where is that written ? We find it in the twenty-second psalm ; and in a moment or two, though John does not record it, Jesus quoted from that psalm on the Cross, its opening words, " My God, My God, why hast Thou forsaken Me ? " I have often wondered, when the Cross was over, if John did not go home and read the psalm, and pondering it, found out the truth about it, that its ultimate value was Messianic foretelling. There he found these words :

" They part My garments among them,
And upon My vesture do they cast lots."

John caught the radiance of the rainbow around the darkness of the tragedy.

There were others beside the soldiers there, four women and one man. Mary the Mother, Salome her sister, Mary the wife of Cleopas, and Mary Magdalene, close to the Cross. One man, the man writing the story. John never names himself in his writings, and he never names the Mother of Jesus, never names His own kindred, never names the brothers of Jesus, and members of the family.

Then something took place that is full of beauty. Evidently the eyes of Jesus,—in the midst of His physical pain, with all the pains of hell gradually getting hold of Him,—fell upon His Mother standing there, and standing close by, John. Those eyes fell upon the face they had first looked into when He came into the world. A sword was piercing her soul. He knew it, and He said to her, " Woman, behold, thy son ! " Then evidently His eyes passed quickly from her to John, " Behold, thy Mother ! " He in the midst of the unfathomable things, in the midst of those hours when all the Divine compassions were toiling to redeem men, and exhibit the everlasting mercy, His heart thought about His Mother, and He provided for her for the rest of her earthly pilgrimage. We are trying to look at the Cross. It will baffle us finally, but as we look we learn that the Christ of Golgotha, of Calvary, of the mystery of the everlasting mercy, has eyes for human sorrow, and cares and provides.

And then John says, "And from that hour the disciple took her unto his own home." One wonders how long she lived with him. There are all sorts of traditions. One is that he stayed in Jerusalem eleven years, until she was fifty-nine, and then she died. Another says that when he went presently to Ephesus, he took her with him.

And so we come to the central Wonder. John says, "After this." How long after? Probably three hours, for the word to His Mother was probably uttered at the beginning. John does not tell us about those three hours. He says, "After this." John's account here is the most revealing of those of the evangelists. Of course Matthew wrote by inspiration, so also did Mark, and Luke unquestionably; but equally by inspiration John has written something in simple sentences that is more revealing than what Matthew, Mark, or Luke were inspired to write about that hour, and what transpired.

John says, "After this Jesus, knowing." What? "That all things are now finished, that the Scripture might be accomplished, saith, I thirst." Jesus did not say "I thirst" until He knew that everything was done. He knew that all things were accomplished. Then there passed His lips the only words in all the process, either of trial or crucifying, or long-continued agony on the Cross, that gave expression to physical suffering. Then He said, "I thirst," but He did not say that until whatever He had gone to the Cross to do was done. When He knew that "all things were accomplished, He said, I thirst." There was a vessel standing there with vinegar in it; and somebody took some hyssop, and saturated it with the vinegar and gave Him, and He received it. At the very beginning they had offered Him wine, mingled with gall, drugged, and He refused it. He refused anything that would deaden the physical pain. But now knowing that all things were finished, He said, "I thirst." They gave Him the simple sour wine of Palestine on hyssop, and He took it.

When He "had received the vinegar He said, It is finished."

But He knew it was finished, before He said " I thirst." Finally He said, " It is finished." John does not tell us, but others, who do not record the words, say that He cried with a loud voice. From them then we know that this thing was said with a loud voice. It was not the voice of One defeated. It was the voice of the Victor. " It is finished." The Greek words mean far more than that something was over. It means that it was rounded out to perfection. Whatever He went to the Cross to do was accomplished.

There is the sea of mystery. We can only stand by it, and listen to the sigh and the moaning of the storms that sweep across it ; but what we learn from John is that the dying by which we are redeemed was not the physical dying. That was necessary as a sacramental symbol, but something deeper, something profounder, something rooted in Deity, into which human intellect peers reverently, always to be blinded by excess of light had been accomplished.

He had finished ; it was over, it was done. The pains of hell gat hold upon Him. All the waves and the billows had swept across Him. He had breasted the storm, and accomplished God's purpose. When He knew all things were finished He said, " I thirst " ; and then He announced His victory, " It is finished." Whatever the " it " stands for, that which brought Him there, the purpose of His going was fulfilled, completed, rounded out.

And then the last act. I did not say fact. I said act. What was it ? He yielded up His Spirit. The eyes closed, the limbs relaxed, and men said, He is dead. Yes, He is, on the human level. The temple is dissolved. They have destroyed the temple of His body. But on the Divine side, before the consummation of their wickedness came, He had completed the work He came to do. And so now John says of Him, He yielded up, He " gave up His Spirit." Again let it be remembered that neither Matthew, Mark, Luke or John says of that final fact that He died. Matthew says, " He yielded His Spirit." Mark says, " He gave up the Spirit." Luke says, " He gave up the Spirit." John says, " He gave up His

[297]

Spirit." It was an act. I go back a little way, and I listen to
Him, when all His enemies were round about Him, and
criticizing Him ; and I hear Him saying, " No man taketh
My life away from Me, but I lay it down of Myself. I have
authority to lay it down, and I have authority to take it
again."

Yes, they had destroyed the beautiful sacred temple. They
have done their uttermost. Sin can do nothing worse. But
the death that redeems was over, before the physical death
took place.

John xix. 31-42.

THIS is a brief paragraph, but it is full of suggestive and
revealing beauty, against a background of appalling darkness.
The ugliest and the darkest days in all the stretches of human
history were the days when Jesus lay dead. The dead Jesus !
The sacred and beautiful temple of His body destroyed,
dissolved, by human malice. During all the process of these
studies we have been following John's account of His ministry,
with its illustrations of His teaching and His power ; but we
have always gathered around Him in the consciousness of the
living Jesus. Now we gather around His dead body. The
dead Jesus ; life ended, light extinguished, love eliminated.

Life ended. Spiritual death universal, and no hope of
attaining to abiding life. The group of His own disciples,
because He was dead, had lost their hope of life. Light
extinguished. The only perfect Light that had ever shone
in human history after humanity had broken with God, was
put out in darkness. Love eliminated. Oh but the world
was full of love. Nay verily, lust, not love. The Incarnate
Revelation of life and light and love had been done to death.
That was the world's verdict ; the dead Jesus !

I have no desire to leave that impression upon the mind

as final ; and if I had, I could not do it. We are all conscious that there is something else to be said, and the light of it is already breaking through for us. For the moment however we are concerned with the dead body of Jesus.

The paragraph falls quite naturally into two parts ; in the first, verses thirty-one to thirty-seven, we see the dead body of Jesus in the hands of His enemies. In the second, verses thirty-eight to forty-two, we see the dead body of Jesus in the hands of His lovers. Yet that statement needs to be amended slightly. I have said that in the first part, we see the dead body of our Lord in the hands of His enemies. As a matter of fact, the hand of an enemy never touched the dead body of Jesus. When once His mighty work was accomplished, and He had dismissed His spirit to His Father with august majesty, no enemy had touched Him. They pierced His side with a spear, the long broad lance of the Roman soldier ; but no hand was laid upon Him. Only the hands of His lovers ever touched that dead body.

First of all, we find the Jews requesting the removal of the dead bodies. There were three. The rulers requested their removal, and the ground of their request was supposed to be religious. The ritual of religion must be observed, however much its principles were violated. According to Jewish law, an executed person must be buried before sundown. (Deut. xxi. 22 and on). They were strictly within the limits of Jewish law when they asked Pilate to grant the dead bodies removal, in view of the fact that the Sabbath was approaching, which was a great Sabbath. The attitude revealed is that of the ritual of religious law being punctiliously observed by men who had violated the very essence of religion. The Roman custom in crucifixion was that of leaving the bodies to putrefy on their crosses. So when these Jewish rulers went to Pilate and asked that the bodies might be removed, they were asking a concession to their religious rites and ceremonies. Pilate granted their request. Pilate let them have their way. Another of the evangelists tells us that he was very careful to enquire as to whether Jesus was dead.　He sent for the centurion, the officer in charge, to find out if He was really dead.　One wonders whether some superstitious fear was haunting him.

That is immediately followed by the account of the response of authority to the request.　The soldiers came, under Pilate's orders unquestionably, and they brake the legs of the malefactors, one on the one side, and one on the other side of Jesus. The breaking of the legs was an entirely separate punishment from crucifixion in the Roman method.　It was however often super-added.　There are different opinions as to the reason for it.　There are those who think it was an act of mercy to hasten death.　It has been shown too, that sometimes they were taken off their crosses long before death, and the legs broken to prevent escape.　Evidently here the intention was to end their lives swiftly, in order to grant the request for the removal of the bodies.　Then we have this most significant statement.　When they came to Jesus, they found He was dead already.　Crucifixion meant a lingering and agonizing death.　Sometimes the crucified hung on their crosses for two or even three days and nights before they died.　Probably the two malefactors would have done so if it had not been for this.　But " Jesus was dead already." When they found He was dead already, a Roman soldier pierced His side.

Then something happened, proving that He was dead. That it was something of vital importance is proven by the way John emphasizes it.　In telling the fact, that when the spear pierced the side of Jesus, straightway there came forth blood and water, he says, " He that hath seen hath borne witness, and his witness is true ; and he knoweth that he saith true, that ye also may believe."　John made this statement because he was desirous of insisting upon the absolute accuracy of what he had recorded.　It is quite possible that that soldier pierced the side of the three.　We are not told that he did ; but it was often done.　If the soldier had pierced the side of either of those malefactors before they were dead, what would have been seen issuing from the wound created by the lance? Blood, red blood alone. That is why John is particular to say when the sword pierced the side of Jesus, there came out blood and water.

Now I have no doubt whatever there are mystical things and symbolic values in the fact, but the first value of it was that the outflow of blood and water, as John calls it, was a demonstration of the fact that He was dead already, and reveals moreover how, on the physical side, He had died. He had died of a ruptured, broken heart. In 1847 a volume was written by Dr. Stroud on that subject. I have a pamphlet given to me eighteen years ago by Sir Alexander Simpson, the father of Dr. Hubert Simpson, called, " The broken heart of Jesus." This pamphlet deals with the subject briefly, but very clearly, quoting from Dr. Stroud, and showing how other men, eminent pathologists took up the work of Dr. Stroud, and investigated it. The finding of these scientific experts is that the out-flow which John calls blood and water might with perfect accuracy have been described as blood and serum ; and the very fact that the two appeared, when the side was pierced, was a demonstration of what John had just said, that He was " dead already." The spear did not put Him to death. Whatever the intention of the spear was, the issue of that action in the case of Jesus was demonstration of the fact that He " was dead already," and that He had died of a broken heart. That breaking of His heart did not take place until He knew all things were accomplished for which He had gone to the Cross, and until He had said, " It is finished," and commended His Spirit to His Father. Then, on the physical side, the whole strain ruptured His heart, and straightway He was dead.

And yet it was a demonstration of the fact, that while the humanity of Jesus was real, the moment of the rupture was within the counsel and determination of His own will, and so we are here also in the presence of something more than human. " No man taketh My life from Me. I lay it down of Myself." Here we have perfect humanity, the strain and the agony, bodily and mentally, reacting upon the physical, until

His heart was broken, but this only taking place when He willed that it should.

John here adds something arresting. He saw in these happenings fulfilment of two words from the past : " A bone of Him shall not be broken " ; and " They shall look on Him Whom they pierced." John saw the over-ruling of God in all these things of human iniquity, and human sin.

His first quotation was from the book of Exodus ; his second from Zechariah. From the law and the prophets he takes out two simple statements. The fact that they did not break His bones was the fulfilment of something found in Exodus ; and the fact that they pierced His side was the fulfilment of something foretold by Zechariah.

As to the first. We search in vain for any such statement in the Old Testament that is explicitly made concerning Messiah. The words in psalm thirty-four,

" He keepeth all his bones ;

Not one of them is broken,"

are often applied to Messiah, and perhaps in some senses justifiably so. As a matter of fact however it is not a Messianic psalm. David is speaking of the righteous in contrast with the wicked. We must go to Exodus to find the reference. John recorded how when Jesus began His public ministry, His forerunner announced Him in these terms, " Behold, the Lamb of God, which taketh away the sin of the world." John was remembering that. When he wrote this, he had come to understand the glory of that introduction of Jesus by His great forerunner, " The Lamb of God." So now he went back to Exodus where instructions were given for the paschal lamb. One definite instruction was that it was to be perfect, and no bone of it was to be broken. They came, the soldiers, and saw Him dead already ; and so there was no need to break His bones. Historically an incidental fact, but in it John saw a fulfilment. Jesus was the true paschal Lamb, and no bone of Him was broken.

Then he remembered the passage in Zechariah, " They shall look on Him Whom they pierced." And now John saw the pierced side. The piercing may have been an act of pity, for in those last moments the soldiers were over-awed. They gibed at Him at the beginning. They joined with the priests in their gibing, but as the hours passed in which He hung upon the Cross, and they listened to Him, the centurion in charge of the business broke out, and said, " Truly this Man was the Son of God," and he broke out also, " Certainly this was a righteous Man." One of the evangelists records one thing, and another another. A spell had been cast upon these soldiers. They found Him dead already ; and then one of them pierced His side. So, the side was pierced, and the prophetic foretelling fulfilled.

That the outflow of blood and water was symbolic to John is seen in his letters, when he refers to blood and water. There we find how presently he came to see a symbolism in that which was purely natural, that it had a supernatural suggestiveness. He came to see that the blood was the symbol of redemption, and the water of regeneration.

There are two lines in one of our hymns which I never sing without a sense of sob in my throat, which merges into a song,

" The very spear that pierced His side,
Drew forth the blood to save."

That was God's answer to humanity's sin. The spear thrust was the last brutality, the last indignity ; and the spear was bathed with the blood, evidence of the infinite and compassionate heart of God.

Now His enemies had done all they could do. So we turn to the second section, in which we see Him in the hands of His lovers. Two of them are here, Joseph and Nicodemus. Joseph a disciple, but secretly, for fear of the Jews. John tells us that definitely about him. From the other evangelists we learn more about him. He was rich. He was a member of the Sanhedrim. He had not voted for the death of Jesus.

[303]

He had not given his consent to their counsel. The finding of the Sanhedrim, when Caiaphas gathered it, and sent Him to Pilate presently, was not unanimous. There was at least one man who did not vote for the death of Jesus. Nicodemus was also a Sanhedrist. I wonder how he voted. I think it is certain that he did not vote for His death, because on an earlier occasion he had raised his voice on the side of justice (vii. 51). In any case we now see these two members of the Sanhedrim acting together, Joseph of Arimathæa was certainly weak. John is very distinct about him ; he was a " disciple of Jesus, but secretly for fear of the Jews." Yet when Jesus was in danger, he manifested his courage in that he did not vote for His death. We are told moreover that he was one who was looking for the Kingdom of God. John does not tell us about the little group which, when Jesus was born, were in the Temple, Simeon and Anna, and a little group loyal to the God of their fathers, waiting for the Kingdom of God. Joseph belonged to that company, and he had come to believe in Jesus.

Nicodemus was one of the earliest seekers. I have no sympathy with those who say he was cowardly. His coming by night proved his commonsense. He came when the crowd was gone, and he could get Jesus alone. He it is now who we see coming, bringing a hundred pounds weight of spices. The Roman pound was twelve ounces ; twelve hundred ounces of spices. What was he going to do ? He was coming to join Joseph of Arimathæa. Certainly they knew each other, for they were both Sanhedrists.

In that supreme hour Joseph did the thing of ultimate courage ; he went straight to Pilate, and begged the dead body of Jesus. He went right to the Praetorium, past all other authority, to Pilate, and begged the body of Jesus.

Then we see those two men acting together. The sepulchre was rock-hewn. It was in a garden. There was a garden near the place where they crucified Him. It was Joseph's garden, and the tomb was prepared unquestionably for his own sepulture by and by. No man had ever yet been buried there. Always in those rock-hewn tombs, there was a porch, into that they carried the dead body. There they brought the body of Jesus, and there we see these two men wrapping it round, with a hundred pounds of spices intermixed with the wrappings. John is careful to say they buried Him " as the custom of the Jews is to bury." That is to say not after the Egyptian manner, or the manner of other nations, which meant embalming, and the mutilation of the body. The Jews never mutilated a dead body, but wrapped it in spices in the cloths, and last of all a final winding sheet. The wrapping of those dead bodies was a work of singular complexity.

Here we see the last ministry of love. Two disciples,— one of them who had certainly been a disciple secretly. The other perhaps so also. Never let us forget that when Peter, the loud talking disciple, and the rest of the crowd with him had all run away, two secret disciples took care of the dead body of Jesus, and buried it with love. In the hour of supreme darkness, it was two fearful disciples who blazed into courage, and buried the dead body of Jesus.

What poetry there is in one little statement here. " In the place where He was crucified there was a garden." Into the garden they carried His dead body. I always seem to see the dead body of Jesus lying where the flowers were blooming, and the birds were singing ; the flowers He loved so well, and the birds He loved so well. Perhaps they were silent for a while ; but I am sure they were blooming, the asphodel of heaven, and the birds of Paradise, when the morning of the first day of the week came. They put Him in a garden.

And yet mark it well. His lovers treated Him as dead. John tells us presently that they never grasped the truth of resurrection (xx. 9). He was dead, and as we see those two men burying Him, we know three things about them. We know they still loved Him. They had not lost their love for Him. We know they still believed in Him personally. They loved Him, they believed in Him. Faith was still there ; love was still there. What was lacking ? Hope. They had lost all hope. They were looking for the Kingdom. They had become His disciples. They had expected that He would realize all their hopes, and all their dreams. They had trusted that it should be He Who should redeem Israel. It was all over. He was dead! He could not do it. He had failed. The world had been too much for him. The forces of ungodliness had triumphed. He was dead! But they loved Him still, and believed in Him. He meant well. So they gave Him burial, the burial of love. They put him in a tomb in which no man had ever lain, and wrapped His body round with an overplusage of spices.

He was dead! His enemies thought they had done for Him, and they were glad. His friends thought He was done for, and they were sad. But heaven watching was preparing the music that should ring around the world declaring the defeat of evil, and the mastery of sin, and the ransom of the race.

John xx. 1-18.

In this paragraph we have the first part of the account of the completion of the Ultimate Sign. The temple of His body had been destroyed by His enemies, destroyed in the sense in which the word was used by Himself, dissolved. They had put Him to death. If that had been the end, there had been no sign, and no authority. However great He may have been in His idealism as revealed in His teaching, however heroic in His devotion to an intention, if death were all, there is no sign of authority. The completion of the sign was His resurrection. The whole story, occupying the twenty-nine verses of this chapter, spans an octave of eight days. The account of the first day is contained in verses one to twenty-three ; and that of the second day—that is, the eighth from the first,—in verses twenty-four to twenty-nine.

We are concerned now with the earlier part of the first day only. John gives an account of the morning and the evening of that day. The story of the morning is found in these first eighteen verses.

These eighteen verses fall quite naturally into two movements. In the first ten we see the empty tomb; in verses eleven to eighteen we see the living Lord.

It is more than interesting, it is arresting, to remark in passing that we have no historic account of the rising of Jesus; but we have accounts of the risen Jesus. It is quite evident that no eye watched Him as He left the tomb. His enemies were not permitted to see that; and His friends were not expecting Him back; and so they did not see it.

As we consider the empty tomb, let us first follow the sequence of events in the early morning. There is much that John does not record. We are simply taking what he does tell us. His principle all through, was that of selection. The same principle obtains here. From the marvellous story of that first day, he makes selections, and he tells us certain things that happened in rapid sequence in the morning.

The first thing recorded by John was that of the arrival of Mary of Magdala, very early, " while it was yet dark." When she arrived, the one thing she saw was that the stone— some of the evangelists say, was rolled away,—John says, was lifted out. The stone which had been rolled to the mouth of the rock-hewn tomb, and upon which the seal of Pilate had been put, to render it secure, was removed from the entrance. Mary evidently did not stay to investigate. She ran to Simon Peter and to John. How long the journey was we have no means of knowing; certainly the tomb was not very far away from Jerusalem.

In passing, notice where Simon Peter was. He was with John, and consequently in company with John and the Virgin Mother of our Lord. John had taken her to his home. This is the only place from which we learn where Peter went after he had denied his Lord. The last picture we have of him prior to this is of the man with a broken heart, going out, having denied his Lord. I used to wonder what became of him during the dark intervening hours between the crucifixion of his Lord, and His rising. Here we find John had taken him in. For evermore blessed be the memory of John, if for nothing else than that he found Peter, and took him in during that dark period.

The next thing in sequence, is the story of how they immediately left their home, and ran to the sepulchre to see if this thing could be so ; and, if the stone were really gone, what it meant. John outran Peter. I think that is our warrant for thinking he was younger than Peter. I am quite sure he was not more eager. When John arrived, " He seeth the linen cloths lying." That was a little more than Mary saw. She had not stopped to investigate. He stooped and looking in, saw the linen cloths lying.

The arrival of Peter is the next incident. He did not stand outside, but went right in, and " He beholdeth the linen cloths lying, and the napkin . . . rolled up in a place by itself."

Then John, encouraged by the boldness of Peter, went in too, and we are told that " he saw, and believed."

Then Peter and John went home. Mary did not. She stayed. We are not told that she had seen what they had seen, but she stayed by, when they went home. Such is the sequence.

The supreme value of this story of the resurrection, as we have it from John, is the care with which he described what these disciples did, what they saw, and ultimately the effect produced upon one of their number. In this way John's account, simple, natural, artless, characterized by truth and poetry, carefully considered, throws a light upon the resurrection, along the line of demonstration, to be found nowhere else in the historic records.

In these few verses John shows that these disciples, Mary, John, and Peter used their eyes, but he uses different words to describe how they did so. It is said that Mary " seeth " the stone rolled away. It is said when John arrived, that " He seeth the linen cloths lying." It is said Peter " Beholdeth the linen cloths lying, and the napkin " in separation. Then it is said that John " saw."

Mary " seeth," and the Greek verb is *blepo*, which means just to see, quite the ordinary word. When John came, and stooping, looked in, he also saw in that way, the linen cloths lying. When Peter came, he beheld. The word for Peter's use of his eyes is *theoreo*. This word suggests far more than mere seeing. It means that he looked critically and carefully. We are not told of any effect produced upon him. I am sure an effect was produced. Then John, encouraged, went in. Now we have an entirely different word. It is the word *eido*. This word, while describing the use of the eyes, always conveys the idea of apprehension and understanding of the thing seen. When John went in, he saw, that is, he understood, and therefore believed. Intelligent apprehension produced absolute conviction.

Let us now consider what it was they saw. Mary saw the stone rolled away, and the entrance unguarded. John saw a little more. He looked in, and saw grave cloths lying, fallen flat, but lying just as they were, except that there was evidence that the body was not there. When Peter came in, he examined. What did he see? In a book written in the year 1900 by the Rev. Henry Latham, M.A., who was then the Master of Trinity Hall, Cambridge, called " The Risen Master," the author has gone into this matter with very great care, and has clearly shown what they actually saw that morning. I have no hesitation in saying that nothing finer has been written on the Gospel of John than Westcott's commentary. But when Bishop Westcott suggests that the description means that everything was left in order in the grave, that there was no haste or hurry in the resurrection ; and that the fact that the napkin was folded together apart shows order without haste, I do not hesitate to say that this is an entirely mistaken interpretation. Peter saw the grave cloths as they had been wound about the body of Jesus, with all the spices

in the windings, undisturbed, except that those wound around
the body had fallen flat. They were not unwound. The most
significant statement is that the napkin was lying by itself,
separately ; and that it was still in the folds as it had been
about the head of Jesus.

A careful consideration of the method of burial in those
rock-hewn tombs shows that the wrapping of the head was
never a part of the wrappings on the body, but was separate.
Into those rock-hewn tombs the body was carried, and laid
the feet towards the opening, and the head further in, the
body lying on a stone ledge ; upon which ledge there was a
slightly elevated place for the head. The napkin about the
head was thus always separate from the wrappings about the
body. When Peter looked, he saw the grave cloths lying.
John had seen that, but that fact had no particular significance
for him, except that it did prove at the first glance, that the
body of Jesus was not there, because they had fallen flat.
He did not see the napkin. Peter saw that also. He discovered
that the grave cloths had not been disturbed. They were
just as they were when Joseph of Arimathæa and Nicodemus
left them. The wrappings were still there ; the spices had
not escaped. Moreover the napkin, wrapped in a peculiar
way about the head, was undisturbed, " folded up." That
word does not mean smoothed out. The napkin was still in
the folds that had been wound round the head.

John entered the tomb, and he saw ; that is, he understood.
There had been no disturbance in that tomb. No rude hand
had gone in and torn away the wrappings. Not even the
hands of lovers had touched the dead body which Joseph of
Arimathæa and Nicodemus had left there. John saw and
believed. His Lord was not there. He was risen !

Remember, that as yet they had not seen Jesus. He had
not appeared to them ; but the demonstration of the resurrection came in a stone rolled away, and in undisturbed grave
cloths. The tomb was empty. He had gone. The Ultimate
Sign was complete.

That is the centre and the heart of Christianity. Deny it,

and we have no Christianity. The historic fact of the Christian Church is the result of the thing that John saw and believed. The angel who rolled the stone away did not do so for Him to leave the tomb, but to show He was gone. He had gone before they rolled the stone away, and without disturbing the grave cloths. John saw, that is he understood, he mentally apprehended the meaning of the sight which fell upon his astonished vision. Therefore he believed.

And now in verses eleven to eighteen, we have the risen Lord. The central value of this is of course the Lord Himself, but the revelation gathers around Mary of Magdala. We see her in three relationships. First alone, in verse eleven ; secondly with the angels, verses twelve and thirteen ; and then with her Lord, verses fourteen to seventeen.

Mary alone. What a wonderful verse this is. " Mary was standing without at the tomb weeping." Standing without. The stone was gone, but she had not understood it. Peter and John do not seem to have stopped and talked to her. A little fellowship might have been helpful, but they had gone away and left her. I can quite understand them from their own standpoint. But she stayed on. What was she doing ? Weeping. The Greek word there means sobbing. It is not merely that tears were trickling down her face. She was convulsed with her weeping. And then what ? " She stooped and looked into the tomb." The word " looked " is not in the Greek, but it is implied. The statement is that standing there, she bent beside, or she leaned over to the tomb, evidently to look in. Peter had been in, and John. It would seem that they had come out and left suddenly, possibly understandably silently. But this sobbing woman wanted to see for herself. I can see her there, Mary of Magdala, out of whom He had cast seven demons ; the woman who through Him had been set free from the appalling domination of seven evil spirits. She had lost Him. She saw them put Him on His Cross. She had tarried longer than anyone else. Other of the evangelists reveal the fact that she stayed all through the first night after they had

buried Him. She stayed by. She was back again the first
day, after the Sabbath, for He was in His grave all the Sabbath.
She was sobbing, convulsed, and she bent over, and looked
in. Then " she beholdeth "—the same word now that was
used for Peter's seeing. What did she see ? " Two angels . . .
sitting, one at the head, and one at the feet, where the body
of Jesus had lain." She knew the body was gone. She had
found that out, but angels were sitting there.

They asked her a question. " Woman, why weepest thou ? "
She replied, " Because they have taken away my Lord, and
I know not where they have laid Him." When she went
to tell Peter and John of what she had seen, she said to them
the same thing, but in a slightly different form. She told
them the stone was rolled away, and this is what she said,
" They have taken away the Lord out of the tomb," using
the absolute term for Him, " the Lord." In her mind He
was dead, but that did not matter to Mary. He was still
for her " the Lord." Now she uses the personal word, " They
have taken away *my* Lord, and I know not where they have
laid Him." Mary of Magdala was true till death, and beyond
it. He was dead. He had cast the demons out, and had
been by her side through the years, and held her by His
love and teaching. During those years He had indeed been
her Lord. But now He was dead. She had lost even His
dead body. That is how she thought of Him. She did not
think of a living Lord. She thought of a dead body. They
have taken away a dead body ; yes, but still she said, " my
Lord." I never read that without feeling rebuked at the
loving loyal devotion of Mary of Magdala. He might be
dead and buried, but He was still her Lord. " They have
taken away my Lord, and I know not where they have
laid Him."

" When she had thus said, she turned herself back, and
beholdeth Jesus standing." She had bent and stooped over
to look into the tomb, and when she had done so, she beheld
the vision of two angels who spoke to her and asked her,
" Woman, why weepest thou ? " She told them through her

sobs, she told her agony, "They have taken away my Lord and I know not where they have laid Him." They did not reply. So she "turned herself back." The wonder of the angels did not satisfy her hungry heart. They had not told her anything about Him. So she turned her back upon the angels. Her Lord was gone, and angels could not fill the gap for Mary's heart.

She turned back; and when she did, there was Someone standing there. "When she had thus said, she turned herself back, and beholdeth"—the same word once more, the word that marks the staring wonder, examination, surprise,—" she beholdeth Jesus." But she did not know it was Jesus.

Then He spoke to her, and He first asked her the same question the angels had asked, and added another. He said, "Woman, why weepest thou? whom seekest thou?" To her at first it was only a man standing there, asking her the questions; a very understanding man, who knew that a woman standing by an empty tomb, weeping, was seeking someone.

Then "She, supposing Him to be the gardener," quite naturally, very beautifully, said to Him, "Lord," or "Sir "— I think it is good to translate "Sir," because, supposing Him to be the gardener, it was not to be interpreted as anything other than a respectful address,—"Sir, if thou hast borne Him hence, tell me where thou hast laid Him, and I will take Him away." That was the splendid language of loyal love. Mary of Magdala may have been a very strong and healthy woman, but hardly equal to carrying a dead man. But love is capable of doing difficult things. Tell me where that dead body is, and I will carry it, she said.

Then He said, "Mary." I cannot interpret that in any tone of voice of which I am capable, so as to reveal the significance of that "Mary." It is possible to utter a name in such a way as to call back all memories, and reveal all endearment. That is what Jesus did. He just said "Mary."

Then she said, " Rabboni." That may be rendered " My Master," but John is very careful to tell us what it meant in her case. " She turneth herself, and saith unto Him in Hebrew, Rabboni." Then John says, " which is to say, Master." No, that is not what John wrote. He used the word *Didaskalos*, Teacher. That reveals how far she had gone. It was very far, it was very wonderful ; but it proved her ignorance of the final facts concerning Him. Immediately she approached Him to take hold of Him.

His words to her here were most significant. He did not say, " Touch Me not." It is unfortunate how that rendering misses the true meaning. The Revised Version, in the margin, reads, " Take not hold on Me." Our Lord did not say, You are not to touch Me. He said, Mary, not that way, you are not to take hold of Me, to cling to Me like that. The old order is changed. Do not so take hold of Me. I have not yet ascended to the Father. He was declaring that the new relationship had not yet been vitally established, but she was to break with the old. All the sobbing of her heart was caused by her grief that she had lost Him in nearness of touch and holding. He said in effect, Mary, there is a new way coming. I have not yet ascended to the Father. He did not then say more. We can run on and see that presently He ascended, and received gifts for men, for the rebellious also. He received the Spirit, and He poured Him out, and linked Mary of Magdala with Himself in a fellowship she never could have known in the days of His flesh.

" I am not yet ascended unto the Father ; but go unto My brethren, and say unto them, I ascend unto My Father and your Father, and My God, and your God." Then " Mary Magdalene cometh and telleth the disciples, I have seen the Lord ; and how He had said these things unto her." What were these things ? What she announced and told the disciples, and revealed to them was not the fact of His resurrection. They knew that by this time. She announced His coming ascension. She told them He was going to ascend. Thus we have seen an empty grave, but a living Lord !

John xx. 19-29.

In this paragraph we have the account of the completion of the final Sign of authority in the mission and ministry of our Lord. Concerning the first day, the day of resurrection, John gives us the story of the morning and of the evening; the records of the morning, the story of the empty tomb and the living Lord. Then he passed at once from those morning incidents to the evening. We know from other writers that other things had happened in the interval. He had appeared to two other women; He had met Peter privately somewhere; and he had joined two walking to Emmaus in sorrow, and revealed Himself to them in the breaking of the bread, when He accepted their offered hospitality. John omits these, and records the story of the evening, in the upper room. Then there is the interval of a week between the things recorded at the beginning of this section and those recorded at the end. We have two appearings of Jesus to the disciples. I said in the upper room. That is not specifically stated, but we take it for granted that is where He came, quite evidently to some place of privacy, and not to a public place; for we are told that the doors were shut on both occasions. The first time we are told they were shut for fear of the Jews. We have the appearances of Jesus, on the evening of the first day, and again a week later. We have no record in John or anywhere else, of anything that happened in the interval between those two days.

In this paragraph then we have three movements; the evening of the first day, verses nineteen to twenty-three; the interval between, verses twenty-four and twenty-five; and the eighth day, and the second appearing, in verses twenty-six to twenty-nine.

On the evening of the first day, let us notice the assembly. " When therefore it was evening, on that day, the first day of the week, and when the doors were shut where the disciples were, for fear of the Jews." Luke referring to this says " the eleven " were gathered together. That was a phrase

used in reference to the apostolic band. Only ten of them
were present. Thomas was not there. That does not mean
that none other were there. We have no means of knowing
how many, but what we do know is that it was a gathering,
all of them disciples of Jesus. Their hearts were filled with
fear, and the doors shut. The fear was perfectly natural.
The hostility to Jesus that had put Him on His Cross was
by no means dead ; and quite naturally this group did not
know exactly what was going to happen. They did
not know where that hostility might break out again ; or
whether it might not manifest itself against them, being His
followers.

But they were gathered together. What brought them
back ? They had been scattered every one to his own. They
had fled when the thunder-storm burst upon His head. But
now they were together again. The only thing that brought
them together again was the stories that they had heard
in the early morning that He was alive, that He was risen
from the dead. They had not understood the fact of His
resurrection. John tells us that in this very chapter at an earlier
point. But there were those who said they had seen Him.
Through the intervening hours, as recorded by other of the
evangelists, others had seen Him. They were afraid. The
doors were shut. And yet inside they were surely talking
of their Lord, and of these strange things. I think I am
warranted in saying that, by the story of the two walking
to Emmaus. They were walking disconsolately away from
Jerusalem when our Lord joined them. He asked them what
they were talking about, and why they looked so sad. They
said, Are you only a lodger in Jerusalem, are you only tarrying
for a night ? Don't you know the things that are happening ?
And He said to them, " What things ? " Then they told Him,
" Jesus of Nazareth . . . a Prophet mighty in deed and
word . . . we hoped that it was He which should redeem
Israel." I am always convinced that the two going to Emmaus
were men, because they said, " Certain women of our
company " say that they have seen Him, as though it were

possibly a delusion. They were all talking about Him. Thus they were gathered, with the conflicting emotions of wonder, of hope, of fear.

Then suddenly the Presence. Right there, in the midst of them He stood. They all knew Him. During these days it was quite possible for Him to appear so that some did not recognize Him. He appeared to Mary Magdalene, and she did not know Him. The walkers to Emmaus did not know Him until He blessed the bread, and they then knew Him at once. On this occasion, however, they knew Him. He was in the midst of them ; and He had come in a strange way,— supernaturally. The door had not been opened, but He was there. Then He spoke to them, and gave them the common, ordinary, everyday salutation, which undoubtedly they constantly used in greeting each other : " Peace unto you."

It is impossible, however, to read this story without knowing that the ordinary and everyday salutation of courtesy took on a new meaning when He used it, that evening, in that upper room. " Peace unto you." The last thing He had said to them in those hours of intimate conversations, as recorded in chapters thirteen, fourteen, fifteen and sixteen, was " My peace I give unto you." They had gone out from these conversations, and had watched Him on His way to Gethsemane and Calvary ; and then they had left Him in the terror and dread. He had said, " My peace I give unto you," and there was nothing like peace to their troubled hearts, as it seemed to them. Now He stood in the midst of them, beyond the tragedy, beyond the agony, beyond the darkness, beyond that which had filled their hearts with terror ; and He used the salutation with which they were familiar. He had said to them, " My peace I give unto you," and now the reason for the dread was over, He was beyond the thing that they had so dreaded for love of Him, and so He said, " Peace be unto you."

Having said this He showed them His hands and His side that they might make no mistake. It was as though He had said, Don't be afraid. I am the very One you saw and followed ; the One you saw nailed to the Cross. Thus the first word of peace, with its accompanying action, was intended to banish their fear. Then John tells us " The disciples therefore were glad, when they saw the Lord." They saw ! The word is *eido*, the same word used of John when he saw and believed. It means more than the mere seeing of the eye, referring to the seeing which produces understanding. When they saw the Lord they were glad. The doors were still locked. The Jews were still outside. Shall I say they were still filled with fear ? For the moment fear was banished ; their hearts were glad. What made them glad ? The risen Jesus.

Then He repeated His formula, again using the common salutation, " Peace unto you." This time we must not stop there. We must read right on, in the closest connection. " Peace unto you ; as the Father hath sent Me, even so send I you." If the first salutation, " Peace unto you " was intended to allay their fears, the repetition of it had another purpose in view. It was to create within them something that was more than the absence of fear, namely a courage in view of the work they were called upon to do. " Peace unto you ; as My Father sent Me, even so send I you." He was bringing them back to the realization of the fact of responsibility that was resting upon them. He had told them that they were to be His messengers to the world. He had left His great commissions with them ; but one can imagine, for the time being, in those days of agony and anguish and despair, when they saw Him die, they would probably forget their responsibility. He brought them sharply back to face it on that first resurrection day. " Peace unto you," look at My hands and My side. Mark My identity, and see that I am the living One with scars, which mean I am Master of death ; there is nothing to fear. Then while their hearts became glad, He brought them back to a recognition of responsibility. As My Father sent Me, so send I you.

It is significant that at this point our Lord did not use the same verb to describe His sending of the Father as He did to describe His sending of them. Here the verb He used for His sending by the Father was *apostello*. The verb He used for His sending of them was the verb *pempo*. They are not the same. He used both verbs at other times about His own mission, and about their mission. It is, however, significant that at the moment, when He was thus bringing them back to face responsibility, reminding them that their own gladness must not be sufficient, their own safety not the final thing, that they were sent ; He used these two verbs.

What is the distinction ? The word *apostello*, from which the word apostle comes, always marked first a setting apart. Now we are very apt to say that an apostle is one sent, and that is true as it reveals a result. The first meaning of the word, however, is to set apart, and therefore to be sent. That is the word He used here about Himself. It is consonant with His constant reference to His own mission, especially as John records it. There are only four chapters in John's Gospel in which He is not recorded as claiming to have been sent. He was the Sent of God. The verb *apostello* stands for delegated authority.

Pempo never refers to delegated authority. It always stands for despatch under authority. God delegated all authority to Him. He does not delegate authority to His Church. He retains it, and His apostles, messengers, are to run errands under Him. Their authority is His. " Peace be unto you." As the Father hath delegated all authority to Me, so now I despatch you under that authority, which is Mine, to carry out My enterprises. And do not let us forget that when He would identify Himself in their presence, He showed them His hands and His side. I cannot affirm it, but I always feel that those hands were still held out to them with the wound prints in them, as He said again, " Peace unto you ; *as* the Father hath sent Me, even *so* send I you." He was not calling them to a soft and easy pathway. The Father sent Him, and those wound prints were the insignia of His authority. When they had become recipients of the new resurrection life, they would be called to go by the way of the Cross, which is always the way of resurrection.

Then " He breathed on them, and saith unto them, Receive ye the Holy Spirit." That, of course, was a prophetic breathing, symbolic and suggestive. They did not receive the Holy Spirit then. Did He not tell them in the course of these days that they were to wait until they received the Spirit ? But while their mission was indicated by the outstretched hands with the wound-prints in them, and His declaration that He had authority, and they were to be His messengers, He symbolically revealed to them the secret of power. " He breathed on them, and saith unto them, Receive ye the Holy Spirit." The word " receive " I think is better rendered by the yet simpler, " Take ye." Take ye the Holy Spirit. He was indicating to them their responsibility in view of the resources at their disposal. My Father has sent Me ; I am sending you. The authority He delegated to Me is the authority under which you will go ; but you cannot go except in one power, that of the Holy Spirit.

Then followed that wonderful word, revealing the reason why they should receive that Spirit, revealing the meaning of their going. " Whose soever sins ye forgive, they are forgiven unto them ; whose soever sins ye retain, they are retained." That was spoken to the whole assembly, to those who were sent, to His disciples.

Is that authority, is that power still with the Church ? It certainly ought to be. It certainly is, when the conditions are borne in mind, and observed. What did the Father send Him into the world to do ? To deal with sin, and so with sins. " Thou shalt call His name JESUS ; for it is He that shall save His people from their sins." He came into the world to face a world morally derelict and bankrupt and paralysed and blasted. What for ? To bear the sins, to break their power, to liberate humanity from the mastery of sins, to remit them, set men free from them. " As My

Father hath sent you, so send I you." The ultimate reason
of the mission of the Church in the world, is to deal with sin.
Of Himself He said in His life-time, " I came not to call
the righteous, but sinners to repentance." That is the
mission of the Church.

Has the Church then the power to remit or retain? To
bring the question down to the individual—have I, not as
a priest belonging to a caste, not as a minister recognized
by the Church, and set apart by the Church to my work,
but have I as sent by Christ, the right to say to any individual
soul, Thy sins are forgiven thee ; or have I the right to say
to any soul, Thy sin is not forgiven? The answer is unquestionably, Yes. To whom have I the right to say, Thy
sins are forgiven? To any man, to any woman, to any youth,
or maiden who, conscious of sin, repents towards God, and
believes on the Lord Jesus Christ. I have done it hundreds
of times. I have looked into eyes hundreds of times, and
after man or woman has said, I do repent, I will trust Him ;
I have replied :—Therefore your sins which are many, are
all forgiven in the name of the Redeemer. And when, for
some reason of supposed intellectual pride, more often of moral
delinquency, the soul has persisted in sin, saying, No, I cannot give this up ; then I have had to say to that soul,
Your sins are not forgiven ; they are retained, they remain
with you.

This was a wonderful hour, and a wonderful word, so
simple, so sublime, so local, so universal, to such a few,
representing such a sacramental host all down the ages.
" Peace unto you." I am alive, behold My hands and My
side. Let your fear be gone. Your work now begins. As
My Father sent Me, so send I you. For this you are only
equal in the power of the Spirit. Take the Spirit. Then
pass out, carry on My work ; face sin, face sins, face humanity.
You will be able to pronounce the remitting word, or the
retaining word.

Then there was an interval of eight days. We do not know
anything about them, except what is revealed in verses

twenty-four and twenty-five. Thomas was not present on that first occasion. Why not ? There can be no dogmatic answer to that question. Yet, as I understand Thomas, I can at any rate make a suggestion. I do not think it was cowardice which kept him away. I think it was anguish. Thomas was the man who said when they were over Jordan, and they heard of Lazarus, Let us go with Him and die with Him. And he meant it. But, he had broken down like the rest. He had not been prepared to carry out his resolution, high and noble as it was. He had run away ; and when he said, " Except I shall see in His hands the print of the nails, and put my finger into the print of the nails, and put my hand into His side, I will not believe," I cannot listen to him without feeling that he was in anguish. He had seen those wounds, and while in a sense he might not have been able to prevent them, he was guilty, he had not been true ; he had run away. I think Thomas said in effect, I cannot go and meet them. We all ran away, but I am the man who said I would die with Him. Yes, Peter had said it too ; but Thomas perhaps had a finer and more sensitive spirit than Peter. But evidently he could not keep away. He got back to them sometime during that week, and they received him at once, and told him the good news, " We have seen the Lord." That is all we are told, but surely they also told him the evidences of identity which He had given them. We have seen Him, and we knew it was He, because He showed us the wounds.

Then Thomas said, I will not believe unless I have your evidences, " Except I see in His hands the print of the nails, and put my finger into the print of the nails, and put my hand into His side I will not believe."

Jesus came back, came back to the man who had come back to the group of His disciples, came back to the man who had been in anguish, and demanding the evidences the others had had. The only justifiable criticism of Thomas is that he was not there on that first occasion. I have tried to account for it. Nevertheless, he ought to have been there.

However, he came back, and Jesus came back to meet him, for who will deny that the coming of Jesus on that eighth day was specially for Thomas.

Then the story which is familiar and straightforward. Again the first day of the week ; Thomas present, probably still unbelieving, but holding on. And again, no door opened, but the Lord in the midst. Again the familiar greeting, " Peace unto you." Then immediately to Thomas, " Reach hither thy finger, and see My hands ; and reach hither thy hand, and put it into My side." He offered him the evidences which the others had received, and which he had demanded ; and warned him, " Be not faithless, but believing " ; or more accurately, " become not faithless."

The with a solemn hush, with hardly any necessity for interpretation, we come to the supreme moment. Thomas saw the wounds, and looked into the eyes of Jesus, and he said two things in close succession, but united. " My Lord," which revealed a conviction of identity. And then immediately the discovery of the ultimate truth, " My God." So Thomas made the greatest confession of any.

Christ acknowledged his faith, as He said, " Because thou hast seen Me, thou hast believed " ; and then there fell from His lips His last beatitude. The earliest were in the Sermon on the Mount. He had uttered others on the way of His public ministry ; He had uttered one to Simon when he made the great confession at Caesarea Philippi, " Blessed art thou, Simon Barjonah." Now the last : " Blessed are they that have not seen, and yet have believed." Of whom was He speaking ? The other ten ? No, they had seen. Their belief was the result of their seeing. Even John at the sepulchre saw and believed. Of whom then was He thinking ? The eyes of the risen Christ were turned from Thomas and the group, and looking down the running ages, He saw the great hosts who should believe on Him, never having seen Him ; and His last beatitude came down the ages for all the sacramental host that make up the Church of God.

John xxi.

QUITE evidently this chapter is an appendix to the Gospel
according to John, a postscript, that is, something that he
wrote after the system of his Gospel was completed. That
system comes to conclusion at the twenty-ninth verse of the
previous chapter. Then followed the paragraph in which he
tells *why* he had done his work, and in which he incidentally
revealed *how* he had done his work : " Many other signs did
Jesus in the presence of the disciples, which are not written
in this book ; but these are written, that ye may believe that
Jesus is the Christ, the Son of God ; and that believing ye
may have life in His name."

Then, how long after none can say, he added an appendix,
which we have in this twenty-first chapter.

It is well to recognize at once that this appendix was not
written to prove the resurrection. The proofs of the resurrection had already been given. This postscript was written
rather to reveal the Person of the risen Jesus in certain ways
and certain applications. This is clearly revealed by the way
in which John introduces the story. Indeed it strikes a deeper
note than that of revealing his own purpose in writing it.
That introduction shows that whatever we have in the chapter,
is a revelation of Jesus, which Jesus Himself desired that
group to have.

Notice carefully the wording : " After these things Jesus
manifested Himself." The voice of the verb is active, showing that it was a manifestation of intention and purpose in
the mind of Jesus. The story is full of pictorial beauty. Let
us imagine ourselves there, at that Sea of Galilee, with which
these fishers were so wonderfully familiar ; on the shores of
which they lived for the prosecution of their old calling of
fisher-folk. As we do so, notice how John tells the story. He
says Jesus manifested Himself. The Greek word there means
to shine forth. That is, Jesus made Himself to shine forth
upon them in certain ways. Whatever we have in the chapter,
it is something which Jesus particularly intended that little
group to see. He manifested *Himself*. And again the state-

ment is made that, "He manifested on this wise." Twice
over the same word, "manifested," shined forth, revealed.
What? Himself. That is the key to everything in the
chapter.

As we take our way through the chapter we see a little
group. They are all named for us at the beginning. We
have met some of them before in the story of the life of Jesus ;
Simon Peter, that is one of the first with whom we came into
contact. Thomas, we have met him also. Nathanael, the
guileless, so named by Jesus. James and John ; we know
them also. Then two others, the nameless ones, the representatives of the great anonymous crowd in the Christian Church,
which constitutes her real strength and backbone. We
remember them all as we go through the chapter, but we shall
not see much of some of them. There is nothing else about
James and Thomas and Nathanael, or the other two. Simon
and John we shall see again. The value of the chapter,
however, is not the revelation of Simon, or of John ; it is the
revelation of Jesus. He manifested *Himself.* He manifested
Himself in two ways, first in relation to the group as representing the Church ; and then in His relation to individuals as
constituting the Church.

In His relation to the group, we see His relation to His
Church, for the group was representative. They were not all
there, even the twelve. Seven are referred to ; five are named ;
and two unnamed. In any group of Christian people, the
whole catholic Church is represented. That is the genius of
Christianity, "Where two or three are gathered together in
My name, there am I in the midst of them." Wherever there
is a gathering of two or three, seven or more, the whole
Church is there in potentiality, and as to underlying principles.
Thus He manifested Himself. That revelation runs on until
we reach verse fourteen. Then we see Him dealing with
individuals in the group, while not separating them from the
group. The individuals are Simon and John.

Now take the first movement, to catch its atmosphere. Let
us look at the group. What was their condition ? They were

restless. Behind them the tragedy of the Cross, by which all their hope had been blotted out. Yet now they knew He was alive. He had already been manifested to them in the upper room. They knew He was alive, but they could not understand. During those forty days between the resurrection and ascension there had occurred the matchless wonder, almost weird, of His appearing and His disappearing. They never knew where they might see Him next. Had He not come through doors without opening? They were down by the sea with which they were so familiar. They were restless, because uncertain. The tragedy had been transformed into triumph by His resurrection, but they did not understand. It was all so perplexing. They were restless, disturbed; nothing seemed settled.

Then it was that Simon, that man of action, said in effect, I cannot bear this; I must do something, I am going fishing; and they joined in and said, We are all coming too. By which they meant, We are all in the same condition. In other words, they sought relief in action from their restlessness.

It seems to me to be a small matter as to whether they were right in going or not. I will leave it. Personally I think they were wrong. He had told them to wait until they were endued with power from on high. Jesus, however, did not rebuke them. They went, restless, seeking relief in action, and they did not get their relief; rather they got a new form of discontent, because they were unsuccessful.

Now to that group of His own, so representative of Christian men and women all down the age, restless, not understanding things in the midst of which we are living, having great certainties in our hearts about Jesus, yet strangely perplexed; trying to find relief in action; and over and over again disappointed even there, how did He manifest Himself? First of all, without a single suggestion of rebuke, either for their going fishing, or for their restlessness or for anything else, He manifested Himself as entering into their immediate experience. All night fishing; no fish, a disappointment. Then, He was there, standing on the shore of the Sea. The

little boat at that time was about a hundred yards; doing
nothing, but drifting in, empty of fish. Then He said,
" Children, have ye aught to eat ? " " No " came the answer.
Then His word, Fling your net " on the right side of the boat,
and ye shall find." It was John who first discovered Who
He was. " It is the Lord." Then Peter, who was stript for
his fishing, when he heard that, flung his coat about him,
" and cast himself into the sea " to get to the Lord.

Luke tells us in his fifth chapter how that once before
He had helped them fishing. On that occasion they certainly
had no business to have been fishing. He had called them
to Himself, and they had left all to follow, and then they had
drifted back to fishing boats. On that occasion He had not
rebuked them. He used the boat for a season for a pulpit,
and then had given them the harvest of the sea. It was
then that Simon said, " Depart from me, for I am a sinful
man, O Lord." What did he mean ? It was as though he
had said, Give me up, I have failed; I had no right to leave
Thee, and come back to these nets.

Now again He had given them a draught of fishes. They
were not called to take dead fish, but to catch men alive.
That He had told them on that earlier occasion. Once
more they had gone back. Yet He came to them, and in
effect said, If you are going fishing, and you have a bad night,
I can give you a good morning. " Thus *He* manifested
Himself," the risen Lord. He entered into their immediate
experience of failure, of being beaten, of a new discontent that had not removed their restlessness. And
there He revealed His power on that lower level of activity.
If it was dead fish they were after, then He could help them
there.

And then what ? When they arrived they saw a charcoal
fire, which unquestionably He had lit that morning on the
shore. Do not read anything supernatural into that. It
was perfectly natural. It was a fire, not of coals, but of
charcoal. Such a fire lights slowly. Very often one had to
bend down over it, and blow it. Jesus did that; He lit

[327]

a charcoal fire. That is how they saw Him. Moreover, there was fish laid upon it. The risen Lord had been preparing a breakfast. When they dare not ask Him Who He was, because by this time they knew, when they did not know quite what to say, He said, Come, and break your fast. I can see the group sitting down on the shore, and looking at Him. What had He done? He made them sit down, and He took the place of a waiter. A *waiter*. Do not be afraid of this. We go to an hotel, and a man or a girl waits on us. That is what Jesus did. He carried the bread round to them. He carried the fish to them. He waited on them till they were satisfied. The whole Church was represented in that group. He manifested Himself as entering into our immediate experiences, providing for our physical necessities, providing breakfast, and serving.

When this first phase of the manifestation is considered in the light of the great enterprise of Jesus which was filling His own mind, as the subsequent conversation with Simon reveals, it becomes the more radiant and beautiful. The vastness of His human emprise did not divorce Him from association with the immediate necessities of His own. Are we baffled and beaten, restless by reason of the times in which we live; beaten in our daily callings in these strange and tumultuous hours, not knowing which way to turn? Thus He manifested Himself. His own purpose and enterprise is vast; but the vastness of it is not allowed to interfere with His interest in His own in the matter of their immediate necessity, and even in the supremely small matter as it seems to us, of physical hunger. Tired men after a night of vain toil, cold and hungry certainly, the risen Jesus will light the fire, and prepare the breakfast. Thus He manifested Himself.

And so we pass, and immediately see Him dealing with two of them, principally with one. Everything that follows is distinctly individual. Yet, the individual is seen, as Jesus deals with him, whether Simon or John, as related to the others, and to the whole of the Master's enterprise.

The real value of personality is never found in personality, but in relationship. The value of a life is not within that life. The value of life is found in what it is in relation to other people, the near, and the far.

It is arresting to observe the contrast between these two. Naturally they did not get on together. Supernaturally, yes; because when the supernatural envelopes them, each finds his need of the other. But temperamentally they were entirely different. Peter was the practical man of affairs, the active, earnest, busy man. Thank God for that man. John was the contemplative man, who would always seem to be a little aloof, because he was dreaming and seeing visions. Such do not get on well together, until they discover that in the supernatural supremacy of things, one is a fool without the other. Presently we shall hear Simon say of John, " Lord, and what shall this man do ? " or more literally, " And this man what ? " Simon, the practical man of action, said about John in effect, What about this fellow, he is always dreaming, what about him ? And yet when I turn over into the Acts of the Apostles, and the Holy Spirit has brought them into a new relationship in Jesus Christ, they are together, the poet and the practical man needing each other. If the practical man had no poet to dream, he would kill himself with his activity. And if the poet had no practical man at hand he would sigh himself away.

Now let us watch Him dealing with Simon, and we must look at Him first, the risen One. What is the position He assumes ? Presently He said to Peter, " Feed My lambs . . . shepherd My sheep . . . feed My sheep." " *My* lambs, *My* sheep, *My* sheep." In these phrases the consciousness of Christ is revealed. If we go back to the tenth chapter of John, in the days of His public ministry, we find Him talking in Jerusalem to His own, and to all, and saying, " I am the Good Shepherd ; the good Shepherd layeth down His life for the sheep." " No man taketh it away from Me, but I lay it down of Myself. I have power to lay it down, and I have power to take it again." The good Shepherd ! The

[329]

thinking of Jesus that morning on the shores of Tiberias
was that of the Shepherd. He was thinking of His lambs ;
of His sheep. That thinking is interpreted by a statement
given by Matthew. In the end of the ninth chapter he tells
us how Jesus saw humanity. " When He saw the multitudes,
He was moved with compassion for them, because they were
distressed and scattered, as sheep not having a shepherd."
Now He was standing on the lake-side, and was looking out
upon humanity the world over, and through all the running
decades and centuries. Of them He said, *Mine*, My lambs.
Mine, My sheep. From that standpoint He was dealing with
Simon. That possessive pronoun marks Sovereignty and
Saviourhood.

Thus He was indicating to him what his work was to be,
Simon's work ; one of the group, representing all. That
work was to be directly related to the enterprise of Jesus as
the Shepherd. " Feed My lambs," " Shepherd My sheep.'
" Feed My sheep."

Once more back to Matthew : " He was moved with
compassion " because the sheep were distressed and scattered,
having no shepherd. Now He told Simon that his work
was to shepherd them. Shepherding the sheep is not always
the sweet and soft pastoral avocation of going through flowery
meadows, and beside still waters ; sometimes it means leaving
the fold, and going out on the mountains wild and bare,
and grappling with the wolf, and allowing the wolf to bury
his fangs in you in order to save the lamb.

The qualifications for the doing of the work are then
revealed. He said, Simon, are you devoted to Me ? The
word our Lord used is far more than emotional. It describes
complete devotion. Simon dared not climb to the height
of the word used by his Lord. He honestly replied that he
loved Him, using the purely emotional word. He asked
him again, Are you devoted to Me ? and again he dared
not climb. He said, I love You. Then with infinite grace,
the Lord came down to Simon's word, Do you love Me ?
Simon did not like that. He did not like Jesus coming down

to the lower word. But still he used it, " Lord, Thou knowest all things, Thou knowest that I love Thee."

The qualifications then for feeding lambs, and shepherding sheep is that of love of the Lord. But do not let us forget that the love He seeks, is the love of absolute devotion.

Having thus spoken in the terms of His emprise, our Lord gave Simon his personal programme. He told him that when he was young he had stretched out his own hands, and girded himself ; that he had gone his own way. It was a portrait of young Simon, a revelation of the sort of boy, and youth, and man he had been until Jesus met him ; self-willed, independent, and able to manage his own affairs. He was not rebuking him. He was describing what he used to be. Then He told him of the differences there would be in him. When he was old, he would be a very different man ; he would be neither self-centred nor self-satisfied. He would stretch out his hands, and another would gird him. Moreover they would take him where naturally he did not want to go. In other words, Jesus in infinite tenderness was saying to this man, that in contrast to what he used to be, the Cross would henceforth be the principle of his life. He also predicted that Simon would be true to that principle. At that point John inserts these words, " This He spake, signifying by what manner of death he should glorify God," thus emphasizing the meaning and value of Christ's words.

After that comment of John, he takes up again the words of Jesus. Jesus said to him, " Follow Me," or more literally, " Travel with Me." In the actual conversation, of course, these words followed in direct connection with what He had said about the manner of Simon's death. He had indicated his work, " Feed My lambs . . . shepherd My sheep . . . feed My sheep " ; and revealed the one qualification necessary, that of absolute devotion to his Lord. One can almost imagine Simon saying ; I shall never be equal to it ! Then the words of Jesus, full of tenderness, telling him that He knew the sort of man he was by nature ; but that now all was changed. He would follow the programme

to the end. Then the command, " Travel with Me," would
remind Peter that his Lord had also gone to the Cross, but
that His Cross had led to His resurrection. And so would
it be with Peter, for Jesus had said in the upper room on
that first day of resurrection, " As My Father hath sent
Me . . . so send I you."

Then followed a scene true to human nature and experience,
and revealing the authority and method of the Lord. At
once the weakness of Simon flames out. He wanted to manage
somebody else. He said, What about this man ? Quick
and sharp, with a touch of acid, the Lord rebuked him,
" If I will that he tarry till I come, what is that to thee ? "
In other words, Mind your own business. Don't spoil your
own soul's condition by fussing about another man. Then
again, and in that connection, He said, " Travel with Me."
Travel with Me, and so carry out life to the Cross. Travel
with Me, and so be delivered from the mistaken fussiness
which attempts to interfere in the life of another. It was
a mystic word and intentionally so. John tells us that men
misunderstood it. Perhaps John did not understand. The
whole point of the reference to John was that our Lord deals
with each of His own separately, and in ways which others
cannot understand, and about which others have no right
to ask questions. It is transparently significant, and of
great comfort to all of us.

Dr. Horton in his poem makes John say this :

" He spoke of me—I do not understand it—
    A tender oracle of love divine,
Which always murmurs through me, and I hand it
    Down to the generations for a sign ;

" He breathed a thought, that haply I should tarry
    Until He came ; and at the welcome word
I saw the winding pathway, dim and starry,
    In which I should accompany my Lord.

[332]

" He said not that I should not die—nay, rather,
　　He did His work by dying, so shall I ;
　He meant not that He would return to gather
　　His Church Elect before my time to die.

" He meant—I know not, but I think I tarried
　　Until He came, for He is very near ;
　Already are the bride and Bridegroom married ;
　　Eternal life is now, and Heaven is here."

That is very suggestive and full of beauty as to what the word
to Peter might have meant to John.

Thus the risen Lord manifested Himself ; as associated
with us in the commonplaces of life, and incorporating all
the commonplaces into the supreme emprise of His Shepherd
heart.

**Books are to be returned on or before
the last date below**

LIBREX—